THE WORLD OF WOMEN

Wetzel, Janice Wood

The world of women

DATE DUE

FEB 0 9 2004	
DEC 1 1 2006	

DEMCO, INC. 38-2931

Also by Janice Wood Wetzel

CLINICAL HANDBOOK OF DEPRESSION

The World of Women

In Pursuit of Human Rights

Janice Wood Wetzel

Dean, School of Social Work
Adelphi University
Garden City, New York

Consultant Editor – Jo Campling

MACMILLAN

First published 1993 by
THE MACMILLAN PRESS LTD
Houndmills, Basingstoke, Hampshire RG21 2XS
and London
Companies and representatives
throughout the world

Copy-edited and typeset by Grahame & Grahame Editorial, Brighton

ISBN 0–333–55030–7 hardcover
ISBN 0–333–55031–5 paperback

A catalogue record for this book is available
from the British Library.

Printed in Hong Kong

With love to my granddaughters, Caitlin and Emily . . .
women of the 21st century . . . .

the future holds promise . . .

my lifetime
listens to yours.
Muriel Rukeyser, "Kathe Kollowitz," 1968

Contents

Acknowledgments

This book would not have been possible were it not for Hunter College School of Social Work of the City University of New York. Their Henry and Lucy Moses Distinguished Visiting Professor Award provided a year long sabbatical with time and finances to study successful women's projects throughout the world. I am deeply grateful for the generosity of the donors and the honor, challenge and opportunity that their gift represents. The International Association of Schools of Social Work (IASSW), headquartered in Vienna, sponsored my research through the efforts of Vera Mehta, Secretary-General of the organization, and Katherine Kendall, the founder and current member of the Executive Board. My thanks to both women, too, for opening doors, along with my eyes and ears, at the United Nations where I continue to be a non-governmental (NGO) representative for IASSW. (Subletting Dr Kendall's Manhattan apartment during my year's sabbatical at Hunter College was an added unexpected pleasure which I will never forget.) Thanks is an inadequate word to reflect the steady support provided by my dear friend, Susan Donner, who accompanied me on the Southeast Asian/Netherlands trip. Her help was invaluable.

It is, however, the women of the world who hosted me and served as translators to whom I must be eternally grateful. I will never forget their kindness and hospitality, as well as the inspiring work that they are doing in every city, town and rural area that I visited . . . particularly in the developing world. I felt proud to identify with them, to share their values and aspirations, and to learn from them. To know that there are kindred spirits throughout the world, both female and male, is to hold hope high on behalf of future generations. I cannot overstate my respect and admiration for these women of the world, and for the men who in partnership are committed to a new social order. Gladys Acosta Vargus, my generous host in Lima, deserves particular thanks, as does Rosemary Underlay, my interpreter while in Peru. Catalina Martinez was most helpful in translating written documents upon my return from Latin America to New York City.

The Social Policy Center at Adelphi University's School of Social Work is including *The World of Women* as one of its research-based books. My thanks, too, to Adelphi University and the School of Social Work for graduate and secretarial assistance with the Index and References sections. I particularly want to acknowledge my fine administrative assistant,

Angeline "Kiki" Kratunis, and graduate assistants, Michelle Lindenbaum, Colleen Barnes and Nancy Miller. Danielle Daum of Adelphi's Computer Center was indispensable.

And even more pragmatically, my thanks go to Judith LaFemina who taught me to use a personal computer by telephone (an amazing teacher!) and to Lorraine Brenner and Linda Scarpelli of L-Com Technology who came to the rescue when my computer crashed, scrambling three chapters. And, of course, I am indebted to my British editors, Jo Campling, Belinda Holdsworth and Anthony Grahame for their professional assistance and support.

Stephen Isaacs, former Director of the International Women's Rights Action Watch (IWRAW) granted generous permission to utilize the instruments developed by the IWRAW as detailed in their booklet, *Assessing the Status of Women.* (See Chapter 10 for a description of the organization.) Their sixteen "articles" provide the blueprint for *The World of Women.* Thanks, too, to Arvonne Fraser, Director of IWRAW and Senior Fellow of the Hubert H. Humphrey Institute, and to Lynn Freedman, the present Co-Director associated with the Columbia University branch of IWRAW. I also want to thank Billie Heller, Chair of the National (U.S.) Committee on the United Nations Convention on the Elimination of All Forms of Discrimination against Women, for her support and assistance (see Appendix).

A special thank you to Charlotte Bunch and her colleagues for their generous use of the comprehensive information and action steps that their international work has produced in the area of prostitution and trafficking. References can be found in the Bibliography. My sincere appreciation, too, to Mary Ballou and Nancy W. Gabalac with David Kelley for their important contribution excerpted from *A Feminist Position on Mental Health* (1985). Courtesy of Charles C. Thomas, Publisher, Springfield, Illinois.

I also appreciate the permission granted by a number of journals which allowed me to reprint portions of previously published articles. They are credited below as follows: Janice Wood Wetzel. "The World of Women Unite in Diversity." This article originally appeared in *Canadian Woman Studies/les cahiers de la femme*, "Post Nairobi," Vol. 7, Nos 1 & 2 (Spring/Summer 1986), pp. 11–14. Janice Wood Wetzel. "Global Issues and Perspectives on Working with Women," *Affilia: Journal of Women and Social Work* (Vol. 1, No. 1), pp. 5–19, copyright Feminist Press, 1986. Reprinted by permission of Sage Publications, Inc. Janice Wood Wetzel. "Feminist World View Conceptual Framework," *Social Casework*, Vol. 6, No. 3 (March 1986), pp. 166–173. Courtesy of Family Service of America,

Publisher. Janice Wood Wetzel. "Mental Health and Rural Women: An International Analysis," *International Social Work*, Vol. 30, No. 1 (January 1987), pp. 43–59.

It should be noted that the Articles listed under "Anti-Discrimination Policy Analysis" (Convention, 1980) and all the assessment items listed under "Pertinent Questions for Analysis" (IWRAW, 1988) in Chapters 2 through 9 are reprinted verbatim from the International Women's Rights Action Watch manual, "Assessing the Status of Women". So, too, is the reporting information reprinted under the same heading in Chapter 10. Permission to quote was granted by Stephen Isaacs, senior author of the manual which is listed in the Bibliography under Isaacs, Holt, and Irwin (1988).

The *Forward-Looking Strategies* (1985) in Chapters 2 through 9 are presented as paraphrased summary paragraphs for the most part. I made as few changes as possible in order to retain the intent of the original writers, while making the content accessible to readers. When I added an occasional thought that they had not introduced in the *Nairobi Forward-Looking Strategies* (*FLS*), I used brackets to indicate that the comments were my own. The content on "Special Populations at Risk" in Chapter 10, excerpted from the *FLS*, is largely quoted verbatim, as is most information extracted from major reports.

The 1955 World/UN Conference, Beijing, China, will write a new Platform of Action. The Convention on the Elimination of All Forms of Discrimination Against Women and their legal rights are expected to be major topics.

Because *The World of Women: In Pursuit of Human Rights* is essentially a global resource manual, all materials should be credited to the original sources whom I have referenced throughout the text. The Bibliography also reflects the extensive contributions of people and organizations to whom I and the women of the world are indebted. At the top of the list is the United Nations Decade of Women's *Nairobi Forward-Looking Strategies*. Thank you, Gracias, Grazia, Efharisto, Danke schon, Shukria, Meherbani, Merci, Spaseboy, Tashakur, Gamsahamnida, Sce sce nin, Cam on, Kob kun . . .

Preface

O world, I cannot hold thee close enough!
Edna St. Vincent Millay, "God's World," 1917

Rationale

As we approach the twenty-first century, a global perspective on social welfare policy and practice is essential to the intelligent understanding of local issues. A multitude of common problems have been found to be too complex and interconnected internationally to be resolved in a domestic vacuum. Profound changes in demographics, technology, and world markets deeply affect the lives of human beings everywhere, and consequently, the services that they require. The education of all people, therefore, must encompass an understanding of the issues that impact the world. Among the most obvious are poverty due to corporate globalization and world debt; energy waste and environmental poisoning; population issues, homelessness, migrants and refugees; hunger and malnutrition; alcohol and drug dependency; sexually transmitted diseases; high rates of physical and mental illness; education deprivation and illiteracy; pornography and sex trafficking; religious, ethnic and gender bigotry; the plight of children, single parents and elderly abandoned by society; and violence in the home, the community and the world. The problems intersect, interpenetrate and merge one with the other on a universal scale. These are enormous human rights issues; and these are largely personal problems that affect individual women throughout the world.

In the few areas where women generally have not represented the majority, such as homelessness and the AIDS epidemic, they are the population in which the problem is rising most rapidly. Yet, regardless of the subject, women continue to be treated as a marginal special interest group by governments, social science disciplines, the professions, and even by most international organizations. This book is intended for all constituencies, for the content is derived from their complementary and mutually enhancing knowledge and skills. There is a need for a global partnership if we are to find solutions to the vast problems of the world of women.

My reasons for writing this book are three-pronged. First, I hope to influence educators and members of the professions to focus their efforts

xi

on the global conditions of women from a human rights perspective. The relevance of the subject matter to social development, political and economic social policy and legislation will be obvious. I want to make equally tangible the connections that must be made between global issues and the personal development and well-being of people. I hope to influence both professionals and involved members of the community who are concerned with the conditions prevalent in our societies to include prevention as a primary focus of their work. This can best be done by incorporating personal and social development programming into their repetoires. Second, I want to provide a comprehensive resource for achieving human rights for women. This is accomplished by making accessible the wisdom and experience of women throughout the world who have contributed to the Conventions, Declarations and Forward-Looking Strategies put forward by the United Nations. Third, I want to provide a resource for women and men who wish to learn from one another, particularly sharing the expertise of women in the developing world. Too often knowledge transfer has focused on that of the more developed countries, denying the leadership of "third world" people. To that end, this book is concerned with the transfer of knowledge, providing ready access to relevant model programs already successfully implemented by the world of women, primarily, though not exclusively, women from developing nations.

This is a book about linkages forged on behalf of women. It focuses on women who are poor, but recognizes the common issues of the more advantaged. It celebrates the leadership of women in the developing world, while honoring the efforts of those in relatively developed societies. It is concerned with making grassroots projects more visible, but does not overlook the work of women in the mainstream. It is a book about human rights policies and programs, but it applies to them knowledge for therapeutic practice, based on psychological theories and research about human development. *The World of Women* is clearly about conditions that are by-products of having been born female, but it acknowledges the negative impact of ethnicity, class, age, sexual/affectional preference, disability, and other differences, on women and men alike. And, finally, although the content is concerned with the problems of women, it should become clear that it is their strength, endurance and resourcefulness that offers hope for the world.

Most of the problems confronting professionals and lay people everywhere are directly related to women. Even when troubles arise affecting children and men, women as their caretakers generally are considered to be chiefly responsible for their alleviation. It is not surprising, then, that helping people around the globe are likely to work primarily with women. In fact, such helpers are most likely to be women themselves, whether they are professionals, or the majority of people in the world who have non-traditional educations.

Awareness of the differential impact of the forces of history on women of disparate cultures serves to enrich the knowledge and insights of all. Rather than dividing women, unity is emerging from their diversity. Domestic problems which have appeared to be culturally unique and overwhelming are becoming accessible through a universal lens. The nuances may vary, but there are common themes that pervade the world of women. The sharing of experience and ideas is not only facilitating progress, but is overcoming apparent barriers. Culturally-based explanations take on new meaning when excused in culture after culture as indigenous reasons for female subservience. The power of the global women's community and the inherent influence of worldwide visibility are not easily ignored.

Because our lives are influenced and controlled internationally, social change can only occur if social consciousness is global, and our commitment to human rights includes the humanity of women on a global scale. Whether in rural Bangladesh, Kenya, or the USA, in urban Thailand, Brazil, or Germany, our local and national actions must be based on a world view that takes into consideration the global context of women's lives. While there are individuals and groups dedicated to this perspective, there is no profession or discipline in the world that is taking on this challenge. Concerned people can reverse the trend, changing the direction that the future holds for women and for the world.

Kugler's (1987) scholarly history of the struggle for women's rights in the western world underscores the importance of lessons learned about the destructiveness of past schisms. His research makes clear that moving forward on the "big, unfinished agenda" of the women's rights movement requires that strategies and tactics of a broadly-based movement be developed, building coalitions and avoiding the narrower issues. Despite the gains in legislation, consciousness, and linguistics, the fundamental fact of women's low status will prevail if this is not accomplished. At this point in history, according to Charlotte Bunch (1987), a leading international feminist, a global partnership can be an important force for change that challenges and transforms the way in which human beings look at themselves in relation to one another, and to the world.

How to Use this Book

Chapter 1 details the conceptual framework for *The World of Women*, beginning with an overview of United Nations' human rights actions as they apply to women. An explanation of the four subsections of the core chapters, 2 through 9, is presented, as well as a detailed explanation of the Person-Environment thesis which provides a blueprint for preventive program analysis, development, and research. The author's Multicultural Prevention and Intervention Assessment instrument (a person-environment inventory), scoring, and score assessment guidelines are detailed for utilization for person-environment program planning.

Each of the core chapters begins with an overview of the focal issue, based upon the sixteen articles contained in the *Convention on the Elimination of All Forms of Discrimination against Women* (1980). The discussion is followed by an *Anti-Discrimination Policy Analysis* heading which includes one or more of the articles with an accompanying section called *Pertinent Questions for Analysis*, developed by the International Women's Rights Action Watch (1988), and relevant *Forward-Looking Strategies*, described below. The analytic material provides a blueprint for a national assessment of the status of women anywhere in the world. It is also an excellent action-oriented teaching tool, for the organization welcomes reports from around the world that serve to keep their information up-to-date.

The *Forward-Looking Strategies* provide summary paragraphs selected for their relevance to the focal topic. This resource document was developed with the universal consensus of member nations at the final Decade of Women conference in Nairobi, Kenya in 1985. It legitimates the human rights issues put forth and provides direction and priorities for both developing societies and relatively developed industrial nations. While the situation of women in developing countries is of particular concern, that of women in the rest of the world cannot be taken for granted. When it comes to women, so-called developed countries are a lot less developed than they wish to acknowledge.

Finally, each core chapter concludes with a section on *Person-Environment Program Models* which includes local programs, reports, research and materials from around the world that are congruent with that chapter's human rights subject matter. Most were acquired through personal interviews in Africa, Southeast Asia, Latin America, The Netherlands, Europe, the United Kingdom, and the United States. Criteria for program selection also required that it address most, if not all, of four major dimensions that research indicates are essential to personal development and mental health. With creative changes to suit local realities, the information provided should be useful to the well-being, social and personal development of women everywhere. Because the experience of the world of women cannot really be separated into pristine compartments, the content of programs is necessarily overlapping. For example, a project selected primarily for its educational excellence may have employment characteristics, role relevance, and legal implications, each of which is addressed in separate chapters. Programming resources, therefore, are cross-referenced.

Chapter 10 provides an overview of common qualities of successful action strategies that are taking place throughout the world – a global zeitgeist; summaries of special at-risk populations of women identified in the *Forward-Looking Strategies*; common errors made in social development; national directives for assessing the status of women, and a global networking resource.

A list of countries that have ratified the UN Convention on the Elimination of All Forms of Discrimination Against Women can be found in the *Appendix*. The *Bibliography* includes personal interviews and communications, and both the *Bibliography* and *Index* include international program and personal interview references.

JANICE WOOD WETZEL

1 A Global Challenge: Human Rights and Women

> . . . women's discontent increases in exact proportion
> to her development.
>
> Elizabeth Cady Stanton, Susan B. Anthony, and Mathilda
> Gage, *History of Women Suffrage*, Vol. I, 1881

CONCEPTUAL FRAMEWORK

United Nations Universal Declaration of Human Rights

The United Nations, more than any other institution, has provided the foundation upon which human hopes and aspirations rest. In 1948, under the leadership of Eleanor Roosevelt, the General Assembly of the United Nations presented to the world the *Universal Declaration of Human Rights*. The document recognizes in its Preamble the inherent dignity and equal and inalienable rights of all members of the human family as the foundation of freedom, justice and peace in the world. And it reaffirms "their faith in fundamental human rights, in the dignity and worth of the human person and in the equal rights of men and women . . . . "

The *Declaration* is unique in that it gave the United Nations the right to ask questions of countries that were previously considered to be internal affairs. Because the human rights declaration has become customary international law, even non-member nations are investigated. It is a civil and political covenant of economic, social, and cultural rights. All citizens everywhere can hold their countries responsible according to human rights principles.

A number of other supportive documents, declarations, charters, and covenants have been created over the years, resulting in an impressive body of international law. The human rights system is built upon the notion of an organized state, a society that is obligated under human rights law to provide its citizens with freedom from violation (either by the state itself or others) of each individual's rights. The state is required to create conditions under which its citizens can fulfill the needs expressed in the human rights system. That includes, but is not limited to, the right to work, to have adequate food, to education, to shelter, and to health. These international agreements require that human rights are expressed concretely in the real lives of the people. The dream remains unattainable if societies cannot overcome the general condition of poverty among its members. Poverty is not only the denial of human rights relative to the fulfillment of basic human needs. It creates conditions which negate all human rights. A poor person has no rights at all, regardless of what is in print (Yunus, 1987). Such is the situation of the world of women who represent the vast majority of the poor in every country.

Women's universal condition, however, is not wholly related to poverty. Although women were included in the *Universal Declaration of Human Rights* as an at-risk population, the truth is that more than forty years after its adoption, the human rights of women remain unprotected. All too often their human rights are viewed, instead, as civil rights which are superceded by cultural and religious family policies which restrict and undermine women.

UN Decade of Women

In recognition of the untenable situation of women, the United Nations proclaimed 1975 as International Women's Year, culminating with a conference to be held in Mexico City. It was not long before they realized that the problems of women could not be addressed in so short a time. A Decade of Women was proclaimed. Equality, development, and peace were priority themes, later to be amended with the sub-themes of health, education, and employment. At the initial conference, a document called "The Declaration of Mexico, 1975" was drawn up by an informal working group of the nonaligned countries. In a revolutionary statement, the document began by recognizing the oppression of women everywhere, linking oppression with inequality experienced by women, with underdevelopment due to unsuitable national structures, as well as a profoundly unjust world economic system, and the absence of rights concerning family matters in regard to choosing whether to marry or to have children. The Mexico declaration mandated the elimination of violence against women such as rape, incest, forced prostitution, physical assault, mental cruelty, and coercive and commercial marital transactions. Men were called upon to participate more responsibly, actively, and creatively in family life.

This landmark document was adopted together with a "World Plan of Action" by majority vote, to be implemented by each nation. As a result, ninety per cent of the world's governments today have some sort of organization promoting women's advancement. The conference in Mexico City has been called the "greatest consciousness-raising event in history." Although it is true that the document was largely ignored by the majority of nations, these revolutionary ideas would prove to be catalytic. With all its apparent conflict, the meeting set in motion the most intricate network of women ever recorded. Women began to realize that collective action was the key to their power and effectiveness. Solidarity links forged over the Decade turned out to be stronger than ever imagined. They formed an unbreakable chain of women throughout the world dedicated to healing and liberating themselves, their children, and, in turn, their men and their nations (Wetzel, 1986).

Convention on the Elimination of All Forms of Discrimination Against Women

At the Decade midpoint in Copenhagen, Denmark, the United Nations endorsed the *Convention on the Elimination of All Forms of Discrimination Against Women* (1980). Often called the "Magna Carta for the human rights of women," it is essentially a bill of rights for women which sets forth internationally accepted standards for achieving their equal rights. Those states that endorse it recognize that discrimination against women is a social problem which requires urgent solution. They are obligated to pursue a policy of eliminating discrimination against women and to report on their progress. A series of corrective measures must be carried out. For example, the legal texts of each nation must incorporate the principle of equality in their political Constitutions; they must prohibit discrimination and provide legal sanctions; they must guarantee women the right to go before tribunals and other public institutions when faced with discrimination; they must take measures to eliminate discrimination against all people, organizations, businesses, and institutions; and they must abolish all legal dispositions which discriminate against women. Not only is the insertion of legislative measures required, but actions are called for which promote the new insertion of women into social and political life. Those who have not endorsed the *Convention* must answer to their citizenry and to world opinion. (See Appendix for a list of ratifying nations.)

Because there are no mechanisms of control to carry out the mandate, for the most part the *Convention* has been a mere formality that has changed the lives of women little or not at all. It will depend on the force of the international feminist women's movement to achieve and ensure its enforcement by demanding of each State and civil society the elimination of every discriminatory norm, procedure, or conduct against women (Acosta Vargus, 1989).

In order that equitable legislative norms and the reality of women are one and the same, every female citizen should know the content of the *Convention on the Elimination of All Forms of Discrimination Against Women* so as to apply it in her daily life. Similarly, attorneys who work on behalf of women should appeal to its specific articles when recognition of their national rights are in conflict with international law, so as to influence their judiciary. New strategies to pressure legislative authorities must be developed to discuss the pertinent changes needed.

In the same manner, the functioning of government organisms should be evaluated so as to raise the issues for necessary rectification. In every case, if actions are to be effective, there is a need for acute global analyses of the formal and the real on the part of women and their organizations (and not just those who are professionally concerned with law). Only organized legal pressure with the support of the populace will guarantee that the distance is narrowed between "lyrical legal texts" and the real rights of women.

If this is true for the fundamental rights of women and men collectively, it is much more true for each woman individually. The social system is often the first enemy against the task. In order to create the necessary conditions for the transformation of patriarchal social relationships, a morass of impediments must be unblocked one by one. They are anchored in the historical periods of every culture, each with its own particular force (Acosta Vargus, 1989).

All judicial orders must be inculcated with the concrete application of the principles contained in the *Convention*, reflected in the daily lives of the people, in their access to mechanisms of appeal, and in their capacity to overcome the situations which violate their rights. The spirit of the law is a necessary, but not sufficient guarantee of human rights. To link these two arenas is to solve an age-old theoretical and practical problem. That is the notion that human rights are ipso facto the rights of all people, automatically including women. Because women have not been incorporated in such a manner, they must be named as a separate entity, with human rights clearly and visibly interpreted globally to include the rights of women. What is more, each right must be examined with precision in light of the question, "how is this right applied to women?" It is "the understanding of the difficult relationship between the today that really exists and the hopeful tomorrow that women are looking for" which is uniting them (10).

Part of the task of broadening the capacity of each woman is the provision of information so that they can make decisions about their lives, whether professional, personal, work-related, political, or social. They have come to realize that working on behalf of one woman is working for all women. What is attained for one woman step-by-step becomes a daily reality for thousands more. Their common experience in their struggle for human rights, though they may not have thus conceptualized it, has forged their solidarity of purpose (Acosta Vargus, 1989).

Forward-Looking Strategies (1985)

The final Decade of Women conference in Nairobi, Kenya in 1985 proved to be an extraordinary event. Despite differing ideology, geography, ethnicity, culture, or age; despite their national differences, more than 15,000 women from over 150 nations stood united in diversity. The Nairobi *Forward-Looking Strategies for the Advancement of Women* (1985), the documented legacy of the UN Decade, reflect their common experience, melded in a consensus at the meeting of the non-governmental organizations at the close of the final conference:

• that women's universal oppression and inequality are grounded in the patriarchal systems that ensure the continuance of female subservience and secondary status everywhere;

• that women do two-thirds of the world's work, yet two-thirds of the world's women live in poverty. Their work is usually unpaid, underpaid and invisible. Their fiscal dependency is perpetuated despite the fact that they do almost all of the world's domestic work, plus working outside the home and growing half of the world's food;

• that women are the peace-makers, yet they have no voice in arbitration. War takes a heavy toll on them and their families as they struggle to hold them in tact, in the face of physical and mental cruelty that leaves more women and children tortured, maimed, and killed than men in combat;

• that there is universal sexual exploitation of girls and women, too often resulting in sexual domination and abuse throughout their lives;

• that women provide more health care (both physical and emotional) than all the world's health services combined. They are the chief proponents of the prevention of illness and the promotion of health. Yet, they have fewer health care services, are likely to experience chronic exhaustion due to overwork, and to be deprived emotionally and physically by their men, their families, their communities, and their governments;

• that women are the chief educators of the family, yet outnumber men among the world's illiterates at a ratio of three to two. Even when educated, they generally are not allowed to lead.

The scenario shifts culture by culture, but the story line remains the same. Despite inherent differences, the common conditions of women prevail. The end of the Decade of Women marked the beginning of an international women's movement the world has yet to recognize (Wetzel, 1985; 1986).

Yet, despite the Decade, a joint comprehensive study by the Carnegie, Ford, and Rockefeller Foundations concludes that little has changed for the women of the world. There is no country on the face of the earth in which women experience equality (Sivard, 1985). In 1989, the United Nations Commission on the Status of Women, meeting in Vienna, Austria, concluded that gains achieving de jure (legislated) equality were not matched by de facto reality. Little had changed at the local level, even when progress had been made in the law. It appears that attending only to legal and economic development, as generally has been the case, without emphasis on equality and peace in the home and in the world, is not sufficient to improve women's condition.

Pertinent Questions for Analysis (IWRAW, 1988)

The framework of the *Convention on the Elimination of All Forms of Discrimination Against Women* (1980) provides the blueprint for each chapter with which to analyze policies and interpret relevant issues and solutions within a women's human rights perspective. It is referenced in the text as Convention (1980). The document includes sixteen substantive articles that form a comprehensive guide for social action. In order to monitor progress, the International Women's Rights Action Watch (IWRAW) developed a reporting manual that addresses each article. It provides a useful framework for analyzing policies and improving the status of women. Written by Stephen Isaacs, Renee Holt and Andrea Irvin, the manual will be referenced in the text as IWRAW (1988).

The International Women's Rights Action Watch was established in 1986 to monitor, analyze, and promote changes in laws and policies that affect the status of women. It is a collaborative project of the Women, Public Policy and Development Institute of Public Affairs in Minneapolis, and the Development, Law and Policy program of Columbia University in New York City. Based in the United States, IWRAW is the only major non-governmental organization focusing on the *Convention* and its relation to women's human rights and development on a global scale. The organization grew out of the international community's shift in emphasis from small social projects towards major legal and policy changes which would have a more lasting, wider impact on women. (See Chapter 10 for their reporting suggestions for *Assessing the Status of Women.*)

In Asian, African, and Latin American countries, the state often relies on neighborhood organizations in order to meet basic needs that they cannot hope to address, given their dire fiscal situation (Campfens, 1988). Women provide the lion's share of the labor in these community projects.

Focusing at the micro-level on their daily problems of survival and their personal development and well-being, they also work at the macro-level in order to affect the causes of women's condition. This model of social action is becoming the norm among women throughout the world. Most of the leadership is coming from developing nations where professional women activists have allied themselves with low-income women.

Person-Environment Program Models

I conducted a global study of these women's programs, focusing on grassroots, non-governmental organizations, universities and other institutions, both educational and service-oriented, and some government sponsored projects. Selected model programs met the following two-fold criteria: First, the program had to address one or more of the issues put forth in the *Nairobi Forward-Looking Strategies for the Advancement of Women* (1985) and the *Convention on the Elimination of All Forms of Discrimination Against Women* (1980). Second, the program had to incorporate most, and preferably all, aspects of human development and well-being reflected in my previous person-environment analysis and synthesis of theories and research described below (Wetzel, 1984; 1989). Those programs that best met the criteria are incorporated as *Person-Environment Program Models* in each chapter of the text, together with relevant research, reports and strategies that are consitent with the theoretical framework.

By integrating what we know about catalysts and barriers to human development and well-being into programming, environmental situations can be created that are non-stigmatizing, personally growth-enhancing and healing. What is more, such programming can be self-directed, as women themselves learn the fundamental principles of health, well-being, and social action for constructive societal change.

The person-environment perspective recognizes the importance of the dynamic interaction between the psychological, internal world of human beings, and their social, external world. Person-Environment model programming reflects a comprehensive perspective based on my analysis and synthesis of a dozen major theories and research concerning human development and mental health (Wetzel, 1984). Four dominant themes emerge that are common to the psychoanalytic spectrum (orthodox Freudian theory, ego-psychology, object relations theories, and self-psychology,) energy theories, life events and role schemas, and person-environment and cognitive-behavioral models, in addition to existentialism and spiritual healing, grounded in Eastern philosophies and major world religions. The major themes (in neutral terminology) are the qualities of Connectedness, Aloneness, Action, and Perception. Each is considered to be on a negative to positive continuum. The presence of negative thematic attributes concerning both individuals and their environments represent vulnerability, while the presence of positive thematic person-environment characteristics reflect the necessary components of personal development and preventive conditions. Hence, for example, those who are alienated (reflecting negative aloneness), overly dependent (negative connectedness), live subservient lives (negative action), and view themselves as powerless (negative perception) are likely to be vulnerable to depression and unhappiness.

Accordingly, those who are able to function autonomously (reflecting positive aloneness), experience close relationship (positive connectedness), are actively engaged in their own advancement (positive action), and view themselves as worthy (positive perception) are in the process of depression-free personal development. This conceptual framework provides a matrix for understanding the impact of variable conditions upon the lives of the world's women (Wetzel, 1984; 1987; 1989). While both negative and positive internal and external realities encroach on everyone's lives, health is not possible unless the positive aspects outweigh the negatives.

The following analysis of the positive and negative personal and environmental aspects of each of the four major dimensions provide possibilities for non-stigmatizing, growth-enhancing person-environment programming on any subject. Programs can be designed to build on existing internal or external strengths, while developing missing attributes. The dimensions also provide the context for analyzing each model program included in the text, and any other programs that are being considered. The following schema, by no means complete, details the theoretical and empirical concepts incorporated in each dimension. A detailed discussion of the concepts presented can be found in Wetzel (1984).

THE PERSON-ENVIRONMENT SPECTRUM

Theory and Research-Based Psychosocial Factors for Personal and Social Development

CONNECTEDNESS

Connectedness Barriers to Well-being (negative aspects)
Negative aspects of Connectedness reflect the concepts of fusion-undifferentiated identity; over-dependence; co-dependence; enabler; symbiosis; excess need for approval from living or dead; too easily influenced; controlling work environment; controlling family environment; enmeshed family; pressure to conform; excess need for external validation; and crowdedness.

Connectedness Catalysts to Well-being (positive aspects)
Positive aspects of Connectedness reflects attachment to people; positive relationship with children, spouse, partner, adults, family, friends, community, world, and/or Higher Power; intimate confidante; empathic relationship; emotional support; interdependence; mutual nurturance; unity with culture (community, world); community with Spirit (higher consciousness, universality); supportive family; supportive employer; supportive peers at work; supportive friends; supportive partner; supportive community; and self-help group.

ALONENESS

Aloneness Barriers to Well-being (negative aspects)
Negative aspects of Aloneness reflects concepts of separation/alienation; unconnectedness; isolation; no opportunity to be alone; loneliness; loner behavior; aloof behavior; inability to relate; no nurturance; fear of being alone; abandoned (orphaned, divorced, separated, widowed, disappearance, runaway, refugee, migrant, exile, ostracized, shunned); non-supportive people (husband, wife, partner, family, friends, employer, peers at work, community); inadequate resources (food, shelter, services, money, language); loss of role, goal, meaning, energy, self-esteem, identity, people, money, appearance; lack of role, goal, meaning, energy, self-esteem, identity, people; and need to be overly self-reliant.

Aloneness Catalysts to Well-being (positive aspects)
Positive aspects of Aloneness reflect concepts of separation/individuation; autonomy; independence; uniqueness; authenticity; inner-sustainment; solitude; alone contentedness; non-attachment; personal development; self-actualization; non-controlling environments; existential Self; personhood; personal identity; and individuality.

ACTION

Action Barriers to Well-being (negative aspects)
Negative aspects of Action reflect aggressiveness; non-assertiveness; negative energy (fragmented, misdirected, dissipated, vicarious living, withdrawal, catatonic behavior, dysphoria, depression); suicidal; negative reinforcement; concerned exclusively with roles; absence of social skills; defensiveness; submissiveness; anxiety; worry; hostility; fear of violence, death, hunger, etc.; conformity; manipulation; punishment/abuse (sexual, rape, incest, clitoridectomy, fibulation, battering, verbal abuse, torture, revengeful/punitive, threatening); alcohol abuse; drug abuse; eating disorders (malnutrition, bulimia, anorexia); lack of interest in the world; lack of interest in self-development; lack of self-reliance; poor work experience; overwork; underpaid; unpaid; inadequate work skills; and oppressed, dominated, or discriminated against.

Catalysts to Well-being (positive aspects)
Positive aspects of Action reflect women's strengths; personal control over life; assertiveness; effectiveness/efficacy; task mastery; work skills; home maintenance skills; education; literacy; numeracy; conceptual analysis; conceptual synthesis; synergy; responsible behavior; caretaking skills; being cared for emotionally/nurtured; decision-making; problem-solving; creativity; resourcefulness; playfulness; focused energy; sharing/collaborating/networking; positive reinforcement; social skills; flexibility; constructive activity; interest development; positive energy (self-development, self-actualization, social action, giving of self, letting go); moderate physical exercise; and receiving resources (income, housing, nutritious diet, clothing, supplies).

PERCEPTION

Barriers to Well-being (negative aspects)
Negative aspects of Perception reflect automatic negative thoughts; negative rumination; negative dreams; negative imaging; lack of self-esteem; negative body image; negative self-representation; negative view of self, others, world, future; hopelessness; helplessness, worthlessness; guilt; shame; loss of "face"; inferiority; sinfulness; inadequacy; fear; sense of failure; identification with the oppressor/dominator; sexist/racist/homophobic/agist attitudes; negative view of physically and mentally challenged people; and phobias.

Catalysts to Well-being (positive aspects)
Positive aspects of Perception reflect awareness; positive cognition about the world, the self and future; absence of negativity; hopefulness; positive self-representation; positive body image; positive self-reinforcement (assertions, affirmations, visual imagery); peace; contentment; consciousness-raising; conscientization; feeling honorable; feeling respected; feelings of prestige; self-awareness; self-acceptance; inner-sight; wisdom; personal power and responsibility; self-defined goodness; personal competence; integrity; personal worthwhileness; and existential/spiritual meaning.

Educators, mental health specialists, and program developers in the formal and informal sector can apply the insights provided by the four major dimensions to the theories, research, policies, and skills that are taught in classrooms, in the field, within organizations and institutions, and in the community. It is expected that the acceptance of gender-specific development on any dimension will be uneven from culture to culture. That is perfectly acceptable, but it is essential that all four areas be addressed constructively to some degree. Each is an important aspect of humanity, the absence of which is debilitating. Moreover, any cultural imperatives that promote negative perception, or the negative aspects of connectedness, aloneness, and action, must be guarded against. Model programs and projects relevant to each of the articles set forth by the *Convention on the Elimination of All Forms of Discrimination Against Women* (1980), described in each chapter, will span the person-environment continuum. They incorporate individual, family, and community contexts, as well as the larger national and international political environment. It is hoped that they will provide a blueprint and stimulus to similar programming, adapted as need be to fit local realities.

The following instrument is designed to assess an individual's psychological and environmental situation so as to intervene in a non-stigmatizing, yet therapeutic way. Scoring and score assessment directives are included.

Wetzel Multicultural Prevention and Intervention Assessment (Person-Environment Inventory)

Please provide the number that best expresses your agreement or disagreement with each of the following statements:

5 = Strongly Agree; 4 = Agree; 3 = Neutral; 2 = Disagree;
1 = Strongly Disagree.

1. I don't think women should always be whom society says they should be.
1a. [Please explain briefly.]
2. I don't think men should always be whom society says they should be.
2a. [Please explain briefly.]
3. I enjoy being alone occasionally.
4. I don't do things on my own very often in our family.*
5. In our family, I am strongly encouraged to be independent.
6. I come and go as I want to in our family.
7. There is very little private space for people in our family.*
8. Family members strongly encourage me to stand up for my rights.
9. I almost always trust my judgment when I have to make a decision.
10. I am a unique person.
11. I am expected to tell my family everything.

+ AL TOTAL

12. I don't need my family at all.
13. I frequently feel isolated.
14. I have difficulty talking to adults in my family.
15. I have difficulty talking to my children.
16. I really don't care much about other people.
17. "Don't count on others" is a good motto.
18. I don't like being alone at home.
19. I don't feel like anyone really understands me.
20. I consider myself to be sociable.*

21. I feel alone in the world.
22. I'm afraid my children will leave me someday.

– AL TOTAL

AL RANGE SCORE

23. When I have a problem, I prefer to take the advice of others in the family.
24. Even when I start out disagreeing with others in the family, I generally end up going along with the majority.
25. I usually take care of everyone else in the family.
26. I don't feel as if I am part of the world.
27. I don't feel like I have a life of my own.
28. At home, I think twice before I say what is on my mind.
29. I spend my life trying to please others.
30. I really don't like to make decisions at home without the help of other members of the family.
31. I usually do what others want me to do.
32. My children shouldn't leave home to live even when they're grown up.
33. The behavior of someone in my family upsets me.
33a. [If so, in what way does that behavior affect your life? Please explain briefly]

– C TOTAL

34. I have friends who back me up when I need them.
35. I nurture others in my family.
36. I have a person in my life to whom I tell everything.
36a. [Specify relationship of person.]
37. My husband (or wife or partner) is usually supportive of me.
37a. [Specify relationship of person.]
38. My children are usually supportive of me.
39. I don't feel like I "belong."*
40. There is a feeling of togetherness in our family.
41. There is plenty of time and attention for everyone in our family.
42. I'm similar to many other people in the world.
43. I am loved and cared for by others in the family.

44. I trust most women.

45. I trust most men.

46. I consider someone in my family to be a good friend.

[Also ask the following questions:]

46a. If so, what is the relationship of this person to you?

47a. What does this person do to express his or her friendship (e.g. share confidences, mutual helping, shared pleasure, etc.)

+ C TOTAL

C Range Score

48. When I have a problem, I feel better if I have a few drinks (or "do drugs").

49. I have gotten so angry that I have even hit a person from time to time.

49a. Explain.

50. I eat more than I should when I feel badly.

51. People in my family act like they don't care about me.

52. My life consists of many roles.

53. Nothing changes, no matter what I do.

54. I often feel like I have to do too many things at once.

55. When others in my family succeed or fail, I feel as if I have done so myself.

56. When I feel sad, I have someone I could call no matter what time of day or night.

57. I have trouble standing up for myself when I am criticized unfairly.

58. I will do anything to keep my children with me when they grow up.

– AC TOTAL

[Also ask the following questions:]

59a. What do people in your family think about females?

——. (What do they expect women to do?)

60a. What do people in your family think about males?

——. (What do they expect men to do?)

61. I am learning to say "no" to too many requests.

62. I have skills that I am proud of.

63. My family criticizes me a great deal.*

64. I know how to maintain a home (e.g. shop for food, cook, clean, wash clothes, iron).
65. I can earn a living.
66. I have been physically assaulted (other than sexually).*
67. I have been sexually assaulted.*
68. I can find people to help me to think through solutions to my problems.
69. I can make decisions to improve my life.
70. I live a fairly healthy life (for example, sleep, exercise, food habits, etc.).
71. People care about me.

+ AC TOTAL

AC Range Score

[Also ask the following questions:]

72a. How do you cope when things are unpleasant at home?
73. I wish I were someone else.
74. Total dependence on others is not really a weakness.*
75. If I were a better person, I wouldn't be so much trouble to my family.
76. If I were to get angry, something terrible might happen.
77. I don't really know what pleases me.
78. If I let people know what I'm really like, they wouldn't like me.
79. I'm physically afraid of some members of my family.
80. Sometimes I worry that I don't love my family enough.
81. Other people expect me to be someone I'm not.
82. It is better to please others than to please yourself.
83. I'm afraid of being separated from my children.

– P TOTAL

84. I am usually hopeful about my life.
85. I won't be satisfied until I change myself.*
86. I trust my perception of things that happen.
87. I am esentially a good person.
88. I can't imagine what a better world would look like.*
89. Even when I am treated as an inferior, I know that I am not.

90. I feel that I am usually a competent person.
91. I believe most people usually perceive me to be competent.
92. Other people seem to be happy doing things that make me unhappy.*
93. Even when I experience stress, I believe I have control over much of my life.
94. I feel that I have a future in this country.

+ P TOTAL

P Range Score

[Also ask the following questions of immigrants:]

95a. Is there anything about leaving your country that you would like to tell me?
96a. Do you ever dream about the country you came from? Explain.
97a. Do you ever dream about your life in this country? Explain.

How to Score the Person-Environment Inventory

Responses on 5 pt. scale (Strongly Agree = 5; Agree = 4; Neutral = 3; Disagree = 2; Strongly Disagree = 1)

* = reverse score   a = written response

1–11	Positive Aloneness (*4, *7)
12–22	Negative Aloneness (*20)
23–33	Negative Connectiveness
+ 33a	written response
34–46	Positive Connectedness (*39)
36a	written response
37a	written response
+ 46a	written response
+ 47a	written response
48–58	Negative Action
+ 59a	written response
+ 60a	written response
61–71	Positive Action (*63, *66, *67)
+ 72a	written response
73–83	Negative Perception
84–94	Positive Perception (*85, *88, *92)
95a–97a	written responses

How to Assess Person-Environment Inventory Scores

After scoring a person's Person-Environment Inventory (dimension and +/- range scores) make the following assessments of all dimensions:

1. Note scores on the negative aspects of each dimension (AL, C, AC, P):
   - very high scores reflect vulnerability to depression (30–55)
   - borderline scores represent possible future vulnerability

2. Note scores on the positive aspects of each dimension:
   - high scores reflect developmental strengths
   - unusually high scores may reflect denial

3. Subtract the negative dimension score from the positive dimension score to get the range score for each dimension:
   - very low positive range scores (0–5RS) and negative range scores (for example – 7RS) reflect vulnerability to depression
   - high positive range scores reflect personal and environmental areas of strength, on a continuum of 6RS and above

4. Explore ways to decrease negative valences on each dimension. (Include interventions with individuals, families, groups, programs, organizations, etc.)

5. Explore ways to increase positive valences on each dimension, building on strengths, both personal and environmental

6. Explore ways to broaden constructively the range between negative and positive scores on each dimension

In sum, systematic prevention and intervention accentuates the positive and if not eliminating the negative, at least reducing its presence both intrapsychically and environmentally. The key is in recognizing risk dimensions and the psychological and social forces that impact on growth and well-being. The catalysts for development and a depression-free life, clinically speaking, as well as the barriers, come from within as well as outside of each person. Both can be culturally influenced.

While we must and should respect multiculturalism, the affirmation of diversity, it is important to educate people of all cultures including one's own, to dysfunctional traditions that do not foster personal and social development and well-being for all. It is possible to retain distinctive and creative traditions, while integrating others. To develop personal self-esteem, to be connected to others in a relational manner, and to act in a personally constructive manner will result in healthy self-perception. If these qualities are not overshadowed by feelings of alienation, extreme dependence, personally destructive activities, and negative thoughts about the self, the world and the future, then vulnerability to depression and dysfunction is unlikely. Within these parameters, there is room for a wide range of beliefs and practices. People who learn about this "blueprint for well-being" are free to design their own programs and plans based on Aloneness, Connectedness, Action and Perception. The Person-Environment Program Models detailed in the text are exemplary.

2 Anti-Discrimination and Pro-Equality Measures

Men their rights and nothing more;
women their rights and nothing less.

Susan B. Anthony, Motto, *The Revolution*, 1868

POLICY AND THE LAW

The three main objectives of the Decade of Women, equality, development, and peace, were followed by employment, education, and health, added later as the Decade progressed and was evaluated. The objectives are broad, interrelated, and mutually reinforcing, so that the achievement of one contributes to the achievement of another. Equality, the first and most basic objective, is interpreted as meaning not only legal equality (the elimination of de jure discrimination), but also equality of rights, responsibilities and opportunities for the participation of women in development, both as active agents and as beneficiaries.

Social welfare and social development can only be created within the domain of the law. Law, however, has a Janus-like personna. It can lead to development or to injustice and discrimination. The law becomes an instrument of society only when both individuals and communities take responsibility for health and welfare. Unfortunately for women, glossing over gender inequities, or ignoring them altogether has been the norm for centuries. The law will not work for the benefit of women if the will of either the people or the state does not allow it.

Transitional eras pose particularly difficult problems for legislative reformers. Economic, political, and social systems must all be involved in the balancing of inherent tensions that are ever present in the complexities of life-enhancing legislation. A balance is needed, for example, between the individual thrust of capitalist nations and the collective orientation of social welfare states. The call of the people in eastern Europe that lead to sweeping historical changes in the late 1980's and early 1990's has provided a clear mandate for such balance. With or without such structural change, women must have protection from the overwhelming forces that rage against them. As they are integrated into society as full partners, they in turn influence structural change. This reality, however, will not be realized until the rights of women are reflected in the Constitutions of their nations.

Constitutions and Social Rights

Constitutions represent the organizing principles upon which the rest of judicial laws which govern the affairs of a country are validated. Their purpose is to structure the life of a nation and define a body of political, ideological, and socioeconomic decisions, principles, and aspirations. The structure of the State, the role of its bodies, and the reaches and rights of its citizens are all affected. The Constitution is a kind of pact that determines the converging interests of constituencies. It is a "provisional peace treaty" among groups that struggle to make their interests prevail and to overcome domineering forces (Acosta Vargus, 1988). Constitutional rights are important to all its citizenry, but particularly so to women who too often have been ignored or specifically subjugated within their texts.

In a study of the rights of women in contemporary, ratified Latin American political Constitutions, Acosta (1988) reported the following common demands of women across cultures:

* No socioeconomic, political, educational, or cultural
  discrimination;
* Equal working conditions;
* Protection of free and voluntary maternity;
* Respect for physical, psychic, and moral integrity;
* Democratization of familial relationships;
* Equality among children.

It is important to evaluate how open the drafters of new Constitutions are to such requests of women, as it is to more established governments when accessing needed revisions to older documents. Both social and personal rights must be taken into consideration.

Social rights imply an active obligation on the part of authorities to create the necessary conditions for their exercise. They are thus distinguished from rights which are strictly individual, that grant the governed person a sphere of liberty, and imply a State's passive obligation to respect that liberty. The personal oppression of women is prolonged in social oppression by the State, whether rooted in laws or attitudes. Their personal rights are not just legal rights, for they are closely linked to the perception of what is important to women as well (Acosta, 1988).

Studies support the fact that the post-1960s emphasis of many countries on economics and the gross national product has had little if any trickle-down effect. The standard of living of the majority of women and men has not improved. There is a growing recognition of the need for laws that ensure basic human needs and other aspects of social well-being. New legislation must be designed to address income distribution, resource allocation, and citizen participation. Human rights laws, together with education and decent standards of living, should be guaranteed.

The law should be a universal social and humanizing service, the instrument of protection of human rights. At the local level, social rights are the expression of each citizen and must be an integral part of social services. The law is significant in that it helps to shape the public sector, to ensure and define the role of voluntary services, and the interplay between public and private sectors. The right of protection of life and survival is not enough. Laws, by definition, should also facilitate democracy, liberty, equality and justice.

In the absence of demands for concrete realization of the international human rights code, social development of the many may become only "sociable development" of the few. In all countries, there are great contradictions in the law of which people are generally unaware. The discrepancy between law and reality is equally great. Mass media plays a major role in the illumination of these questions, as well as keeping them in the shadows. Women generally do not know their rights when they have them, think they are protected when they are not, and the human and civil rights "guaranteed to all citizens" are blithely circumvented when it comes to women. Without knowledge of one's rights, development, whether personal or social, is a moot point.

Political Involvement

Comprehensive and sustained campaigns at local, national, regional, and international levels should be launched if discrimination is to be abolished, a goal that was targeted for the year 2000 by the Decade of Women. The mission must be extended with the deadline. Target groups should include policy and decision-makers, legal and technical advisors, politicians, business and labor leaders, professionals and the general public, with priority attention given to women. The education of women should enhance the probability of their being elected to public office, participating in the political process on equal terms with men. Educating action-oriented professions, such as social work, where needed, and developing relevant educational curricula are fundamental to contemporary and future social change. The same mandate holds true for the education of lawyers and business people. Schools of social work and schools of law and business should provide courses to educate each other's students for practice in the 21st century. Collaboration between the public and private sectors is becoming a cliche, but it, too, is an essential factor. Only then will possibilities for the interaction of law with private initiative and social responsibility become a reality.

Women must find greater expression in political life in order to influence the social, economic, and legal decisions which affect them. The right to vote is indispensable, but not sufficient. Women as voters help to shape their governments, but they must also participate as candidates. Barriers are often formidable because political systems are mostly male. They do not easily share power with a new political force. Until women have decision-making power, their plight will not change measurably.

Affirmative Action

Affirmative Action, special measures to ensure equal opportunities for women, is fundamental to overcoming the barriers that have closed off women throughout the world from full participation in society. Affirmative Action on behalf of women's human rights requires that efforts be made to build unity among women and women's groups, and among those who support them. Governments should be pressed to take action so that women gain equal partnership with men in all aspects of public life. The creation of laws is primary, but the implementation of those laws is crucial. Organizations and professions can take responsibility by endorsing the United Nations *Declaration on the Elimination of Discrimination Against Women* (1980) as outlined in each section of this book under the heading, *Anti-Discrimination Policy Analysis*, and by endorsing the *Forward-Looking Strategies* correlated with each issue.

Anti-Discrimination Policy Analysis: Political and Legal Measures

Articles 1–3: Policy and Legal Measures to Eliminate Discrimination and to Ensure Full Development and Advancement of Women (Convention, 1980)

Article 1 defines discrimination as "any discrimination, exclusion or restriction made on the basis of sex which has the effect or purpose of impairing or nullifying the recognition, enjoyment or exercise by women, irrespective of their marital status, on a basis of equality of men and women, of human rights and fundamental freedoms in the political, economic, social, cultural, civil, or any other field."

Article 2 requires governments to eliminate discrimination against women and sets forth their obligations to promote equality through constitutional, legal, and other appropriate means.

Article 3 requires governments to take positive measures to ensure the full development and advancement of women.

Pertinent Questions for Analysis: Political and Legal Measures (IWRAW, 1988)

- Are there policy statements or laws that define discrimination against women? What do they say?
- Is the definition of discrimination sufficiently broad or interpreted broadly enough to cover practices which are discriminatory in their effect, even if they are not intended to discriminate?
- Does the constitution, if there is one, include a guarantee of nondiscrimination on the basis of sex or a guarantee of equality? If not, what work is being done to amend the constitution and what are the obstacles to such an amendment?
- What laws or administrative provisions, if any, discriminate against women? Are they in the process of being repealed or changed?
- What legislative or administrative measures have been adopted to prohibit or to eliminate discrimination against women?
- Are there any penalties, such as fines or loss of government contracts, imposed for discrimination against women? If so, what are they? Have they been applied?
- Do courts or other tribunals affirm or protect the rights of women? How many cases of discrimination have been brought before the courts or other government bodies in the last four years? How were they decided?
- Are there policies or practices of government or other public institutions that discriminate against women?
- What measures, if any, have been adopted to advance women or to guarantee women fundamental freedom and equal rights?
- What are the practical obstacles that prevent women from attaining their full development, fundamental freedoms, or equal rights?

Anti-Discrimination Policy Analysis: Affirmative Action

Article 4: Temporary Measures (Affirmative Action) to Accelerate Equality between Men and Women
Article 4 states that temporary measures to accelerate defacto equality should not be considered discriminatory (Convention, 1980).

Pertinent Questions for Analysis: Affirmative Action (IWRAW, 1988)

- What positive temporary (affirmative action) measures, if any, have been adopted to achieve equality between men and women? What are the inequalities that they were meant to correct?
- How are these affirmative action measures enforced? What have their effects been?
- Are they considered to be non-discriminatory under the law?
- What enforcement mechanisms have been established? How do they operate?

Forward-Looking Strategies: Anti-Discrimination and Pro-Equality Measures (1985)

The world cannot afford to approach development in the absence of a social and economic framework that ensures universal environmental safety for all. A moral dimension is required of development to ensure that needs and rights of individuals are responded to in a just manner. As more and more women participate successfully in societal activities as legally independent persons, their rights to equality will become ever more visible. The role of women in comprehensive economic and social development is fundamental to the development of all societies.

Women's Political Development

Development should be conducive to providing women, especially those who are poor and destitute, with the means that are required if they are to achieve, enjoy, and utilize the equality of opportunity to which they should increasingly lay claim as a legitimate human right. Contrary to past practices, development should be defined as total development. Political development and other aspects of human life must be incorporated along with economic, social development, and material resources. Nor can moral, physical, cultural, and intellectual growth be ignored.

Policy and program formulation and analysis has been difficult because there has been insufficient awareness and understanding of the multifaceted and complex relationships between development and women's advancement. In the early years of the Decade many believed that economic growth would automatically benefit women. Experience and evaluation research has shed considerable doubt on this over-simplified premise. Consequently, research gathering, analyzing, and disseminating information for the more effective formulation of policies, programs, and projects has increased.

Importance of Structural Change

It is important to note that the problems of women in developing nations can take a different form from those of women in more developed countries. This is particularly true of their integration in the development process. Even though problems of poor women everywhere are often a matter of survival, in so-called developed and developing countries alike, it is essential to work toward structural changes, as well as increased participation. Scientific and technological capabilities must be accelerated, and attention to an equitable distribution of national income should be promoted. Without it, the eradication of poverty cannot be realized, a reality that is disproportionately experienced by women and their children throughout the world. An encompassing strategy is needed that will eliminate hunger and malnutrition, working towards the construction of more just societies.

To truly achieve the goals of development, which are inseparably linked to the goals of equality and peace, women's issues should be incorporated and institutionalized in all areas and sectors at local, regional, national, and international levels. Action should not be confined to statements of intent or to small-scale transitory projects relating to women. It is vital that the link between socio-economic and political development and the advancement of women be emphasized for the effective mobilization of resources to women.

It is important that there be direct, specific attention to effecting positive change in the attitudes of traditional male decision-makers and those few females who are aligned with them.

When passing new legislation of any kind, care should be taken to ensure that discrimination, however indirect, is not implied. Many societies have multiple and conflicting legal systems which should be thoroughly understood by all concerned if women's right to equality is to be fully respected in law.

PERSON-ENVIRONMENT PROGRAM MODELS:
ANTI-DISCRIMINATION AND PRO-EQUALITY

Association for the Advancement of Feminism – *Wan Chai, Hong Kong*

The Association for the Advancement of Feminism works with low income women. They analyze social policies and conduct group discussions, helping women to become aware of the connections between their personal issues and discriminating legislation and other social policies. The women themselves, working together, thus become activists in their own behalf, utilizing facts as well as feelings. Analyses have been conducted concerning family life education, community care (the mentally retarded and elderly), social security, battered wives, child care services, labor, law and housing policies as well. Underlying assumptions are being challenged, and their investigatory research has revealed that social welfare policies ignore or discriminate against women (Cheung Choi Wan, 1989).

Asian Women's Resource Center on Culture and Theology – *Kowloon, Hong Kong*

A structural approach to the societal analysis of women's situation was used as a workshop model at a conference in Singapore attended by women from sixteen Asian countries. Developed by Sister Mary John Mananzan of Manila in the Philippines, the model provides a way of organizing data concerning women that is observable in society. Because the structure and function of systems are thought to be unconsciously produced, the objective of structural analysis is to discover the conscious logic of the social phenomena observed by analyzing the system that undergirds it. This approach is based on the assumption that society is made up of interrelated systems, the most basic of which are the economic, political and socio-cultural, including religious institutions. The economic system has been thought to be a fundamental determinant, providing the infrastructure on which the others are built and maintained. In truth, they all infuse each other. Formerly confined to the concept of class, the awakening of women's consciousness has added a new dimension to this analysis. It is important to consider how each system affects women, and what the non-conscious structures are that are behind discrimination, subordination, and oppression of women. These structures not only exist within a given class, but also transcend all classes and cultures. The study of the genesis of the structures, particularly the patriarchal system, is essential to understanding the contemporary situation of women. It is considered to be the result of concrete forces and events, and not just the cumulative historical effects of abstract actors in society over time.

The Process

Conference participants were asked to write papers to bring to the workshop, thus ensuring more thoughtful consideration of the issues. The primary paper concerned their national situation – economic, political, and socio-cultural, including religious traditions. Next, they were asked to write about the situation of women within each of these contexts. Finally, they were asked to reflect on the religious texts and their teachings in relation to each area of concern. Their third paper was a theological thesis, based on what they had learned in the first two assignments and on their own personal spiritual experience, rather than on what they had perhaps been taught in religious education, the family, or community. Thus, through awareness of their own spiritual identity, as compared to that taught by institutions, they embarked on a journey of personal growth. The following process can be generalized to any group:

Over a five-day period, brainstorming on the economic, political, and socio-cultural facts of life observed is carried out in groups of not more than ten. Each group is provided with newsprint, markers, and tape so that the information can be recorded for all to see. The participants are asked to determine (1) the core symptoms or data that would explain other symptoms or data; (2) who or what groups of people benefit or do not benefit from the system; (3) a summary statement that would characterize each system; and finally, (4) the interrelation of the systems to each other, summarizing the relationships.

To ensure consideration of the women's perspective, the following questions should be raised when replicating the workshop:

Economic

- How is domestic work regarded in the society?
- What are the conditions of work of rural women, women in factories, and professional women?
- What are the contributions of women in the economic activities in the society?
- How much do women benefit from the economic activities in society?

Political

- What percentage of women are represented in the different policy making bodies of the society at the local and national level?
- Are there laws in the society that are discriminatory to women?
- What is the state of organization of women in the society?
- What is the extent of political consciousness of the women in the society?

Socio-cultural

- What religious and cultural practices in the society do you consider oppressive or discriminatory to women?
- What forms of trafficking of women exist in the society?
- What is the status of women in the family in the society?
- How are women treated in the arts and media?

Structural analysis is not done just for its own sake, but as a basis for each individual's and group's involvement in transforming societies. It also provides a basis of evaluating an already existing group to establish whether or not it is working to reinforce the existing system, or to effectively challenge the established social order. It is important to discern who those who control the economy are; who those who do not control or own the means of production are, and whose labor is used to run the economy and receive subsistence, or subsistence pay; who the unemployed are; and who has a tendency to identify with those in control; as well as who is unaware, passive, and vacillating. This content is imperative in planning strategies, setting priorities, and structuring substantive programs for societal change (Mary John Mananzan, 1987; Yvonne Dahlin, 1989).

Social Research Institute – *Bangkok, Thailand*

Since 1985, the Social Research Institute at Chulalongkorn University has concerned itself with qualitative, participatory studies of social issues impacting on women. Their research is both policy and action oriented, and designed to provide base line data. Women's position within the society and gender relations provide the focus for these interdisciplinary studies which incorporate sociology, anthropology, economics, history, and culture. The objectives of the Institute also include collaboration with other individuals and institutions who conduct studies on women; disseminating and distributing findings through publications and seminars; and improving the conditions of women as a result of the research.

The women of the Institute have conducted comparative studies of religions and the social values which inhibit women's social progress. Attention is given to the texts to discern whether or not the prohibitions are documented; comparative research on rural and urban women in slum areas; gender relations and the situation of women working in rubber plantations in Eastern Thailand, women in resettlement areas, in agriculture, and in factories.

The Institute also assesses the indirect impact of development projects, working closely with non-governmental organizations. Having explored a given issue, the Institute develops conscientization models, bringing women's individual experiences to light in a group format. It is important to focus on practical matters in order to attract the women to such programs, for they will not come voluntarily for purposes of awareness. The concept of consciousness raising for its own sake, popular in western nations in the 1960's, is not culturally accepted in Thailand (Amara Pongsapich, 1989).

Asia Pacific Forum on Women, Law, and Development – *Kuala Lumpur, Malaysia*

In December of 1988, at their regional conference, the Asia Pacific Forum on Women, Law, and Development declared and adopted a *Charter of Values for Policies and Laws Affecting Women* that will guide their political and legal action initiatives into the 21st century. The women of the Asia-Pacific region acknowledge the diversity and richness of their cultures and religions; recognize that a woman is a full human being with an individual identity in her own right; and contend that patriarchal structures and existing socio-economic political forces continue to subordinate women and impede the exercise of their right to development. They, therefore, assert that changes in values are necessary for social transformation towards equality and justice for women. Their declared principles are based on the Asia-Pacific experience, arising out of their needs and vision, accept only those traditions that promote their right to development "in the true spirit of justice, equality and human dignity."

International Congress for the Elderly (EURAG) – *The Netherlands*

The XIIth International Congress of the European Federation for the Welfare of the Elderly (EURAG) met in The Netherlands in the spring of 1988 in order to focus their attention on the situation of older women in Europe. As a result, they adopted a declaration of the Rights of Older Women, affirming their right to security and independence in their later years; affordable housing and safe environment, accessible by public transport; the right of older women who need care to obtain community support systems, keeping in mind that, in many cases, families are not present, or are not in a position to take care of them, including a health care system which respects their differences, which emphasizes prevention of health problems, access to rehabilitation, which avoids over-medication, and which takes into consideration the realities of the woman's life situation.

3 From Sex Roles to Sex Industries

PART I

SEX ROLES AND STEREOTYPING

The knowledge that the personalities of the two sexes are socially produced is congenial to every programme that looks forward towards a planned order of society. It is a two-edged sword.

Margaret Mead, "Sex and Temperament in Three Primitive Societies," 1935

Sex Role Identification

It has been recognized for some time that sex role identification is a universal aspect of human development. Three aspects are involved in the process: (1) sex role preference, the desirability of one sex over another (2) sex role adoption, sex-related behaviors, and (3) sex role identification, the incorporation into one's personality of characteristic sex role responses (Lynn, 1959). Despite years of intensive research, it is impossible to assert that behaviors are intrinsically female or male. What has become clear is the fact that the environment is a major factor in sex role stereotyping, regardless of the tendencies of a person of either gender.

Growing up female anywhere in the world inevitably leads to subordination; the rights of women are seldom conceived as human rights. Early explanatory theories were based on biological grounds, social reinforcement, modeling behavior, and cognitive-developmental theory (Williams, 1977). In more recent years, many feminists have argued, though not without controversy, that the innate experience of mothering leads to an ethic of caring which is antithetical to the male's more alienating experience that separates him from his mother at an early age (Miller, 1976; Chodorow, 1978; Gilligan, 1982). There is little doubt, in any case, that in most cultures women are obliged to be compliant, nurturant, and dependent, while men are expected to be aggressive, dominant, and autonomous – if one ignores their dependence on home maintenance and care. Historically, women and men have consensually accepted these norms, not based on sophisticated, deliberate policies, but as natural. Even when painful, women suffered silently. The swelling numbers of protestors throughout the world is one of the major phenomena of this century, and probably the next. More and more people feel that it is unfair that privileges accorded to human beings are based on having male bodies (Bernard, 1987).

Social Class

The social class or income group to which a woman belongs is very important in determining their role status as women in relation to men. The repercussions of class, however, are not stable across cultures. Despite women's inferior status, in countries like Thailand, poor women and men work side by side in the fields, often doing the same work. It is not unusual to find men in rural villages taking care of children when women find wage work and they do not. In Bangladesh, women work in the fields, but it is not acceptable for them to work on urban streets; only extremely poor women do so. In better off families, the women retire from work outside the home. Their work in the home, like that of all women, is not acknowledged as "real work." The result is that poor women have more rights than their sisters with more means. Consequently, wealthier women are no more secure emotionally than poor women.

The same holds true for women in the Arab world where the higher the social class, the more likely it is that they are confined to the home in purdah. The women themselves in these cultures consider themselves to be weaker and more delicate than men, not their equals. (The situation is not unlike that of housewives in the western world less than two decades ago. Indeed, in some western circles, the condition remains unchanged.) In India, poor and wealthy women are more likely to see themselves as equal to men. The poor because they must work side by side to survive; the rich because they are more likely to be educated, to work in the professions and have household help. It is middle-class women who are most oppressed in their roles as housewives. As in industrialized nations, those who work outside the home carry the dual burden of home maintenance and child care (Sathe, 1989).

Reproduction

There is a world trend toward exclusionary work policies based on women's reproductive capacity. Discriminatory sex-segregation and wage disparities are being excused on protective grounds, as they were in some industrialized nations decades ago (Finlay, 1986). Women are handicapped even when they gain benefits, such as generous maternity leave policies. There is strong evidence in The Netherlands, for example, that women are not being hired because they may become pregnant someday.

Strengths of Women

Just as the issues and problems of women have an impact on the world, so, too, do their strengths. The personal power and responsibility of women include recognition of their resilience, flexibility, endurance, and courage, as well as the care and consideration that has become their forte, however stereotyped. It is important to advance women as role models for our world, their finest attributes – nurturance, relationship, and family responsibility – to be rewarded and emulated by all, rather than relegated to one sex, idealized on the one hand and demeaned on the other. Women's qualities must become public values (Wetzel, 1986).

Eisler (1987) has provided a dynamic, comprehensive history of sex roles and civilization in which the "Chalice and the Blade," the title of her book, are used as metaphors for female and male functioning. She makes a case for female partnership models (cooperative relationships) over male dominator/female dominated patriarchal models which have prevailed for seven thousand years. It is not that all men are aggressive and all women servile, but rather that the universal system of patriarchy does not allow men to behave in a gentle, caring manner and women to reject the stereotype of compliance without being ostracized. The idea of the "war of the sexes," she notes, is now being exposed as a consequence of this dominator world view, the result of seeing the other as the enemy.

The emerging growing awareness of a global partnership is integrally related to a reexamination and transformation of the roles of both women and men. Women must not be given the sole responsibility for the welfare of others, at the expense of their own well-being. And men must not be socialized to pursue their own ends, at the expense of their ability to relate to the needs of others, whether within the confines of the family or in world encounters. Gender roles are fundamental to a dominator model of social organization on all fronts. (See "Role Restructuring and Training" in Chapter 5, *Education for the 21st Century*.)

Anti-Discrimination Policy Analysis: Sex Roles and Stereotyping

Article 5: Sex Roles and Stereotyping
Article 5 addresses social and cultural patterns that lead to discrimination

and to stereotyped roles for men and women. It emphasizes the responsibility of both men and women in raising children (Convention, 1980).

Pertinent Questions for Analysis: Sex Roles and Stereotyping (IWRAW, 1988)

- What cultural and traditional practices, if any, hamper women's advancement in society?
- Does religion or custom impose practices or beliefs that interfere with improving the status of women?
- What roles are men and women expected to play in society and the family?
- What measures have been taken to change social and cultural patterns that lead to stereotyping or reinforcing the idea of the inferiority of women?
- Are males and females stereotyped in school books or in the media?
- What efforts are being made to eliminate the stereotyping of men and women? What are the obstacles to eliminating these stereotypes?
- Who is considered, by law or custom, to be the "head of the household?"
- Are there certain kinds of work that are considered as "men's work" or "women's work"? What are the percentages of men and women in these kinds of work?
- What kinds of work are women forbidden to do, either by law or custom?
- Are girls and boys expected to do different tasks in the home or at school?
- Who is responsible for the care of the children?
- In divorce cases, who is typically given custody of the children and why?

Forward-Looking Strategies: Sex Roles and Stereotyping (1985)

Women continue to be regarded as secondary to men because of the historical devaluation of their productive and reproductive roles. Their participation in development is universally limited, in turn limiting their access to education, employment, and health resources, among others. Because of these barriers, the effective integration of women in decision-making is seriously affected. The process is circular, leading nowhere. The second class status of women imposed by cultural constraints of such a socio-economic reality necessarily limits progress, regardless of gains.

Further, the double burden for women who participate in the labor force, while carrying major responsibility for domestic tasks, inhibits efforts to promote equity in all spheres of life. The lack of adequate supportive services as an obstacle for women is echoed throughout many developed and developing countries. Complementary strategies for the elimination of women's secondary status, therefore, are needed. Equal recognition of women's informal and invisible economic contribution to the mainstream of society must go hand in hand with the sharing of domestic responsibilities by all family members, including men.

Restructuring the Family: Re-Visioning Stereotypes

Concerted actions should be directed toward the establishment of societal and family systems of shared parental responsibilities. Priority should be given to the development of an infrastructure to enable both the society and families to do so. Changes in social attitudes will be required so that new or modified gender roles will be accepted, promoted, and implemented. Males, as well as females, need to attain self-reliance in regard to their new roles. It is particularly important that young people, as future parents, be educated and mobilized to act as stimulators of changes and attitudes toward women.

Measures can be taken that are designed to make the societal context more supportive by reducing or removing obstructions. The elimination of sex-based stereotyping, the root of continuing discrimination, is such a measure. The ripple effect that such measures to improve the situation of women would make would facilitate the establishment of a human and progressive society. The advancement of women is considered to be a pre-condition of such a world.

The different life styles of women and the constant changes in their life cycle, in addition to their numbers and socio-economic heterogeneity, will affect the feasibility of policies, programs, and projects concerning women. In order to guarantee that their different aptitudes and capacities will be developed, governments should take the necessary steps to ensure that both men and women enjoy equal rights, opportunities, and responsibilities. Access to all types of education, training and employment is key.

In order to eliminate stereotypes and to make progress toward full equality, timely and reliable statistics on the situation of women are needed. Governments should help collect them, making periodic assessment in the identification of stereotypes and inequalities, the provision of concrete evidence concerning the many harmful consequences of unequal laws and practices, and in the measurement of progress in the elimination of inequities. Governmental and private national research institutions are urged to undertake investigations of the problems associated with the law and the role, status and material circumstances of women. Relevant educational institutions should integrate the findings into the curricula so as to promote general knowledge and awareness of the law.

It is important that young people and children, as future parents, be educated and mobilized to act as stimulators of changes in attitudes toward women, monitoring progress at all levels of society. The need for greater flexibility in the assignment of roles between men and women is of particular importance.

PERSON-ENVIRONMENT PROGRAM MODELS: SEX ROLES AND STEREOTYPING

United Nations Population Fund/Gender Role Analysis Model – *New York, New York, USA*

The Technical and Evaluation Division of the United Nations Population Fund has adapted a Gender Role Analysis model to be used in all programming. Roles to be analyzed should include the individual roles, kinship roles, domestic roles, parental roles, conjugal roles, and occupational roles of females and males. The areas for analysis of each role includes (1) the opportunity for creative activity and expression; (2) activities and time spent in them; (3) control over resources; (4) access to money, materials, goods, and services; (4) decision-making power; (5) access to knowledge and training opportunity; and (6) free time for leisure and relaxation (Mallica Vajrathon, 1989). (See Chapter 7 for a detailed discussion of emerging needs and issues in population communication and education, focusing on women's concerns.)

Indicators of Social Well-being (Dixon, 1980)

Ruth Dixon's comprehensive evaluation of development projects lead to her conclusion that social change must upset a particular status quo if the roles and rights of women are to be advanced. Included in her "Bill of Rights for Women" is their physical, economic and social well-being. Social well-being includes knowledge, power, and prestige. *Knowledge* encompasses specific skills, as well as general knowledge as reflected by literacy, numeracy, vocational skills, and understanding of the "interplay of socioeconomic and political forces in the household, the community, and the larger society" (71). Conscientization is part of the process and includes strategies for change. *Power*, Dixon's second component of social well-being, includes autonomy as expressed in self-reliance, freedom from coercion and physical movement, and especially "participation in the household and community decision-making . . . and mobilization for group action" (73). The benefits of group action are related to the "number and strength of linkages among individuals and groups, the degree of shared self-consciousness, and the capacity for group action" (73). *Prestige*, the third ideal, is in reference to a newly emerging recognition of its denial as part of female oppression, and the demand spreading through the female world. Self-esteem, the subjective belief in one's value as a person, is necessarily a part of prestige, as is the esteem of others. Such esteem is measured by the degree to which a person or group is valued by other household or community members (76). Data must be interpreted in light of the fact that female infants are considered less valuable than males in many parts of the world. Their births and deaths are not thought important enough to be recorded. Female infanticide and abortion of fetuses because they are female are increasing, including in the United States. In other parts of the world the implications are less overt, but insidious nonetheless.

Based on Dixon's findings, project designers should incorporate in their planning how the project affects women's feelings about themselves. Lack of sensitivity to possible negative consequences regarding self-feeling, status, or prestige are related directly to unanticipated deleterious consequences, in her study. While compromises are to be expected because one cannot effectively move on all fronts simultaneously, it is essential that the costs are not paid disproportionately by women, those least able to afford them.

Dixon provides a guideline for analysis of the treatment of women's roles. She uses three measures: (1) the extent of women's participation in project decision-making (with project staff or participants analyzed separately, (2) the extent of women's direct access to project benefits, and (3) immediate and long-term effects of the project on their social and economic status. Participation in decision-making includes project design, implementation, and evaluation. Direct and indirect access to project benefits refers to the extent to which girls and women are direct recipients of goods and services such as vocational training, credit, or membership in cooperative organizations. While indirect access is commendable, direct access is the only real avenue to personal development. The effects of the project on the status of women encompasses the variety of ways in which women's position in the family and the community may be affected by participation in the project, in absolute terms, and relative to the men in their society. Immediate effects should be distinguished from long-term impacts, indicating that process and follow-up research is essential (Ruth Dixon, 1980).

Save the Children-USA/An Expanded World for Women – *Dhaka, Bangladesh*

Although founded in 1972, Save the Children – USA in Bangladesh did not focus on women until 1981. Their experience over the years taught them that the lives of children would not improve unless their mothers' lives did also. Despite the many responsibilities and skills of the women of Bangladesh, they feel that they are useless, worthless commodities, helpless and dependent members of society.

Changing perceptions of women and by women about themselves is the main objective of Save the Children's three-part program, "An Expanded World for Women." The concepts were first tested and refined during an orientation workshop for village women leaders. Their individual perceptions and group discussions were recorded, contributing to the final product. An artist translated their ideas into pictures as the discussion took place. The women participated actively in the process, suggesting the content for some of the pictures, modifying others, and giving final approval for each. The final product reflects images of how their days are spent from early morning to bedtime. It documents the activities of the women that were disregarded as if invisible, as well as those for which their husbands took credit. (For example, agricultural products that were raised and crafts that were created by women were sold by men as their own.)

A set of three silk-screened cloth flip charts were produced, based on this participatory research, together with an accompanying "Women's Awareness Training Guide." Each represents a different phase of women's personal and social development. The purpose of these materials is (1) to increase awareness in village workers and women of female development issues; (2) to present ideas through pictures, thereby making them more interesting and easier to understand and remember; and (3) to help village workers transmit ideas to village women more effectively. The materials are used in small group discussions in which the trainer and participants are seated in a circle, creating an intimate setting. Each flip chart has a set of ideas which together convey the meaning and significance of women's awareness. The facilitators undergo training in three working sessions, learning to demonstrate the flip charts, memorize the information, and lead groups.

Part I: The first flip chart depicts the village women as they carry out their everyday work in the home and in the field, growing, preparing and cooking food, serving the family, caring for children, cleaning the home, and helping their husbands in their work. Time is spent discussing their multiple roles and their importance to the family and the community. When their consciousness is raised concerning how much they are actually doing, they begin to recognize how essential they are to the well-being of everyone.

Part II: The second flip chart helps them to see that their world can expand. Depicting seeds and their growth as analogous to women helps them to understand that their own growth requires a suitable environment, time, and nurturing. Due to socialization, the women are not otherwise aware of their personal needs, but they are very knowledgeable about the necessity of tending nature. In fact, women throughout the world are socialized to nurture others, yet no one is socialized to nurture them. Self-development is typically viewed as selfishness. These phenomena are highly correlated with depression (Wetzel, 1984). A tree analogue also helps them to understand the paradox of diversity within unity – how different each woman is from the other, at the same time that they share universal needs. Respect for individual differences and the importance of all women, given their unique gifts and potential promise, become part of the consciousness-raising discussion. In the process, they are taught the importance of visualizing their desires for the future realization of their expanding world.

Part III: The third flip chart is utilized to broaden their perspective even further by introducing the concept that "changing our world begins with us." They review their discussions of how women are perceived, what hampers their growth, the isolation and restrictions that society places on them, and the poverty, hunger, poor health, child bearing, and lack of opportunity and security. They encourage the women to think about what can be done to change their reality, concluding, "If we want society to view us differently, we must first view ourselves differently. If we believe we have the potential for growth, then we must begin to develop that potential." The women are encouraged for the first time in their lives to recognize their right to a share of the money that is earned by their labor. They are organized into Savings Groups to finance the development of income generation projects through individual efforts and collective savings. As they become aware of being strengthened by their unity with one another, they begin to learn about a women's movement so big that it is beyond their village, and even beyond their country. Mutual cooperation brings them out of isolation, sharing happiness and sorrow with one another, as well as work.

Over time, the women learn to become managers of their own enterprises, making decisions, planning, and implementing new projects. (To date, they have harvested kitchen gardens, raised poultry, built new roads, and established a play school. Many have become independent entrepreneurs with the help of loans from their group savings bank. Participants receive instruction in literacy, numeracy, and bookkeeping, as well as programs on pregnancy monitoring and immunization. As community organizers, their circle of influence and support widens as they reach out to their neighbors and even neighboring villages. Barriers that once existed are breaking down. Because change is being brought about slowly, people accept it. The development activities benefit all – children, husbands, and families, as well as the women themselves.

The participants are encouraged to talk with their husbands and families about their new functioning, role-playing conversations in advance. When women are not allowed out of the house, their support group helps them to maintain self-esteem, providing suggestions for convincing their husbands by showing them how it will strengthen the family and help the men as well. Follow-up evaluations have revealed that they are being better treated by their husbands, that daughters are beginning to be valued as much as sons, and that the children are being taught new perceptions about the worth of males and females, and what they are capable of doing. Sex-roles are changing, slowly but surely.

Save the Children has found that women have the same cultural issues, whether rich or poor. In fact, the wealthier women often are in the more difficult position since their families are more conservative, not allowing them to leave the village. Yet, they are at risk of being expelled from their homes by husbands who are better able to afford second wives. Both rich and poor women work together in the project, contributing the same amount to the investment pool. Care has been taken by the trainers to be certain that the richer women do not overpower the others, but to date it appears that poor women have been more likely to emerge as leaders who go on to organize new groups in the community (Jobunnesse Lily, 1989).

Education Center for Community Organizing/Women Organizers' Collective – *New York, New York, USA*

ECCO, the Educational Center for Community Organizing, is located at Hunter College School of Social Work of the City University of New York in the United States. The organization was founded in 1982 (1) to strengthen the effectiveness of organizers in neighborhoods, human service agencies, and the workplace; (2) to enhance the knowledge and skill of organizers through the provision of workshops, seminars, conferences, and training; (3) to raise timely issues of concern to those engaged in progressive social change; and (4) to promote communication and networking by providing a place for the exchange of ideas, information and experiences. The steering committee of ECCO is comprised of community and labor organizers, human service workers, students and faculty. While some of their activities have been for both women and men, the Women Organizers' Collective will be the focus of this discussion.

The Women Organizers' Collective is concerned with the urgent need to develop female leadership on behalf of women in poverty. They have based their project on the fact that women are rarely taught to be leaders, and that often the role is in conflict with the expected female image. Sexism, racism, classism, ageism, and homophobia also inhibit women's potential leadership, even though they are often the mainstays of organizations in which they are involved. Moreover, criticism and isolation are often very real experiences when women find the courage to step into the leadership role.

Ecco's Feminist Organizing Principles

Value Base: Feminist organizing is based on belief in the dignity and strength of the individual and respect for life; belief in the individual and collective human capacity to grow and to change; the interconnectedness of problems and solutions; the distinct perspective, experiences and histories of women based on their functions and socially defined roles; cooperation rather than competition; belief in the interdependence of people and their need to seek mutuality and community; and acceptance of different ways of thinking and knowing.

Goals: Transforming society to a democratic, egalitarian structure through the reduction of class, status, and power differentials; meeting human needs through resource recovery and development; eliminating racism; building community (cooperative economic, social, and political arrangements); eliminating sexism; recognizing and respecting diversity and differences (of color, class, sexual preference, and ethnicity).

Methods, Approaches, Strategies and Tactics

Community involvement: Validating resident's, consumers, and/or constituencies' reality, knowledge of "community," and women's abilities to plan for themselves; identifying risks as well as benefits of participation; recognizing recipients', residents', and members' vulnerability, and facilitating informed choice; recognizing differential abilities and willingness to commit time and facilitate varying degrees of involvement.

Emphasis on collective problem-solving: Assessing and building upon strengths, personal natural informal networks and relationships; demystifying planning and organizing processes; and respecting and utilizing different kinds of expertise.

Emphasis on process as part of the product (goal): Building in social and emotional supports; recognizing different types, levels, and styles of leadership; creating opportunities for leadership and skills development; struggling between vision of the organizer and the group's vision; struggling against potential group dependency on the organizer, and the possibility of rejection and hostility towards her at different points in time; acting with people, rather than doing to or for them; building in the time to work issues and difference through, and making it a priority; creating a safe environment; and recognizing complex needs, functions, and responsibilities of many women (for example, recognizing women's connections to family and neighborhood, and planning meeting space, time, and agendas accordingly.)

Utilizing consciousness-raising: Naming feelings of self and others; building confidence and self-respect; identifying how women have been kept out, isolated from others, and separated from their inner voice.

Emphasis on consensus, cooperation, collaboration, and coalition-building: Assuming the principle of least contest; anticipating conflict and working towards a conflict-resolution model (willingness and skill in bargaining, negotiating, and compromising); assuming common cause and common social reality on the part of the participants and/or workers in a system; and assuming power is not a limited or fixed quantity, but is mutable through collective action.

Emphasis on unity and wholeness: Minimizing compartmentalization and segmentation of functions and roles; recognizing difficulties in splitting the public and private self and arenas; minimizing dichotomization or polarization, seeking continuity and making connections.

Emphasis on a collective, shared problem-solving approach: Recognizing that there are multiple definitions of the problem; recognizing that the definitions of the problem shapes the solution; recognizing that there is no such thing as objective, value-free planning, yet there is need to be logical, systematic and consistent; recognizing that tension between meeting survival and immediate individual and group needs and organizing for structural basic, comprehensive social change.

Emphasis on the use of praxis: Building in mechanisms for developmental feedback, evaluation, criticism and self-criticism; and building in mechanisms for evaluation of theories, approaches, strategies, and tactics (Terry Mizrahi *et al.*, 1989).

Lesbian Collective/Collectiva M.U.L.A. – *Mexico City, Mexico*

The Collectiva Mujeres Unidas por Lesbianismo Autonomo (M.U.L.A.) grew out of the lesbian movement in Mexico which dates back to 1971. The Collective is made up of professional women, most of whom were previous members of feminist groups, and some of whom are lesbian mothers and/or sexual educators. They work primarily with lesbians or in coordinated workshops with heterosexual feminists. A few of the members participated in the First Gathering of Latin American and Caribbean Lesbian Feminists which was held in Geneva, Switzerland in 1986. M.U.L.A.'s Lesbian Identity and Sexuality Workshops are two examples of their activities. The following description is in the words of Lourdes, one of the workshop leaders:

Lesbian Identity and Sexuality Workshops

Initial Purposes: At first, we were mainly concerned with creating a space from where we could discover and analyze ourselves and find out the common things that identify us. What do lesbians have to say to each other? What do we have to say to the world? We wanted to provide a space for the work of history's renegade women whose words have been silenced, their lives invisible to the eyes of most people. We wanted to propose a mutual process for the interchange of personal experiences, to analyze our everyday lives (emotional, sexual, and work) where what is personal becomes political and what is political becomes personal – the encounter, the description and discovery of an identity that we had to construct together.

The goals of both workshops include analyzing and reflecting on the sexual-political condition of lesbians as women and as lesbians; seeking our identity in the critical exploration of our daily lives; and finding together some alternatives to live [our lives more fully]. We consider what our daily lives are like in relation to our development and experience as lesbians who function outside of what is socially established. Some of the topics we considered were: Who are we? How do we see ourselves? How do others see us? If we have been invisible in history, we have been in more than one way invisible to ourselves. That which is not named does not exist. We wanted to begin to whisper our existence.

PART II

TRAFFIC AND PROSTITUTION OF WOMEN

Upon these women we have no right to turn our backs . . .   They
have been created by the very injustice against which we protest.
Carrie Chapman Catt, "Is Woman Suffrage Progressing?"
Stockholm, 1911

A systematic study, mandated by the United Nations as a result of feminist
initiated pressure, reveals that prostitution, like slavery, has an economic
base. It has become a multi-national sex industry. The special rapporteur
who was assigned to the investigation reported:

> While being a cultural phenomenon rooted in the masculine and femi-
> nine images given currency by society, it is a market and indeed a very
> lucrative one. The merchandise involves men's pleasure, or their image
> of pleasure. This merchandise is unfortunately supplied by physical
> intimacy with women or children. (United Nations, 1983, para 18)

Traditional patriarchal ideology universally demands that women should
not allow more than one man to have access to their bodies. Women who
cannot fulfill the requirement have low self-esteem and often feel worthless
after having lost their virginity to lovers or husbands who abandon them.
Their bodies, already considered worthless, are then transformed into
instruments to earn a living. This form of degradation makes it possible
for them to become more independent than they would be otherwise.
The reality is that economic exploitation goes hand in hand with sexual
exploitation (Skrobanek, 1983).

At the *Global Feminist Workshop to Organize Against Traffic in Women*,
held in Rotterdam, The Netherlands in 1983, participants concluded that
sexual violence in all its forms (pornography, incest, rape, battering, sexual
mutilation, and torture) are all related to prostitution and trafficking. At
the core is the objectification, manipulation, exploitation, and control of
female sexuality. Traditional customs and female dependency, particularly
economic dependency, often contribute to the vulnerability of women to
sexual abuse. The facts ring true throughout the world. Violence against
women is inherently connected to the male-female power relationships
that exist in patriarchal societies, engendering fear and psychological and

emotional dependency. (The group's strategies to combat trafficking and prostitution are detailed in the *Person-Environment Programs: Traffic and Prostitution* section of this chapter.)

Though the workshop participants urge that prostitutes themselves should not be blamed for their behavior, they point out that viewing prostitution as a woman's choice reduces all women to contemptibility in any male dominated society. Free choice is a specious claim when one recognizes that most young girls and women in prostitution have been victims of prior sexual abuse, particularly incest. Further, the majority of these women have turned to prostitution as a result of extreme poverty, with no other choice, given the low wages of women in all unskilled fields (Barry, 1984; Bunch, 1984).

The Children's Rights Protection Centre of Thailand estimates that two million Thai women, including 800,000 children under sixteen are in prostitution in that country alone. Women's organizations throughout the world report that young rural women are often enticed by procurers to go to urban areas to obtain "good jobs" which turn out to be in the flesh trade. Many other girls are knowingly sold to sex tourism procurers by their parents. Sales are motivated by money and benefits. The rural poor are tempted by the "luxuries" of the good life they cannot afford, luxuries that bring them social status in the eyes of their neighbors. The money sent home by their daughters in the cities buy their parents television sets and cars, but leave these young women in perpetual poverty. They become slaves to prostitution as they mount new debts. To compound the tragedy, their status as decent women is lost forever to their families, despite their service to them.

In Thailand's Pattaya, a center of sex tourism, even girls who have not reached puberty are forced to dance naked before tourists and locals alike, their bodies offered as an "exotic experience" to any man who pays the fee. There is a general acceptance among officials of child, as well as adult, prostitution. The government has been reluctant to accept the fact that trafficking is ruining their tourism business, as people begin identifying their country with the sex industry rather than with its inherent beauty (Bangkok Post Editorial, January 17, 1989, 6). The story is not limited to one nation or region; the sex tourism and trafficking industry has global dimensions.

Kathleen Barry (1984) warns that "Severing child from adult female prostitution has been part of the tradition of silence which has cloaked female sexual slavery in invisibility" (24). Acts which are degrading and humiliating are violations of the human being, regardless of her age, culture, race, or situation. While the physical and psychological effects of such sexual exploitation on the young are likely to be more severe and must be condemned, relativity should not obviate the human rights of adult women.

Anti-Discrimination Policy Analysis: Traffic and Prostitution

Article 6: Traffic and Prostitution of Women
Article 6 requires states to take measures to suppress all forms of traffic in women and exploitation of prostitution of women (Convention, 1980).

Pertinent Questions for Analysis: Traffic and Prostitution – *IWRAW, 1988*

- What is the prevailing social attitude towards prostitution?
- What are the laws on traffic in women and exploitation of prostitution?
- If prostitution is legal, how are prostitutes and their clients treated under the law? Are prostitutes licensed or regulated in any way? What laws, if any, are there concerning child prostitution?
- If prostitution is illegal, is the law enforced? Is it enforced only against women or against men as well?
- Is the selling of sexual services by a third person illegal? Is it illegal to sell women to other countries to be prostitutes? If yes, how are these laws enforced?
- What obstacles are there to eliminating the exploitation of prostitution and traffic in women?

Forward-Looking Strategies: Traffic and Prostitution (1985): Violence Against Women

Effective measures should be taken by governments to identify, prevent, and eliminate all violence, including family violence against women and children. But government responsibility is not sufficient. Community resources should be mobilized to make women and children aware that maltreatment is a curable phenomenon, as well as an assault to their physical and moral integrity. (Too often, those who have been subjected to years of violence believe it to be a incontrovertible fact of life. Some even think it is a sign of caring, having experienced minimal attention in other forms.) As an urgent and protective measure, they must be taught that they have the right and duty to fight against it, whether they are victims or witnesses. Long-term supportive mechanisms should be set in motion to aid and guide maltreated people, whatever one's sex or age, as well as those who maltreat them.

Criminology training should include special attention to the particular situation of women as victims of violent crimes. The violation of women's body's and the serious physical and psychological damage that results is one of those crimes. In every nation, legislation should be passed and laws enforced to end sex-related crimes of degradation to women. Law enforcement and other authorities should be given guidance concerning the need to deal sensitively to survivors of such crimes.

The rising tide of violence, drug abuse, and crime related to prostitution must be stemmed at all levels by strict enforcement provisions. Increased and coordinated efforts by police agencies internationally are essential to combatting the complex and serious problems of exploitation and violence that are associated with prostitution. Many countries have signed the United Nations *Convention for the Suppression of the Traffic in Persons and of the Exploitation of the Prostitution of Others*. The provisions dealing with the exploitation of women as prostitutes should be implemented by those parties. Such international measures should be given urgent consideration. Without global cooperation, world scale prostitution will continue. On the individual level, attention must be given to resources for prevention and assistance in the personal, social, and professional reintegration of prostitutes, focusing on economic opportunities. Training, employment, self-employment, and health facilities for women and their children should be included if it is to be viable. The cooperation of governments and non-governmental organizations will create wider employment opportunities.

Vulnerability to Prostitution

Forced prostitution, a form of slavery imposed on women by procurers, is a result of economic degradation. Even in the best of times, women are dependent upon men. Processes of rapid urbanization and migration, resulting in further underemployment and unemployment, compounds their condition and sometimes leads to prostitution.

More difficult to combat are the social and political pressures that produce refugees and missing persons which often include vulnerable groups of women who are victimized by procurers.

PERSON-ENVIRONMENT PROGRAM MODELS: TRAFFIC AND PROSTITUTION

Foundation for Women/Women's Information Center – *Bangkok, Thailand*

The Foundation for Women has focused for years on women and children trafficking and domestic violence. The membership works at all levels of society, serving the general public, professionals, and the government. The Foundation cooperates with lawyers who are supportive of women and require accurate knowledge upon which to base their claims. The members conduct qualitative social action research which they disseminate through professional and governmental reports, as well as posters and bus advertisements targeted to the public sector. Training models are designed for health centers and social workers, and handbooks are written for women-at-large. With government support, a beautifully illustrated book has been written and distributed to faculty and students in 400 schools throughout nine regions in the north of Thailand. Young women are provided straight-forward information about the sex industry that may counter their decisions to leave their rural homes to earn money in urban Bangkok. The literature also is designed to influence poor and middle class families who are tempted to sell their daughters to the sex industry in urban areas in exchange for commodities.

The Foundation recognizes that personal conscientization is as important as the government's awareness of the issues and development of new policies. They work with trade union women workers to raise their consciousness about their self-worth, attending meetings,and conducting weekend workshops. The training center evaluates, tests, and modifies materials each time they are utilized. Teaching modules for two-day sessions are developed for factory rural and urban women and youth. All of their work is interdisciplinary, a perspective that the foundation finds essential to the advancement of women. They emphasize that addressing poverty, violence against women, sexual exploitation, and family planning issues, for example, in the absence of socio-economic and other political factors is not only futile, but destructive to women. Theories and interventions must be congruent with such analyses.

The Whistle Blowers

"The Whistle Blowers" is presented as a role play to raise women's awareness of their problems regarding wife abuse, to show that these problems are common to many women, and to develop an awareness of the potential of women to act. Several whistles are needed.

The Whistle Blower technique is successfully utilized by women in Peru and other countries in Latin America, Southeast Asia, and Africa. As a role play, it is one of the methods of helping women to become aware that their problems are the product of destructive social values, that battering of a woman is not just a "personal" problem. It is the natural outcome of a universal viewpoint that women are the natural property of men. When women become aware of this, they find solutions together. Collective action and the formation of groups are necessary in working to solve women's problems.

Role Play

Women in a poor neighborhood in Lima, Peru were active in a community group. One of the issues they discussed frequently was the problem of wife-battering. Many of the women were victims of their husbands' violence. Neither the police, nor any other agency, was effective in stopping men from battering women. The women decided that one possible way of stopping the battering was to expose to public embarrassment the men who were beating their wives. They developed the following strategy: All of the women bought whistles. If one woman's husband started to beat her, she would get her whistle and blow it. If she could not get to the whistle, but another woman heard the battering taking place, she would blow her whistle. In any case, when one whistle was blown, all of the other women would come out of their houses and start blowing their whistles. They would all walk to the house where the battering was taking place and stand outside blowing their whistles, thus alerting the entire community and embarrassing the abusive man.

Issues for Discussion
- Is being battered just a personal problem of each woman?
- What are the causes of wife battering?
- What steps do the women take to solve their problems in the story?
- How could the above method be used in solving other women's problems? (Siriporn Skrobanek, 1989)

(See Chapter 9 for further discussion of the Whistle Blowers and violence against women.)

Program for Adolescent Punk Girls – *Mexico City, Mexico*

In Mexico City, a woman called Lourdes is working with heterosexual teenage girls in the punk movement. They have been violated by gangs who have introduced them to drugs. Pregnancy is common, and the boys who are the fathers desert the girls when they learn of it. The young women have become aware that they are being sexually oppressed by the gangs, and are expressing themselves through political street and indoor theater. Abortion and violation have been subjects of the plays that they write and perform. Also composing their own songs, such as "I Feel Humiliated," the girls are putting an end to their masochism. As each develops a personal sense of identity for the first time, rather than living vicariously through the identities of the boys, their health, self-esteem, and feminine sexuality has a chance to develop and flourish (Lourdes, 1989).

Global Feminist Workshop/Organizing Against Traffic in Women – *Rotterdam, The Netherlands*

Under the leadership of Charlotte Bunch, Kathleen Barry, and Shirley Castley, comprehensive strategies for action were developed at the *Global Feminist Workshop to Organize Against Trafficking in Women*, held in The Netherlands in 1983. The network of participating women considered the ways in which identified issues are connected to the treatment of women in all areas, to cultural attitudes towards female sexuality, and to oppression, whether related to class, race, militarism, or neo-colonialism. Three major areas were identified: (1) Violence and Sexuality; (2) Institutionalization of Female Sexual Slavery; and (3) Legislation and Prostitution. Their strategies for action are summarized below within each category.

Violence and Sexuality

In order to devise a common strategy to eradicate female sexual slavery, it is important that women throughout the world recognize that patriarchal oppression is experienced by all women. To that end, the different forms of violence against women and their relationship to female sexual slavery must be made more visible in all countries, facts that are frequently kept hidden. Different tactics must be used to raise issues often deemed "undiscussible." For example, if in a particular country the discussion of a certain form of sexual violence or other demeaning sex-related behavior is taboo, a woman in that country might disseminate the information to a neighboring country, thus opening possible avenues for discussion in her homeland.

In order to reach people with information and methods to combat sexual slavery, resources of other local and regional groups and organizations must be utilized. For example, working with immigrant women who could provide information about the situations of women in the countries they had to leave provides an important alternative resource. Immigrant women also can become channels of information back to their countries of origin concerning the exploitation and violence against women.

Training centers in non-traditional fields should be established for women who are prostitutes, or at risk of becoming one. Shelters should be created as intermediate havens for prostitutes in order to provide them with protection from pimps and other practical services. Governments and other groups should be pressured to support such centers and to help ensure employment following job training.

Non-sexist, coeducational education should be available from primary school on for all people; the content of textbooks, especially in regard to attitudes towards women and girls must be revised. Throughout the world, women's groups should establish communication with parent associations and teachers regarding these issues.

Through contact with women in the media, strategies for using it to expose violence against women and its prevention can be devised. The global network of women could coordinate campaigns on specific issues of violence and female sexual slavery on an international scale. Organization of the network, however, should be congruent with the specific conditions of each region and country. International and National Days Against All Forms of Violence Against Women could be adopted, thus creating a greater sense of solidarity among women globally. (This strategy has been utilized successfully in Latin America on November 25th for several years. It is the date commemorating the death of three sisters from the Dominican Republic who were raped, tortured, and murdered during the Trujillo regime. The group invites others to consider joining them in recognizing this date, or selecting one appropriate to their region if they prefer.)

Institutionalization of Female Sexual Slavery

The political right of women to determine the nature and extent of their sexual activity should be internationally recognized. Those who seek to escape from enslavement or sexual violence should be considered a political refugee with commensurate protection and asylum; and a woman's right to self-defense, too often denied, should be honored.

The international trafficking of women in the sex industry, the procurement practices (such as deceptive advertising for employment and phony marriages), and the exploitation of women in particularly vulnerable situations (such as migrants, refugees and displaced persons) should be investigated and exposed. Human rights and church groups should be enlisted to assist in this exposure of transnational institutions which invest in trafficking directly and which control development options in developing countries.

The creation of alternative plans for the development of national economies that do not exploit women's bodies should be demanded, challenging the national interests which profit off sexual exploitation. Public education campaigns should be conducted concerning these practices. Again, media and dialogue groups can be utilized. Lists of sympathetic media and those who exploit sexual topics can be shared with network women, as well as media guidelines about who to debate and under what circumstances it should be done.

It is extremely important to create domestic and international awareness of the connections between sexual enslavement, violence, militarism, and the torture of women. Peace, labor, and political groups particularly should be made aware of the situation in jails. Women who are incarcerated as political or regular prisoners, by police or terrorist forces, as prostitutes controlled by pimps or brothel keepers, in refugee camps or hamlets, in military or war settings, and on the job as workers and union organizers, are all at risk.

Direct action must be taken with the sex industry at points of contact, such as airport demonstrations where tours leave or at travel agencies; picketing and harassing agencies and individuals who are involved; and campaigning against and removing racist and sexist advertisements, posters, and publications.

Legislation and Prostitution

The existing legal system regarding prostitution, in particular, and women in general, should be studied in each country in order to compile a complete picture of the legal situation regarding prostitution and female sexual slavery on a national and global level. The abolition of discrimination against women should be sought in all laws dealing with employment, education and other areas of life, including legislation developed to guarantee women equal rights in marriage and divorce laws.

The decriminalization of prostitution and the strengthening of laws that oppose the enslavement of women by pimps should be worked for, together with the prosecution of those involved in all forms of trafficking of women. Efforts to combat police harassment and other discriminatory measures against women in prostitution should be initiated and supported, as should efforts that promote the prosecution of violent crimes against women in prostitution.

Refuge centers and supportive services should be provided, aimed at assisting women to escape or leave prostitution. There must be cooperation with organizations which are committed to addressing these issues from a feminist-oriented perspective compatible with the network's position.

Permanent relationships should be established with international governmental and non-governmental organizations which deal with the problems of prostitution, trafficking of women and children, and female sexual slavery, and the necessary information and consulting services should be provided to nations that are requesting such services, seeking to make improvements in their legislation and services related to prostitution and violence against women. Investigation in international trafficking of women, sex tourism and the like should be promoted (Charlotte Bunch in Kathleen Barry, Charlotte Bunch, and Shirley Castley, Eds, 1984).

4 The Politics of Oppression and Action

> Women's rights, men's rights – human rights – all are threatened by the ever-present spectre of war so destructive now of human material and moral values as to render victory indistinguishable from defeat.
>
> Rosika Schwimmer, Speech, Centennial Celebration of Seneca Falls Convention of Women's Rights, 1948

GLOBAL AGENDA SETTING

The problems of women will not become visible if they are not sustained over time on local and national agendas. But women's issues will continue to be fragmented as individual, local, and single issues if an international human rights perspective is not added to the political agenda. Separation of local and global politics on behalf of women is possible only in a geographical sense. In large measure, the essence of the political agenda is astonishingly similar; only the details differ with the locality. Agenda setting is the means by which issues are selected and adopted for governmental consideration and solution.

The process can be approached from an economic or issue-oriented perspective; or it can be undertaken as an organizational decision-making process, coupled with intensive media involvement, and pressure on legislative bodies. When issues are noncontroversial, engendering a universal response, it is generally because they are conceptualized as related to individual deviance, require relatively inexpensive, incremental remedies, and sustain an unchanged power structure. Since politicians are becoming aware of the social and economic antecedents to the problems of women, controversy is becoming strong. It is only under such conditions, however, that support can be found for more comprehensive, structural social change.

The response of governments and the media to the United Nations Decade for Women provides an excellent example of the evolution of political response. At the start of the Decade, the United States, for example, was openly supportive, declaring an International Women's

Year of its own in 1977, at which time state and national conferences were instituted. The massive response of women in the U.S. caught officials off guard. While feigning support, the dozens of recommendations agreed upon by the nation's women in Houston, Texas have been relegated since to file cabinets. The global UN conferences have not fared any better.

When political decisions are being considered, politicians need to be tested against the facts. The testing must be factual, logical, and clear. Since the facts about women have been skewed and denied for so long that intelligent people are ignorant of them, the decision to become informed must be an ethical choice in the service of humanity. This is a challenge particularly well-suited to the mission and responsibilities of social workers throughout the world.

To ensure social change, once facts are gathered, they must be repetitively stated, visible in mass media, and in behind-the-scenes lobbying efforts. Goal and strategy setting, coalition-building, face-to-face lobbying, letter writing, and verbal and written expert testimony are action tools that are fundamental to the political influence process (Haynes and Michelson, 1986).

PART I

Anti-Discrimination Policy Analysis: Political Activities

Article 7: Political and Public Life
Article 7 requires governments to take all appropriate measures to eliminate discrimination against women in politics or political life (Convention, 1980).

Pertinent Questions for Analysis: Political Activities (IWRAW, 1988)

- Do women have the right to vote in all elections on equal terms with men? If so, what percentage of women vote as compared to men?
- Are there any property or literacy or other requirements for voting? If so, do these requirements eliminate women or have a greater effect on women's ability to vote than on men's?
- Are women eligible to be candidates for elected positions on the same terms as men? What percentage of candidates are women?
- List the high public offices and political positions held by women. Include both appointed and elected positions.

- Do women have the same right as men to participate in political parties, in non-governmental organizations and associations concerned with the public and political life of the country? Do they participate in fact?
- What are the obstacles to women's full participation in political and public life?
- What measures have been taken to ensure that women participate in the design and implementation of development planning at all levels?
- Are women discriminated against or subject to human rights violations because of their political activities as member of women's organizations? If yes, please give details.
- Are women political prisoners or detainees subject to sexual abuse? If yes, please document.

Forward-Looking Strategies: Political Activities (1985)

Political Will and Unity
The promotion of effective participation by women in the development of their countries continues to be retarded by a lack of political will and commitment. This is being recognized in the developing world, but it is just as serious in countries that consider themselves developed, yet effectively absent women. Because women throughout the world are excluded from policy and decision-making activities, it is difficult for them and their organizations to incorporate into their preferences and interests the largely male-dominated choices of progress and development. What is more, the issues of women in development are often viewed as welfare problems, a cost to society, rather than a contribution. Consequently, they have received low priority, and the formulation of targets, programs, and projects concerning women have received little attention. Too often, women are told to await the attainment of their country's development, a trickle-down ideology proven to be inadequate. Rather than being instrumental to development, such policies cause parallel weakness in the institutional, technical, and material resources devoted to the promotion of activities geared to women's effective participation. Such policies must be reversed.

Political will is needed to promote development so that strategies for the advancement of women seek before all else to alter the present unequal conditions and structures. Without that will, women will continue to be defined as secondary and given low priority. To move development to another plane, their pivotal role in society must be recognized and given its true value. Only then will they be allowed to assume their legitimate and core positions in the promotion of change and development. Unless major measures are taken, there is no doubt that numerous obstacles will continue to retard the participation of women in political life, in the formulation of policies that affect them, and in the formulation of national women's policies.

Whether or not women succeed will depend largely upon whether or not they unite to help one another change their poor material circumstances and secondary status. Unless they unite, they will not have the time, energy, and collective experience required to participate politically. They must help each other to exercise their right to vote, to be elected, and to participate in the political process on equal terms with men and at all levels.

Awareness of the political rights of women should be promoted through many channels . . . among them education, both formal and informal, political education, non-governmental organizations, trade unions, the media, and business organizations. A deliberate effort should be made by political parties and other organizations, including trade unions, to increase and improve women's participation within their ranks. Measures regarding the selection of candidates should be instituted to activate women's constitutional and legal guarantees of the right to be elected and appointed. They should be given equal access to organizations' political machinery and to resources and tools needed to develop skills in the art and tactics of practical politics, in addition to effective leadership capabilities. Those women who are already in positions of leadership have a special responsibility to assist them.

Women's Rights and Peace

The full and effective promotion of women's rights can best be realized when there is international peace and security. Rhetoric aside, this can only occur when there is respect for the legitimate rights of all among nations great and small, and when there is respect for independence, sovereignty, territorial integrity, and the right to live in peace within one's own borders. As with all freedoms, such self-determination must be coupled with respect for the human rights and dignity of all its members, including women. Preventive measures must be taken to reduce the use or threat of force, aggression, military occupation, and interference in the internal affairs of others. [Autonomy of nations, however, does not imply permission for them to infringe on the human rights of women.] The elimination of domination, discrimination, oppression, and exploitation of women is the first step in countering the destructive dynamics between nations.

Because of their gender, women experience discrimination reflected in denial of equal access to the power structure, a structure that both controls society and determines issues regarding development and peace initiatives. In most countries, additional differences such as race, color, ethnicity [and class] may have even more serious implications, since such characteristics are used as further justification to compound discrimination, justify poverty and deny peace.

Peace, so often conceptualized as the absence of war, hostilities and violence, must also include the enjoyment of economic and social justice, equality, and the entire range of human rights and fundamental freedoms. Sexual inequality obviates the possibility of peace, as does economic inequality, the deliberate exploitation of large sectors of the population, unequal development of countries, and exploitative economic relations. Without peace and stability there can be no development, for they are interrelated and mutually reinforcing.

The direct participation of women in peace efforts has always been limited. Their work goes unnoticed, even when they have been involved overtly, such as in the struggle to eradicate colonialism, neo-colonialism, imperialism, [communism marred by dictators], totalitarianism (including fascism and similar ideologies), alien occupation, foreign domination, aggression, racial discrimination, apartheid, and other violations of human rights. The mutual support and encouragement of women, therefore, is essential as they develop initiatives and action relating to either universal issues, or specific conflict resolution between or within their own countries.

PART II

Anti-Discrimination Policy Analysis: International Participation

Article 8: International Representation and Participation
Article 8 states that women should have equal opportunity to serve as representatives of their country and as participants in the work of international organizations (Convention, 1989).

Pertinent Questions for Analysis: International Participation (IWRAW, 1988)

- Do women have the right and the opportunity to represent the government on an international level and to participate in the work of international organizations?

- What percentage of ambassadors are women? What percentage of other representatives to foreign governments or international organizations are women? Where do they serve?
- Are there instances where women, because of their gender, have been denied their opportunity to represent the country or to participate in the work of international organizations? Please describe.

Forward-Looking Strategies: International Participation (1985)

While national activities regarding women can be limited to domestic concerns alone, more often there is an interactional national and international impact on causes and solutions. Although nations speak metaphorically of three or four worlds, and the world of poor women was accurately labeled an "invisible fifth world" by Elise Boulding in 1980, in reality there can be only one world, that in which we all live. Most people have become aware that the world has become a global neighborhood, its people and institutions increasingly interdependent and involved with one another. The inability to wall off poison air and contaminated water, to contain transmittable diseases, and the very real possibility that a single nation could destroy the world, have made all nations aware that they either have a common security or none at all. For the first time in the late 1980s, the United Nations began to work as it was envisioned from the start. International peace, which lies at the heart of women's human rights, may not be a utopian dream after all. Still, 117 wars still raged throughout the world in the early 1990's, wars in which even more civilian women and children are killed, tortured and maimed than are men in combat. They were all civil wars from the perspective of the aggressors, yet embroiled many of the nations of the world. The existence or absence of peace directly affects the advancement of women. The continuation of widespread international tensions diverts policy makers from development to the military. This is true, regardless of the global segment in question, and regardless of whether the threat is nuclear catastrophe or localized conventional warfare. In either case, the improvement of humanity is on hold for the duration.

Economics

If current trends continue, the prospects for low-income and the least developed countries is grim. In order to redress imbalances that are predicted to be even greater than in previous decades, policies should be reoriented and reinforced to promote world trade, in particular, market access for the exports of developing countries. Other non-inflationary growth-enhancing policies, such as the lowering of interest rates, should be pursued as well. Coercive measures of an economic, political or other nature which are adopted by certain developed countries should be stopped. (To their credit, debt forgiveness, once a radical idea, is being recognized as a reasonable policy. Given the extreme conditions prevalent in the developing world, it should be offered to them on a priority basis.)

The objectives of the Decade – equality, development and peace – are inseparable and interdependent. Each goal must be integrated in economic, political, social and cultural development in every country of the world. When identifying the foremost obstacles to women's advancement, different socio-economic and cultural conditions should be taken into account. Programs designed to deal with the current economic situation within the world monetary and financial systems should not adversely affect women who are disproportionately represented among the most vulnerable segments of society. Regional and international technical cooperation among developing countries should be extended and strengthened to promote the effective participation of women in development.

PART III

Anti-Discrimination Policy Analysis: National Participation

Article 9: Nationality
Article 9 grants women equal rights with men to acquire, change or retain their nationality (Convention, 1980).

Pertinent Questions for Analysis: Gender-Specific Rights (IWRAW, 1988)

- Do women have equal rights with men to acquire, change or retain their nationality? What social, cultural or economic factors affect a woman's exercise of these rights?
- Does marriage to a non-citizen or a change of nationality by the husband affect a woman's nationality in any way?
- Is a person's citizenship determined by birth, by parentage, by marriage, or by some combination of these factors? If citizenship is determined by parentage, does a mother's citizenship carry equal weight with that of the father?
- Can minor children travel on their mother's passport or only their

father's? Is the father's consent required to name children on their mother's passport or to leave the country with them?

• Can a woman obtain a passport or travel without her husband's permission?

Forward-Looking Strategies: National Participation (1985)

Efforts should be congruent with the specific problems of diverse categories of women in different regions and countries. Everyone should be made aware that development prospects will be improved and society advanced through the full and effective participation of women. This includes the right to dissent publicly and peacefully from their government's policies. Such rights are presently denied women in many countries, while in others women are simply derided when they protest. Whatever the form discrimination takes, it is unacceptable.

As economic conditions have deteriorated nation by nation, the progress of women accrued in the Decade has deteriorated with them. Not only has equal participation of women slowed, but in some cases, benefits to women are not commensurate with their increased participation. The fact that mass poverty constitutes a major obstacle for women in the least developed countries comes as no surprise. But the fact that it is women who are at highest risk of poverty in more developed nations comes as a shock to some. In the United States, for example, the government itself predicts that elderly and young women will comprise the total poverty population by the turn of the 21st century. Because women everywhere are marginalized, those belonging to the lowest socio-economic strata are likely to be the poorest of the poor. They should be given priority; women are an essential productive force in all economies. It is important in times of economic recession that programs and measures designed to raise the status of women not be relaxed, but intensified. [To perpetuate poverty among women and their children in order to ensure corporate profits is a reality that must be revealed and rejected in the interest of human rights.]

Government machinery for monitoring and improving the status of women should be established where lacking at high levels, receiving adequate resources, commitment, and authority to advise on the impact of all government policies on women. Interestingly, the older the constitution, the less likely it is that such departments exist. The newer constitutions are more likely to include women's rights, thanks to the efforts of activists. Such legislation can play a vital role in the dissemination of information to women on their rights and entitlements, through collaborative action with governmental departments and agencies, and with non-governmental organizations and indigenous women's groups. These special offices preferably should be headed by a woman [who is pro-women], charged with monitoring and accelerating the process of equitable representation.

The right to take part in national and international decision-making processes includes the right to dissent publicly and peacefully from their government's policies, as well as having equal input into the formulation of more equitable policies. At the national level, the review and appraisal of obstacles encountered and progress achieved in the realization of the goals of the Decade identifies some hard truths. As economic conditions deteriorated throughout the world, by the mid-1980's women's initial progress deteriorated with them.

Nationalism

Too often, nationalism emphasizes national security, unity, and stability based on the preservation of existing structures, and in opposition to constructive change. The suppression of human rights on a small scale, as well as mass action, is justified wrongfully on the same grounds (Takenaka, 1988). This is particularly likely to be manifested in reaction to social change on behalf of women. In the early 1990s, as communism's authoritarian control in the East gave way to democracy, capitalism and nationalism, the new found vision of freedom was marred by the steady retrenchment of women's rights. Not only were their few gains eroded, but the ideal of equality for women was increasingly viewed by men in power as a destructive legacy of the old regime. The women's movement was recast as the enemy of democracy. "Double speak" is clearly not relegated to a single ideology. (PART III, consistent with the *Convention on the Elimination of All Forms of Discrimination Against Women* format, is concerned with women's basic right to acquire and retain national citizenship. Other national participation issues will be addressed in subsequent sections of this chapter.)

PERSON-ENVIRONMENT PROGRAM MODELS: POLITICS OF OF OPPRESSION AND ACTION

The Ford Foundation – *Dhaka, Bangladesh*

The Ford Foundation, centrally headquartered in New York City in the United States, is influencing funding policies worldwide by making their granting policies consistent with progress toward diversity and equity. Not only did they double their original appropriation for women's programming in 1980, but their guidelines for prospective grantees assess the nature of their commitment to pluralism and equal opportunity by an evaluation of diversity and equity in its programs, governance, and staffing. Any special characteristics of the environment in which the prospective grantee works that either favorably or adversely affect progress toward the goals of the Foundation are considered. This may encompass the demography of the field or region, the state of the economy and its social consequences, educational requirements and opportunities, and regulatory or contractual obligations. Gender statistics and, when known, patterns of change in recent years are collected on white males and females, and men and women of color. When appropriate, data are requested concerning ethnicity, race, and national origin (Ford Foundation, 1987). By so doing, Ford is influencing governmental and organizational structure and policies throughout the world.

Their work in Dhaka, Bangladesh, the world's second poorest nation, provides an excellent example. Although ninety percent of Bangladesh's income is from foreign countries, in 1988 less than ten percent was given to women's projects, and ten percent of that figure targeted population control. Less than a fourth of the ten percent total went toward skill-training for women. Ford's staff points out that the rhetoric had changed due to the Decade of Women, but the dollars have not. Their influence in Bangladesh is impressive, as they have underwritten most of the quality programs for women's personal and social development at some point in recent history. In some instances, they are allocating lump sums to women's programs, rather than requiring approval of line item funding. Provided the larger goal of equity and diversity is adhered to, the women's agenda is negotiated internally, with the funding agency no longer the authority on specific content. The process facilitates personal and social development, and makes the Ford Foundation's commitment to women's self-direction and responsibility consistent with its policies. Women who are sponsoring the programs are given control, as are the women participating in them (Susan Davis, 1989).

INSTRAW – *Santo Domingo, Dominican Republic*

INSTRAW (International Research and Training Institute for the Advancement of Women) is the United Nations research and research-training arm for women in development efforts. INSTRAW has found networking to be cost effective, as well as mutually supportive and enriching. They suggest, however, that objectives should be professionally formulated, based on sound knowledge of mainstream practices, never losing sight of the changes that women want to introduce. To that end, the organization advocates the following ten principles of networking:

1. *Formation of broad functional coalitions around well-defined tasks:* Coalitions should encompass mainstream organizations and their decision-makers, development officials, academic institutions, professional associations, and any other bodies that can contribute to developmental changes for women's benefit;

2. *Continuous and consistent advocacy and reporting to the mainstream:* This is a never-ending task that must be done to gain allies in influential places;

3. *Wide dissemination of results of research achieved at the grass-roots level:* Information flows must not be sporadic or limited. Communication must be based on systematic exchanges through well-designed information networks;

4. *Establishment of new criteria for network management:* This is a complex, difficult task because it requires decentralized programming of a highly participatory nature. In order to secure the linkages necessary to incorporate women's issues and participation at the micro and macro levels of the economy, some traditional methods should be adapted or adopted as well; for example, linear programming, critical path and input-output analyses;

5. *Intensification of training of all participants about women and development issues:* Training and consciousness-raising must encompass men and women who are responsible for passing and implementing developmental decisions;

6. *Exploration of innovative venues of network financing:* For example, joint programming, cost sharing, and combining public and private funds can be effective. Efforts also should be intensified to assess the portions of national budgets devoted to women and development objectives;

7. *Future expansion and consolidation of networks:* Women in development should be made an integral part of the educational process at all levels. A professional approach to women in development should be integrated into all relevant study programs, in addition to Women's Studies. Social sciences, cross-cultural fields of studies, and other social and economic interdisciplinary disciplines are legitimate and necessary to the development of new inroads;

8. *Greater use of new communication technologies:* Rural radio, low-power television, and computer training have enormous potential for

women yet to be explored. Appropriate content which would help in expanding networks of women in development are urgently needed as well.

9. *Greater interaction among countries and regions*: Women in development networks should contribute to building bridges across the southern hemisphere in economic cooperative efforts among developing countries, working on behalf of women and their self-reliance. (This is also an important principle for the northern hemisphere and industrialized nations.)

10. *Building bridges to the mainstream:* Bridges between grass-roots women and the establishment must be built, so as to ensure implementation of proposals based upon women's experience (Pastizzi-Ferencic, 1988).

Women for Life – *Santiago, Chile*

Women for Life (Mujeres por la Vida) is a coordinating group that was created in response to the double oppression of Augusto Pinochet's dictatorship and the dictatorial policies that impinge on women as wives and mothers. In Chile, when women marry they are considered to be legal nonentities, "incapable beings." Since President Salvadore Allende's assassination, improvements that were being made have been reversed. Without their husbands' consent, women cannot sell their belongings even if they have inherited them; they cannot open accounts, or travel out of the country. If they work outside the home, their salaries are considerably less than those of men who do equivalent work. They have no access to contraception, legal abortion, or maternity health care. As in all countries, as the economy declines and pressures mount, abuse against women escalates. Many of the women of Chile have not yet become aware of their rights as women, but they are aware that their society must be restructured for the good of everyone. One famous shanty-town organizer has a sign above her soup kitchen that says it all: "Democracy in the Country and Democracy in Bed."

The lives of Chilean women are spent maintaining family cohesion and searching for loved ones who have disappeared, been detained, imprisoned, tortured, or murdered. The oppressive political climate has created the impetus for women's organizing efforts. In December 1983, with less than three weeks' notice, Women for Life called its first meeting. Although 80 percent of the women did not have telephones, 10,000 members representing hundreds of women's organizations attended, united against the "system of death" that they experienced. As in many countries, only the women are organized. They publicly declare their demands for freedom to live under democracy in non-violent demonstrations. Their activities have included symbolic excursions to the Presidential Palace to ask Pinochet to resign, and to the National Security Council to ask the generals to return to their barracks (1984); holding a "Somas Mass" (We are More) demonstration for peace, justice, and democracy (1985); organizing international hunger strikes, and silent street demonstrations where they carried life-size cardboard silhouettes with the names of the missing on them (1986). In the same year, they organized a "Right to Vote" day in which all of Santiago participated, "voting" for democracy. They organized over 200 demonstration throughout Chile on International Women's Day (1987); surrounded the former National Congress, presently a center for persons under arrest (1987); and organized a celebration of International Women's Day where 30,000 women attended, filling the stadium in Santiago (1989). At all of these events, women have been sprayed with power hoses and toxic chemicals, beaten, detained, and imprisoned. Their courage and spirit are indomitable as they join forces to be certain that the men, women and children who are missing are not forgotten (Carman Rohland, 1989).

National YWCA of Bangkok – *Bangkok, Thailand*

The National YWCA of Bangkok provides primary health care services to detainees in the Suan Phlu Detention Centre. Children, adolescents and adults are imprisoned because the government considers them to be illegal immigrants, refugees awaiting resettlement in a third country, or Thai nationals who cannot prove their birthplace. Women and children comprise the largest group of participants in the program. They remain locked in their cells, held in captivity for reasons they do not fully understand; there are no facilities to meet the educational or developmental needs of either the adults or the children. The YWCA program enables them to leave their cells five times a week, teaches them reading and writing, and provides instructions on prenatal and child care for expectant and new mothers. They also provide transportation for the sick to visit nurses and doctors. The chief problems of the women are malnutrition and mental illness. They are confined to a small space and cannot leave, leading to infighting, depression, hallucinations, and suicide attempts. There are no church services and Buddhist spirit houses that are important to many are not allowed in the camp. The work that the YWCA has been able to do is limited; still, they provide the women with a sense of community concern and hope (Boonchuan Hongskrai and Wasana Sukasan, 1989).

UNHCR Program for Refugee Women – *Geneva, Switzerland*

Conclusions of the thirty-ninth session of the Executive Committee Pertaining to Refugee Women of the Office of the United Nations High Commissioner for Refugees (UNHCR), emphasize the interdependence of the problems and special needs of refugee women in regard to assistance, protection, and durable solutions. Their report is ground breaking, given the relative invisibility of the plight of refugee women, even among those who work with them daily. The committee report recognizes that refugee women should be protected because they face particular hazards, especially threats to their physical safety and sexual exploitation. They call for the reinforcement and strengthening of preventive measures on behalf of refugee women-at-risk. The report supports the High Commissioner's recognition of refugee women as a vital economic force, and of the need to promote their participation as agents, as well as beneficiaries in the planning of protection and assistance programs. The committee requests the High Commissioner to introduce further effective measures towards the integration of women's issues within the program planning cycle at all stages.

Oxfam America – *Boston, Massachusetts, USA*

Oxfam America is an international development and disaster relief organization. Because building self-reliance is their chief purpose, they concentrate on funding local grassroots groups in twenty-one developing countries in Asia, Africa, and Latin America. Oxfam informs policy-makers and distributes educational material to the general public, including people in the United States, about the root causes of world hunger and poverty. The condition of women is central to their mission. They have devoted all of their resources in India and Bangladesh to meeting the needs of poor women because they consider them to be the most marginalized population. They note that women are subject to triple oppression – as citizens in underdeveloped countries, as peasants living in the most disadvantaged areas of those countries, and as women in male-dominated societies everywhere.

Poverty compounds the disadvantages of womanhood, yet they are excluded from most of the world's programs. Government and international aid agencies that do sponsor women's programs limit them to traditional handicrafts and family planning activities. In contrast, Oxfam supports six basic strategies for women's programming: (1) removing barriers to financial credit; (2) access to technology; (3) training; (4) management and marketing skills; (5) health and day care services; and (6) the formation of women's support groups. Countering the paternalistic, welfare approach of governments which they believe does not improve the fundamental condition of women, they focus on women's long-term self-reliance and control over their own economic activities. They fund local, non-governmental programs that are more likely to combine economic projects with group organizing, and are open to experimenting with progressive social change. Such organizations are the linchpins of Oxfam America's programs in India and Bangladesh (Oxfam, 1989). (Oxfam America program evaluation methods are described in the *Person-Environment Program Models* section of Chapter 5, regarding education.)

5 Education for the 21st Century

> The widening of women's sphere is to improve her lot. Let us do it, and if the world scoff, let it scoff – if it sneer, let it sneer . . .
>
> Lucy Stone, "The Lot of Women," 1855

The challenge of contemporary higher education is in its changing role, its involvement in the affairs and problems of the community, the nation and the world. Education must be involved with personal and social development and services, while maintaining its classical role, the cultivation of the mind, and the promotion of fundamental research in natural and social sciences and the arts. Confronted by serious social, economic, and political issues, a university cannot remain an ivory tower. It must become an "intellectual powerhouse for development and an instrument for social transformation" (Narayanan, 1988, 14). While we need to pursue the material advantages of science and technology, we need also a value-based society with human beings who are not insensitive automotons. We need well-rounded, integrated individuals who combine "the qualities of the heart and soul with those of the head and stomach" (16).

Whether teaching future students in institutions of higher learning or people in their communities, the curriculum must place an emphasis on the role of women as primary actors, co-equal with men in decision-making regarding their own welfare, and in taking action to improve their own standard of living (Estes, 1988). It goes without saying that the education of men remains an important factor in the evolution of the world. But until women's roles are shared by men, it is women who are crucial to the development of citizens, who combine the qualities that are considered priorities for civilization. It is more likely to be women who concern themselves with the well-being of the community. It is women who provide basic education for their children on a day to day basis. It is they who model the behavior that children in their formative years emulate. But when women themselves are denigrated, when it is they who are most likely to be illiterate (at a ratio of 3:2 in the world), their ability to educate is demeaned. Girls internalize their mother's perceived inferiority, and boys reject at great cost the culturally demeaned feminine qualities lying dormant within themselves. The world loses.

Despite such a salient argument, it is important to be committed to social justice, human rights and development for women, regardless of their roles of mother, nurturer, and educator. Their rights are tied to their existence as human beings and all the respect due them, regardless of any socio-demographic factors. Development education is fundamental to the realization of such a perspective.

Development Education

Development education, relevant across the lifespan, is learning which creates a global world view. The basic tenets, according to the American Association for International Aging (1989) hold that poverty in a world of plenty is unnecessary and unacceptable. The world has the resources and the human capability to eliminate poverty, and people must be empowered to bring about their own change. Although national well-being is dependent upon global well-being, individuals can make a difference even where basic societal changes are needed.

Conscientization

Paulo Friere, the Brazilian educator who has done more than most to influence progressive global education for the 21st century, came to the forefront in 1974 with the initial publication of *Pedagogy of the Oppressed*. The key elements in the first stage of his model are consciousness of one's own oppression and its causes, which he called "conscientization." The primary purpose of this stage is to identify the oppressor within oneself, the predictable outcome of socialization. In the second stage, the focus is on the pedagogy of all people, ensuring the process of permanent, on-going liberation from oppression. The pedagogy of the oppressed requires a non-hierarchical dialogical relationship between the educator and the learner, learning and acting together about their social reality. The second major aspect of dialogical education is that no one person or group owns knowledge. It is not private property to be guarded jealously, but information to be shared and reflected upon together. Third, authentic educators do not focus their energies on trying to change the oppressed. Instead, their role is to work with them to organize and reframe the existing social reality in order to change it together. The focus must be on the existential, concrete situation of women, focusing on the "great generative themes of the epoch," the most salient being "domination."

Domination implies the need for its counterpart, "liberation," another great generative theme. Before women can identify with these themes, they must be given time to develop a critical consciousness. Only then will they be able to participate in the transformation of their own reality, creating their own liberation. Many of the governmental and non-governmental projects included in the *Person-Environment Program Models* section of this book use Friere's pedagogical schema. The sponsoring leadership, time and time again, have found their development projects failing and even destructive to women when conscientization was ignored. Still, the following insights about the poor by Fuglesang and Chandler (1987) should be kept in mind. (The adaptation to poor women is my own.)

The Assets of Women in Poverty

Before all else, one must be certain not to assume that poor women are limited in their horizons. They often have a sophisticated understanding of the origins of their socio-economic conditions, well before conscientization programs are established. Researchers and educators must guard against irrelevant questions and condescending statements, however unintended. Although the theory and praxis of conscientization has taken us to new levels of social insight, the approach is not always economically sustainable. Poverty as a label wrongly implies poverty in all things; it denies dignity. Women in poverty should be viewed as a culture that should be appraised in terms of their assets, resources and skills, including the following possibilities:

- *Listening skills.* Poor women reflect the perceptual and conceptual ability to "read" reality through the ear, interpreting social situations accordingly. Poverty is an oral tradition, a communal culture that does not survive without the spirit of the community.
- *Memory skills.* When women who are illiterate have no other means of storing knowledge and information, they often develop exceptional memories, lost in those who read and write.
- *Survival skills.* Poor women learn of necessity how to economize the use of their own energy, extending even to qualities such as patience and perseverance.
- *Resource utilization.* Every source of energy and material object is explored for its particular qualities and applications. Available resources are used in a remarkable variety of ways and combinations to maximize their potential. (Slum dwellers' shelters are excellent examples of such ingenuity.)

- *Occupational skills.* A high degree of labor division, common among poor women, often leads to a command of several skills, for survival is based on their competencies.
- *Economy of poverty.* The culture of poverty is also the economy of poverty, a sub-system which serves to sustain the national economy, although its productivity is not reflected in the national accounts. ("Women's work" is an excellent example of this reality.)

Participatory Research

A participatory approach to research on women is a major, relatively recent, global trend. It arose as a reaction to the lack of tangible results in traditional social science research approaches. Participatory research redefines the relationship between theory and practice by making the research itself action producing. It is not just an academic exercise whereby the researcher is a data collector, and the people studied are indices. Instead, participatory research calls for an interaction between the researcher and those who are studied. The undertaking becomes an educational process for all involved, offering skills and services that are needed. According to INSTRAW (the United Nations International Research and Training Institute for the Advancement of Women), the major components of participatory research are:

- that it promotes the active participation of the constituents in the collective investigation as well as a collective action;
- that it is problem-centered, "thematic investigation," and therefore is goal-oriented and action-oriented;
- that it has the advantage of being applicable to small groups, and is of relevance to a whole community; and
- that it develops a sense of social responsibility and shows the participants the link between discussion, research, and identification of solutions (Marei, 1985, 16).

This approach brings to research the concept of conscientization which utilizes a variety of group involvement methods, such as public meetings and small discussion groups. A major departure from the top-down approach to research, participatory studies provide the methodology for women to become active agents in the environment, participating in the design and implementation of policies and programs that influence their lives, rather than being passive objects to be investigated (Marei, 1985).

A Sociology of Women

Canadian sociologist, Dorothy Smith (1987), points out that women's experience generally has not been represented in the making of knowledge, culture, and ideology. The organization of society has been developed from the standpoint of men, what interests them, and is relevant to them. Until recently, it has been written by, about, and for men who listened to one another. Women have been systematically excluded, having had no written history, no poetic or artistic tradition, no share in religious ideas, no political philosophy, nor representation of society from their perspective. The means available to women to think about, image, and put into action their experience has been manufactured for them, not by them.

Smith refers to such exclusion as "the brutal history of women's silencing" (22). She cites research that makes clear the submersion of women's folk art tradition as true art, the appropriation of women's discoveries and work, and the subordination of their genius where it has existed. Even knowledge of their own sexual and procreative func- tions have been coopted by male physicians who usurped the domain of midwives. Smith speaks of such male authority as "relations of ruling," a power bestowed only on men. She explains that such power exists for men simply because they are a member of a ruling social category, not necessarily because of any individual characteristic. When they speak, they speak with the authority of the category, never standing alone as each woman in every society must do.

The concepts, methods, topics, and what is relevant within any discipline are accomplished in the social organization of discourse. Because women are "outside the frame," until recently they have had little influence. To learn about women, Smith asserts, we must learn about the experiences of women as knowers located in actual lived situations. She calls this the "problematic of everyday," a sociology of women. Analyses, descrip- tions, and understanding of their situations can be developed, along with determinations made in the wider socio-economic organization to which their situation is related. This is not meant to obviate scientifically rigorous methods and procedures. Rather, it is an alternative that turns the method "on its head" so as to make the everyday world the locus of sociological inquiry, rather than preordained theory. Care should be taken not to confine the inquiry. Rather, the everyday world must be seen as organized by social relations that are not observable in it. Because the method is designed to discover how things work and are actually put together, being faithful to the actualities and organization in question is required.

Women's work has been essentially invisible, conceptualized as maintenance activity that makes possible men's occupation of the conceptual, abstract mode of action. Whether in the home, the community, or the world of work, at all socio-economic levels, this fact holds true. Women's knowledge must begin to include their own conceptualization, analysis, and synthesis. In defining the everyday world as the problematic as a method of guiding and focusing inquiry, the questions one asks are the means of developing the model. This is not a transparent, obvious everyday world, for it is generated by a variety of organized social relations that originate elsewhere. Events and changes outside of the setting influence the reality of everyday life. The "personal is the political" forms the basis of the model, an equation which locates an oppression invading women's most intimate relationships, the immediate particularities of their lives, the power relations between persons anchored and sustained by a patriarchal organization of ruling.

Women throughout the world are becoming aware (some for the first time) that there is no distinction between the powers of public and private domains. This method of study is thus intended to systematically develop consciousness that traces these relations from women's own standpoint. The abstractions that ordinarily limit awareness are clarified in the actual practices of actual people as they are both expressed and concealed. As women's local space is examined, they learn from one another. But even more important, the model analyzes that experience that is anchored in the political, economic, and social processes that shaped them. Woman as subject is preserved as "active and competent and as the knower to whom our texts should speak" (Smith, 1987, 142). It is this method of sociological ethnology that is being utilized by activist women throughout the developing world in the educational training projects described in the *Person-Environment Program Models* section of each chapter.

A Feminist World View of Professional Education – (*Wetzel 1986*)

Within recent decades, there has been an information explosion regarding women's problems and concerns. Research has accumulated along with experiential knowledge and a proliferation of literature. Those educators throughout the world who ideologically agree with the need to integrate women's content into the curriculum have found it difficult to apply that knowledge and perspective. At best, they have initiated a few electives, or they slip their viewpoint into their courses. What is needed is a feminist world view, a restructuring of curricula that is grounded in human rights principles. Given that the problems of women are the problems of the world, a feminist world view conceptual framework would be relevant to all people.

It is important to recognize, in this era of daily compounded information, that the ability to process and apply information, rather than to memorize theoretical concepts and "facts" that are rapidly changing, must be a primary consideration. Analysis has long been the method of choice for problem-oriented professions. It requires breaking up the whole into parts, to partialize problems and expose components and functions. Analysis, unlike synthesis, is not a connecting process; nor does analysis provide a context in which all aspects of human functioning can be understood. The lack of synthesis may provide yet another reason why more progress has not been made on women's behalf.

The core of the feminist world view involves three organizing principles: (1) the unity of all living things, events, and knowledge; (2) the uniqueness of the individual; and (3) personal power and responsibility. (Translating these principles into the dimensions that are included in this book's conceptual framework, unity and uniqueness represent positive connectedness and aloneness, while personal power and responsibility represent positive action. Together, the three principles result in positive perception.)

Unity of Living Things, Events and Knowledge

The feminist principle of unity enhances context-building (Broudy, 1980). It involves the awareness that one's personal characteristics can interact with the situations in which one finds one's self. What has been lacking is a framework in which the person-in-situation can be evaluated from a human rights/feminist perspective.

There is no need to dichotomize relevant variables into either-or, right-wrong, true-false views to "prove" something. Such partial viewpoints only lead to artificial choices (Ferguson, 1984). Some class analysts conclude that these win-lose paradigms are based on a masculine mode of thinking, which they consider linear, in contrast to the feminine mode of thinking, which they consider global (Schaef, 1981). Other analysts have spoken of the parallels between feminism and quantum physics that refutes single, linear ways of knowing and acknowledges the centrality of connectedness (Imre, 1982).

Seeing patterns and wholes is essential to understanding context and detecting meaning. Learning to learn, then, must include learning to see connections. An interdisciplinary perspective allows synthesis of the fragmented knowledge of fields of inquiry, multiple disciplines, and areas of specialization. The integration of multiple perspectives can allow cognitive growth and understanding to occur. This capacity to consider many perspectives, to move coordinately beyond a single focal point, allows a more accurate perception of reality. In a search for common truths and complementary paradoxes, depths of knowledge, which are only superficially tapped when assessed competitively, can be explored. Women have long respected the collective wisdom of all cultures and eras, and consciousness-raising or conscientization has made them aware that the personal is the political, the interrelationship of all events and policies.

Professional women must go public – to teach the people-at-large and to learn from them. In Freire's words, this is praxis, unity, communion – a two-way dialogue of reflection and action – not a cultural invasion, but rather a cultural synthesis, not another oppression, but rather a liberation, trusting in the purposeful dialogue for mutual evolution (1974; 1985). This is a synergistic concept, combining energies to become something finer and stronger and more enduring. Whether we are concerned with fulfilling basic human needs, understanding existential philosophy, eliminating poverty, enhancing mental health, facilitating human development, or securing world peace, we are connected. The paradox is that despite this interrelationship, persons remain uniquely individual personalities, even in cultures that are inherently more concerned with connectedness.

Uniqueness of the Individual

Belief in the uniqueness of the individual, of self-worth, and of dignity, generally has been translated as respect for personal rights and a consideration of differences. Although these attitudes are exemplary, interpretation of them is often limited to benign noninterference. More dynamic is the feminist perspective on uniqueness that respects intuitive knowing, personal knowledge, and subjective experience; these are qualitative, nonobjective ways of knowing. Personal participation of the knower is essential, for knowledge cannot exist apart from the knower. Social science cannot be reduced to a collection of facts; it is, rather, a truth-seeking endeavor that comes alive only through individuals (Polanyi, 1974). Uniqueness of the individual, then, becomes part of the human effort to find coherence in the world.

Each individual is a combination of genetic history, experiences, and thoughts never before or ever again to be replicated exactly. Still, recognition of one's uniqueness is not static. It comes from experiencing one's self in the world and can be altered by ongoing experience-education, objective knowledge, interpersonal interaction, and different life events. Valuing the subjective does not mean abandoning objective information. There is no reason to polarize the two perspectives or to deny that each is informed by the other (Berlin, 1982). To split knowledge arbitrarily unnecessarily polarizes ideas. Qualitative research, for example, is often compared to quantitative research and denigrated. Yet, there is nothing inherently less valuable or less legitimate in qualitative research. In fact, quantitative data, rather than being used to confirm the high risk associated with women and their concerns, has too often abstracted women's experiences and silenced their voices. That silence can be broken by means of research that informs policy by documenting the reality of individual experience. In a feminist model, research is thus a method of action for change, not an end in itself. Such action is inherently therapeutic and leads to personal change.

Personal Power and Responsibility

The third organizing principle is action-oriented and pervades the concepts of unity and uniqueness. It refers to feminism's allegiance to a single standard system whereby all human beings have personal power: the power to be and to become, while no one sex, race, or culture has power over another (Dougher, Pirtle, and Wetzel, 1976). This egalitarian concept espouses noncontrolling participative psychological, social, and economic environments within the family and the larger community. That does not mean that one should settle benignly for a self-determination that masks and perpetuates socially internalized self-limitations. Development and well-being require nurturance and reinforcement. Commitment to one's values, and social action in their behalf, means that everyone has a responsibility to take an active role in the growth and freedom of others, as well as their own. Personal power as a value affects relationships, whether wife-husband, student-teacher, worker-employer, organizer-community, or client-professional. Even child-parent relationships are relevant within development-appropriate limits. Partnership is a given, and shared decision-making is a fundamental value. Personal power, then, is seldom experienced in isolation.

Anti-Discrimination Policy Analysis: Education

Article 10: Education
Article 10 requires governments to take all appropriate measures to eliminate discrimination against women in education (Convention, 1980).

Pertinent Questions for Analysis: Education (IWRAW, 1988)

- Have legislative or other measures been taken to ensure equal access to education for men and women?
- Is there equal access to education in practice?
- What percentage of primary, secondary, and university graduates are female?
- What are the overall literacy rates for males and females? Between ages 15–24? Ages 25–44? Ages 45 and above?
- In schools [or units within schools] that are not coeducational, are the curricula, examinations, teaching staff, school premises, and equipment of the same quality for boys and girls? If not, describe the differences. For example, compare student-teacher ratios, subjects taught, per capita expenditures for male and female students.
- If the educational system places students into different branches or "tracks" of studies, are girls and boys equally represented in such tracks? Are girls encouraged to pursue traditionally "male" studies? How?
- What is the percentage of women graduating in the fields of medicine? Engineering? Law? Sciences? Agriculture?
- What percentage of all available scholarships, awards, or grants are given to women at primary, secondary, and post-secondary levels?
- What percentage of the students in adult education and literacy programs are women?
- Are there laws and policies that attempt to keep girls in school? Please describe.
- What educational programs are available for girls and women who have left school before graduation?
- What are the dropout rates for women at all levels of education? What are the major causes of girls or women discontinuing their education?
- What percentage of all teachers at the primary level are women? At the secondary level? At the university level?
- What percentage of school principals and heads of departments are women?
- Do women have the same access as men to family life education, including family planning?
- Do girls have the same opportunities as boys to participate in sports and physical education in the schools? Is it culturally acceptable for them to participate?

(When reporting on this topic, it is important to indicate both the situation at the present time and progress, if any, over the past years. It is appropriate to begin this section with a description of your nation's educational system.)

Forward-Looking Strategies: Education (1985)

Although the *Forward-Looking Strategies* are addressed primarily to government, international, regional and non-governmental organizations, a spirit of solidarity must be developed through education of the public. In particular, women and men who now enjoy some improvements in their material circumstances, or who have achieved positions where they can influence policy-making, development priorities, and public opinion have the means to change the current inferior and exploited condition of the majority of women in the world.

Education is the foundation for the full promotion and improvement of the status of women. It is the basic tool that they should be given if they are to fulfil their roles as full participants in society. Governments should strengthen their participation at all levels of national educational policy and in the formulation and implementation of plans, programs, and projects. Mechanisms also should be instituted to monitor and evaluate the effectiveness of institutional and administrative arrangements to promote equitable participation. But participation is not enough. Women's education must be revised and adapted to the realities of the developing world. Special measures are required to accomplish this goal. New and existing services should be directed to women in their capacities as intellectuals, policy and decision-makers, planners, contributors, and beneficiaries. Increased equal access to scientific, technical, and vocational education is called for, with particular attention to young women. Evaluations should include the progress of the poorest women in urban and rural areas.

Illiteracy

Special measures should be taken by international organizations and governments to eliminate the high rate of illiteracy. While literacy is important to all, priority programs for women are still required to overcome the obstacles that result in their higher illiteracy rates. It should be noted that literacy should not be limited to reading, writing, and arithmetic (numeracy). Efforts should be made to promote functional literacy as well. Health, nutrition, and viable economic skills and opportunities are areas of special emphasis. In low-income urban and rural areas, programs for legal literacy should be initiated and intensified. Raising the level of education among women is not only important for them, which is reason enough, but for the general welfare of society. There is an inextricable link between education, child survival, and child spacing.

Research and Statistical Methods

Training for producers and users of the significant statistical methods and concepts that have been advanced in recent years should be implemented by national institutions which are engaged in statistics and women's issues. Such institutions should improve their capabilities in regular statistical programs in order to make effective use of these data in the policy-planning process. Monitoring and evaluation efforts also should be strengthened, with particular regard to indicators on the situation of women as compared with men, over time and in all fields.

Such gender-specific information and statistics should be compiled by governments, developing and reorganizing their information systems to make decisions and actions in behalf of women and their advancement. They should also support local research and experts who can help identify mechanisms for women's advancement. Their focus should be on women's self-reliant, self-sustaining, and self-generating social, economic, and political development.

Strategies for social change must include in-depth research undertaken to determine when customary law may discriminate against or be protective of women's rights. Studies also need to access the extent to which customary and statutory law interface to retard progress in the implementation of new laws. Particular attention should be paid to the abolition of double standards in every aspect of life when they are revealed. Discriminatory practices in education and training should also be investigated in order to ensure equality in both arenas. The impact of sexual discrimination on the development of human resources is of particular interest.

Special Supports

Where it exists, the causes of high absenteeism and drop-out rates of girls in the educational system must be attended to. Appropriate incentives to ensure that they have an equal opportunity to acquire education at all levels, and to apply it in a work or career context, require that relevant measures be developed, strengthened, and implemented. Such measures should include the strengthening of information and communication systems, the implementation of appropriate legislation, and the reorientation of educational personnel. What is more, governments should encourage and finance adult education programs for those women who have been forced to interrupt their studies or never completed them, owing to family responsibilities, early pregnancies, or lack of financial resources.

Efforts should be made to ensure that scholarships and other forms of support are available to girls and boys equally from governmental, non-governmental and private sources, and that they are expanded and equitable distributed to them. Boarding and lodging facilities should be equally accessible as well.

New teaching methods should be encouraged, ensuring that programs, curricula, and standards of education and training are the same for females and males. Audio-visual techniques that demonstrate clearly the equality of the sexes are of particular importance, as is the ongoing evaluation of textbooks and other teaching materials. When necessary, they should be updated, redesigned, and/or rewritten in order to ensure that they reflect images of women that are dynamic and participatory.

Role Restructuring and Training

It is equally important to present men as actively involved in all aspects of family responsibilities. Educational programs at all levels of the system should be introduced to enable men to assume as much responsibility as women in the raising of children and the maintenance of the household. In order to eliminate all forms of discriminatory gender stereotyping, educational institutions should also be encouraged to expand their curricula to include studies on women's contributions to development.

Public and private institutions are urged to include in the curricula at all levels of education, courses and seminars on women's history and their roles in society. Research institutions are asked to strengthen Women's Studies by promoting indigenous research and collaboration. Women's Studies should be developed to reformulate models to influence knowledge and create a value system that reinforces equality.

Governments and non-governmental organizations should address the needs of both older and younger women. The contribution of older women should be recognized, with attention to the importance of their input in those areas that directly affect their well-being. Accordingly, special retraining programs, including technical training, also should be developed for both urban and rural young women who lack qualifications and are ill-equipped to enter productive employment. Steps should be taken to eliminate any exploitative treatment of them in their work. Counselling services, as well as encouragement and incentives, should be provided for girls to study scientific, technical and managerial subjects at all levels in order to enhance their aptitudes for decision-making, management, and leadership in these fields. (See Chapter 3, *From Sex Roles to Sex Industries*, PART I, "Sex Roles and Stereotyping.")

PERSON-ENVIRONMENT PROGRAM MODELS: EDUCATION

Social Research Institute – *Bangkok, Thailand*

The Social Research Institute at Chulalongkorn University conducts research throughout Thailand in cooperation with two of the country's other universities, Thammasat and Khon Kaen, and Canada's York University. They have conducted a number of studies on women in Islam, including comparative studies between rural and urban Islamic women, and observations for medical schools on care of their children, for purposes of diarrhea prevention and intervention, a leading cause of childhood mortality throughout the world. Their research has revealed that governmental income generation projects focusing on skills building are appreciated by women who live in poverty. But the women in their studies, like so many others in the world, are exhausted by their double burden.

The consortium's research also has been instrumental in exposing the exploitation of women in subcontracting work, as compared with factory employment. Factory work has been shown to be dehumanizing, and the situation of women who now do piece work in their homes is equally shocking. The research has lead to the development of conscientization and organizing of woman in factories and in the community.

Studying the complex situations of political refugees, displaced persons, and those who have been selected to find asylum in a third country, the researchers have found that women represent the majority of refugees and suffer the most severe consequences. This is because of their status as refugees, their responsibility as mothers, and their subservient status as women. The Director of the Social Research Institute also works with the Institute on Asian Studies where they have investigated refugee conditions in twelve countries. They have found that those women who are in polygamous cultures are in a devastating situation. Their husbands do little work and continue to have intimate relations with other women. Many of these families do not leave even when given the opportunity because the men view maintaining a nuclear family, which is a prerequisite of acceptance into a third country, as a loss they do not wish to accept. (See Chapters 4 and 10 for further discussion of refugee women.)

The Social Research Institute translates their findings into social action at many levels. They make certain that all training projects include conscientization about sex roles and impact on development projects. Recommendations are made to the government at the highest levels, utilizing their research to substantiate their claims. A series of papers on women's issues have been published (Amara Pongsapich, 1989).

Women for Women – *Dhaka, Bangladesh*

Women for Women was established in 1973 at the time of Bangladesh's postwar reconstruction. This group of highly educated professors, researchers, lawyers, and other professional women generally target the elite, heads of government and non-governmental organizations, and attorneys. They are a "sounding board" for governments and other opinion leaders, conducting seminars for them, such as *Women and Economic Development, Gender Differences, Policy, and Vital Issues of Dhaka*. Women for Women publishes and disseminates the results of their studies from embassies on down. The first research-oriented women's group in their country, the information they present is always data based, thus increasing their credibility. While they do not pretend to be a grassroots organization, Women for Women communicate with their constituencies through a free quarterly newsletter which is published in Bengali, the language of the people. Women from all walks of life throughout Bangladesh are also included in their Annual Conventions. These conventions have themes, such as *Women and Media, Health, Mental Health, Law, and Disaster.* During the nineteen-eighties and nineties, they engaged in women in development planning for the year 2000, and the inclusion of women's viewpoints in their government's first five-year plan (Shaheen Ahmed *et al.*, 1989).

Oxfam America/Project Evaluation – *Boston, Massachusetts, USA*

Oxfam America regards evaluations of projects as an opportunity for project partners and the Oxfam staff to learn the lessons of the project experience. Rather than a judgement, evaluations are designed to attest to how the parties involved can do better what they are already doing well. To that end, most evaluations are participatory from the planning stage on, ensuring that the questions asked will be useful to them. An agreement is usually made at the outset as to how the results of the evaluation will be presented to both the grassroots members and the local staff.

There are several levels of monitoring, beginning with annual project reports explaining disposition of the funds and outcomes of the work. At the second level, Oxfam staff visit the projects, writing their own reports, describing what has transpired since their last visit, and what has been learned from this experience. One major research project, carried out by the local women, is planned for each region, focusing on a common theme or a case study of a project that exemplifies the development strategy for that region. Finally, research themes of cross-regional significance are identified, such as projects that involve peasant organizing.

Oxfam America research and evaluations focus on strategies and impact. They are interested in learning how the project set out to accomplish its objectives; whether or not the objectives were accomplished; what happened as a result of what was accomplished; who benefited and how; and who was overlooked. The organization believes that quantitative data may be useful information, but that it does not give much evidence about impact or effectiveness (Snow, 1987).

Literacy in Action – *São Paulo, Brazil and Boston, Massachusetts, USA*

Education in the next century, according to Friere (1988) will not be a neutral act. Rather, educators must take an ethical stand, openly and without apology standing up for a dream – a perspective or idea. They must clarify political options, not to impose a particular position, but to walk critically. One then cannot speak in a generalized fashion about the role of the educator. They are not neutral agents, technicians, or specialists remote from the discord of society.

Friere and Macedo (1987) call for a view of literacy that is a form of cultural politics. Literacy, they contend, cannot be reduced to the mechanical treatment of letters and words as currently practiced. Rather, we need to go beyond this rigid comprehension of literacy, and begin to view it as a relationship between learners and the world. It should serve to empower people by promoting democratic or emancipatory change. Friere identifies eight qualities of a progressive educator:

1. Educators must not be racist or sexist, view others as incompetent, or view themselves as better than others. There must be coherence between what one says and what one does. To diminish the gap between oneself and those who are served is a daily effort.
2. Educators must stimulate and develop a permanent curiosity in the

world, as well as stimulating the same in others with whom they are working. Finding answers is not the point; asking the question is.

3. Educators must utilize science, not mystify it. They must consistently express competence that is responsible, disciplined and rigorous, that is curiously critical and scientifically based.

4. Educators should embody the virtue of tolerance – the art of living with those who are different in order to struggle against those who are intolerant. Those with similar objectives, even though different, are to be tolerated.

5. Educators should make a disciplined effort to be "armed with love" – not sugar-coated, dulcified love, but available love.

6. Educators must be "impatiently patient." (Patience alone is disastrous because it aids and abets the dominator and slows history.)

7. Educators must understand the limits of their practice (social, ideological, political, cultural, and historical).

8. Educators must recognize the importance of critical and creative participation in the act of knowing. It is possible to reinvent society, thus creating our own history, rather than allowing history to manipulate us.

The Latin American Social Work Center/CELATS – *Miraflores, Peru*

The Latin American Social Work Center (CELATS) was established in 1975. The tremendous accumulation of social problems and the development of the social sciences towards more structural approaches permitted Latin American social workers, in schools as well as other institutions, to revise their mission to encompass social awareness, training, and technical support for organizations. Their purpose is to enable the people, including social workers and technicians, to take control of their lives, responsibly and efficiently, and begin to solve their problems. As a profession which emerged from the problems of poverty, it is an effort to confront the suffering of poor people. The common challenge in the many countries that they serve in Latin America has favored attempts to organize social workers on continental, as well as national levels.

Through investigation, training, and the sharing of significant experiences, CELATS seeks to make effective projects linked to the living and working conditions of the poorest sectors throughout the continent. Their policies are pluralistic in that their work is designed to respond to the professional necessities of social development, while ensuring relevance to the specific realities of each country or region. CELATS' charge is divided into four structured components: research, training, communications, and practical experiences. Each forms a programming area which has its own objectives, programs, and personnel. In practice, however, they are tightly linked and interdependent (Margarita Rozas de Fernandez, 1989).

The research area deals with theoretical problems and the practical intervention of social work. It also scientifically analyzes the characteristics of the poorest sectors with which social workers operate, as well as analyzing the characteristics of the social policies within which the profession unfolds.

The practice area seeks the theoretical collection of practical experiences so that once analyzed, those experiences can be offered to Latin American social workers.

In the training area, CELATS reinforces and deepens the theoretical, methodological formation of social workers (over 3000 in 21 countries, as of 1989) in their various fields of action. National characteristics are emphasized in order to respond to the demands of each concrete situation.

The communication area publishes and distributes CELATS' work, as well as that of its collaborators in different countries. They also produce instructional material which is used in the training and practice of social work.

The manner in which CELATS orients the work of this four-pronged structure is marked, from start to finish, by the fundamental purpose which inspires the creation and development of the Center – service to deepen and enrich professional action in the neediest sectors of the continent, and to the professional training for that job. The objective is clear throughout the CELATS programs – from the selection of research themes, to the practical experiences which are supported and encouraged, and the content of training.

Women's Projects

Many CELATS efforts involve women because they are likely to be the poorest and most marginal of all, and because they have been charged universally with the responsibility of caring for their families and communities. In 1988, they conducted a political analysis of gender in a comparative study of Nicaragua, Chile, and Peru – three countries in crisis. Case studies utilized a participative research model in which the women not only were invited to the presentation of the findings, but the proposals were their own. For example, the women leaders of the Lima federations proposed that they must make the decisions in their families and communities if they are to have the responsibilities (Marcela Chueca, 1989).

Community kitchens in the poorest Peruvian zone of El Algustino were created by women in 1979 when the food crisis became so acute that individual families could not afford to buy food for themselves. The women organized collective services, at first for children and breast-feeding and pregnant women, and then in a short time extended to entire families because of the dire need. At first thought to be temporary, they have become permanent. CELATS works with the women as trainers to educate them to the fact that what they are doing is more than just eating better. They are involved in growth as women and as Peruvian citizens. They learn what it means to be a grassroots organization and to coordinate efforts with other organizations. To that end, needs identified by the women are developed into proposals for action (Norma Rottier, 1989).

Thirty women established a neighborhood nursery school for 75 children, involving 20 teenage girls and boys who run it and work with a team of four CELATS staff – a primary school teacher, a psychologist, a skills craft teacher, and a social worker. CELATS is interdisciplinary in its approach, recognizing the expertise of allied disciplines and professions, as well as the people themselves (Esperanza Reyes, 1989). Friere's Popular Education model is basic to all projects, including in the area of health. For example, CELATS works with the women's Glass of Milk program in one of Lima's districts; they are conducting health policy research to evaluate whether or not the government is allowing authentic community participation that they espouse in regard to their health concerns. Recognizing that health is more than just food or reproduction (as important as they are) CELATS has developed a program to address community services and ecological issues that impact on health. They have developed a course for 28 shantytowns designed to strengthen the women's organizations without creating dependency. The ultimate question is how education can become a tool for the creation of autonomy (Monica Escobar, 1989).

6 An Employment Imperative

> The story of women's work in gainful employment is a story of constant changes or shiftings of work and workshop, accompanied by long hours, low wages, unsanitary conditions, overwork, and the want on the part of woman of training, skill, and vital interest in her work.
>
> Helen L. Summer, Senate Report, *History of Women in Industry in the United States*, Vol. X, 1911

It has become widely recognized that women contribute generously to the gross national product, as well as to the well-being of their families and their communities. Women are the main providers for one-third of all families in the world, and two-thirds of the poorest. If truth be known, more women than men are solely responsible for their families. Three-fourths of the world's micro-entrepreneurs are women, and in low-income countries women produce between sixty and eighty percent of the food for local consumption. In nearly every part of the world, women work longer hours than men and perform a wider variety of tasks (International Women's Tribune Centre, 1985). Though fiscal resources differentially affect support services for them (provided by poor women in most countries) and the availability of labor saving equipment, women who work outside the home, regardless of class or ethnicity, are likely to carry the dual burden of responsibility within it. Still, neither men, women or their governments call women's exhausting contributions "work."

Because women's efforts have continued to be invisible, unpaid, underpaid, and limited to low-skill, dead-end jobs, two-thirds of the world's women live in poverty. (By the time they are elderly, the figures jump to over eighty percent.) The feminization of poverty has reached global proportions. In the United States alone, based on statistical projections, the government has predicted that all people in poverty by the 21st century will be old women, and young women and their children. Yet, they are doing little to stem the tide. While there were some abstentions, the United States, for example, was the only country in the world to vote against a comparable worth proposal at the Decade of Women conference in Nairobi, Kenya in 1985.

Since women also do almost all of the world's domestic maintenance work and family caretaking on a voluntary basis, the United Nations acknowledges that they provide two-thirds of the world's work. Women in low-income societies are not only exhausted mothers of malnourished children, they are providers of food, water, fuel, and the family income. They are the sustainers of life, the developers of their families, communities, and countries. Thus, a critical determinant of the fate of entire societies is the fate of its women.

Corporate, Cultural, and Political Exploitation

While the situation of women in industrialized nations does not appear to be linked as clearly to their countries' progress, at closer range, the picture grows sharper. The global recession in the 1980s and 1990s validated once and for all that there is a global economy, and that women throughout the world play a central role in it. By 1989, many United States corporations were visibly shedding their national identity, proclaiming themselves to be global enterprises whose fortunes no longer depended on the economy of their mother country; nor did they view the U.S. as having an automatic call on their resources. Globalization, in fact, was emerging as corporate America's strategy of choice (Uchitelle, 1989). Their far-reaching perspective might even be applauded as enlightened were it not for the less than honorable motives that drive their policies. Multinational corporations are exploiting women of the developing world, recruiting them as cheap, foreign labor. Because they lack labor organizing experience, can be paid low wages, and will tolerate frequent job turnover with no security, they are hired by the thousands. In industries such as electronics, garment manufacture and assembly work, they constitute the majority of the work force. Research suggests that these women are not even conscious of their exploitation, despite the fact that they continue to live in poverty while working long hours in extreme conditions (Duley and Edwards, Eds., 1986).

The situation of women in the developing world is replicated when they become immigrants in countries like the United States. (Their shocking working conditions harken back to that of the mill girls of Great Britain, Europe and the United States at the turn of the twentieth century.) The international division of labor continues to be shaped by capitalist economies that cash in on cheap raw materials and cheap labor. Governments are as responsible as the corporate sector. The United States Department of Labor, for example, wants to legalize industrial homework in the women's apparel industry for the first time in nearly half a century. Virtually all women, they have been among the most exploited workers in the nation.

Most are non-English speaking Asian and Hispanic immigrants who work in thousands of sweatshops that are already operating illegally in cities across the country. As they did a century ago, sweatshop bosses force their workers to take home "piece goods," the unassembled parts of a garment, and sew at home for a few pennies per garment. They receive no benefits or protection, and just one or two dollars an hour for endless drudgery. Women comply with their bosses' demands because their appallingly low wages perpetuate their need. As in the past, their children also get involved. Industrial homework inevitably leads to child labor, also an illegal practice. The legal rights of these women and children are not only not being enforced now, but if legalized, their employers will be given implicit sanction to continue to exploit them. The Coalition for Working Women's Rights (1989), arguing that it is impossible to enforce worker protections in the home, have coalesced to fight government pressure, using the media to inform the people.

The home health care industry in the United States, in which 350,000 women are employed, provides a classic example of the economic exploitation of poor women of color. In their efforts to contain nursing home costs, the government is saving millions of dollars by creating a sub-employment system that is designed to reduce labor costs by keeping wages low, and severely retarding or restricting benefits. Donovan's (1987; 1989) study of home care work in New York City, for example, reveals that the system promotes job insecurity, along with the lack of opportunity for advancement. A ghetto of women in poverty is thus created, the vast majority of whom are African-American or Hispanic. Dominated by white male physicians and administrators, the industry is characterized by clear patterns of racial and gender segregation. Nearly half of the respondents in Donovan's study are immigrants from twenty-six Caribbean and Latin American countries. Despite long hours, they remain in poverty, facing severe economic hardships. Their health benefits are minimal and money even for food is often lacking. Their problems are deeply rooted in patriarchal gender discrimination and racism that segregates women in undervalued and underpaid jobs. Caretaking and home maintenance work, traditionally considered to be "women's work," are viewed as something to undervalue in the first place. The main mechanism by which control is achieved and maintained is the sexual division of labor of the patriarchal system which permits men to reap disproportionate benefits, placing them in positions of authority. The system ensures that women of color are relegated to the worst jobs of all.

By treating race as a parallel system of stratification between women and "minorities" or "people of color," issues of women of color, as women, are ignored. Race, gender and class issues become depoliticized through categorical homogenization. Economic exploitation and political domination are global issues so enmeshed that they must be understood in the context of national planning, policy development and resource allocation in all countries (Bourque and Warren, 1987; 1989). Still, a capitalist critique alone will not suffice.

It has become clear to women throughout the world that socialist countries have done little more for women's advancement. Class analysis without an examination of gender relations within and between classes (and racial and ethnic groups) has only perpetuated the subordinate status of women. Regardless of the dominant culture or political party, when women are included in the labor force, the majority of them are integrated at the lowest levels, thus remaining a secondary, poorly paid, expendable work force. Institutional cultures, power relations, social values, and stereotypes must be understood so that obstacles can be reversed, in addition to lifting legal and official barriers to entry. The status quo has systemic implications, for women themselves do not select occupations that are culturally off-limits, not even realizing that their socialization has restricted their development and negative or limiting self-perceptions.

Cultural-Political Systems Change Model

The challenge of the cultural-political systems model is to change the perspectives of people in arenas that have long resisted change. Changes in education and the workforce obviously require the cooperation of governments. But less obvious is their presence in the family, despite protestations to the contrary in most cultures. The private power-ridden gender conflicts within households are dynamics fundamental to those operating in the public world. The treatment of women as inferior or of secondary importance is widely perceived by governments to be justified because women's contributions are considered to be marginal or subsidiary. Attention, then, must be given to changing family structures and the decisions made within them, as well as to women's access to technology and the marketplace. They are all linked to an interdependent global economy. The real key to equalizing opportunity is the understanding of the political, economic, and cultural contexts of access (Bourque and Warren, 1987; 1989).

Access to Credit and Opportunity

Access and opportunity must include access and opportunities for earning money. In order to break out of the cycle of poverty, women must be able to use money to generate more. The absence of credit is one of their greatest barriers to advancement. Because women have a valuable contribution to make to the economic well-being of their families and their countries, pressure groups are needed to promote change in the policies of formal lending institutions and government agencies. Given their knowledge of social policy and human development in the social environment, social welfare organizations and social work educators can provide such leverage. Although the language of business has been used, the majority of income-generating projects involve community development professionals. Generating profits is one measure of success, but should not be the only one. Increased awareness and mutual support through the formation of groups and collective activity is also important to the well-being of women, families, and their communities, whether or not the project is an individual or group effort. It often takes years for an enterprise to become profitable, even in the most sophisticated arenas (International Women's Tribune Centre, 1985).

If human rights are to be recognized, the development of women should be supported, regardless of immediate outcomes. That said, it is important to know that alternative cooperative lending institutions have found that ninety-eight percent of women borrowers repay their individual loans, and their collectives make up the difference. What is more, women in development projects have used their profits for the benefit of the family and community. The fact is that this has not been true of the men who have a much lower repayment record and often use their money for their own private enjoyment, rather than the well-being of others (Davis, 1989).

Credit as a Human Right

The myth that credit is the exclusive privilege of a few fortunate people needs to be exploded, according to the Bangladeshi's Grameen Bank, an internationally respected credit institution which largely serves rural poor women. The logic behind the notion that the poor should not have access to credit has always been considered infallible. It is argued that because they cannot provide collateral, there is no basis for making loans to them. If collateral alone can provide the basis for the banking business, the Grameen Bank contends that society should, without hesitation, identify banks as the harmful engines for creating economic, social, and political inequality by making the rich richer and the poor poorer. Without the support of credit, dispossessed persons are beaten mercilessly in their fight against economic odds that surround them. Credit is a human right to which all people are entitled, not on the basis of charity, but within realistic, but disciplined parameters (Yunus, 1982; 1987; 1987).

Women's access to credit must be strengthened everywhere in the world, at the same timing being certain that they are involved in highly productive activities. The Gramcen Bank rccommcnds thc following successful elements based on their years of experience: (1) provision of collateral-free loans; (2) formation of small homogenous groups for group guarantee of loans and supervision of loan utilization; (3) taking credit services to women; (4) participation of bank staffs in social development activities for the borrowers; (5) recovery of loans in small regular installments; (6) developing institutions for collective savings for the mutual benefit of the borrowers in timcs of distrcss; (7) providing intensive practical training for developing a well-motivated dedicated cadre of workers and organizers who would deliver credit to women (Hossain and Afsar, 1988). (See *Person-Environment Program Models* in this chapter for further discussion of the Grameen Bank project.)

Winds of Change

Canadian sociologist Dorothy Smith (1987) provides a credible critique of the conceptualization of women's everyday work. Typically, she observes, their work processes are reconstructed as social or psychological practices, depriving them of their necessary anchorage in an economy of material conditions, timc, and cffort. Thus, thc helping professions, borrowing from the conceptual analyses of sociology and psychology, have assessed families in terms of their interpersonal relations and roles. Such terminology has rendered invisible the institutional presence of the home as an economy and a work setting for women.

Even foundations and corporations are beginning to address the dual burden of work at home and in the world, and the corresponding need to balance and defray conflicting demands. The Ford Foundation, for example, also has studied its organization and concluded that their employees have many of the same problems as working women in the programs they are asked to support. Expecting no less of themselves than they do of potential grantees, they are revising their own administrative policies and restructuring employee services to address these needs (Davis, 1989).

Du Pont, a corporate giant, created an Employee Relations Work and Family Committee to study the issues and modifications needed within their industry, recognizing that as women and men of the corporation benefit, so too will their organization. The committee's recommendations for action include improved communication, sensitivity of management, flexible work schedules, options and benefits, re-examination of the career process, and leadership in stimulating community and business initiatives to improve the supply and quality of child care (Wilkinson, 1988).

Corporations are coming to the realization that they must make other marked changes as well if they are to meet the challenge of the 21st century. "Workforce 2000," a study by the Hudson Institute for the United States Department of Labor, concludes that eighty-five percent of the 25 million people joining the world of work in the U. S. will be women, most of whom will be immigrants of color. Managing diversity will no longer be confined to social welfare institutions. Businesses and other institutions that cannot manage diversity will find themselves at a competitive disadvantage (Schmidt, 1988; Du Pont,1988). Corporations, unfortunately, often consider gender relationships within each culture as "givens" that should not be tampered with at risk of being intrusive. The rights of women will continue to be jeopardized in the absence of enlightened corporate awareness in regard to the misuse of the concept of self-determination.

The Paradox of Self-Determination and Oppression

Professionals are often guilty of this same unintentional discrimination. Women's concerns are usually invisible in texts on cross-cultural issues, and the noble "ethic" of self-determination of individuals, families, and governments obviates commentary. However well intentioned, self-determination has become a euphemism for women's overt oppression at worst and invisibility at best. Established to protect minority cultures from ethnocentric majority ideas, the well-intentioned ethic has led instead to silent collusion. In good faith, people are taught that it is not the business of professionals to interfere in the mores of others. The intent is non-intrusiveness, but the result is the perpetuation of a passive oppression of women.

Self-determination is a viable concept only when knowledge and possibility are present. Because personal development and awareness are both hampered and made possible by one's environment, the concept of self-determination is limiting when the environment is oppressive. Interventions that require closing one's eyes to subservience are damaging wherever they occur, resulting in an abdication of an even higher principle, that of human rights. A global analysis of women's position in the context of human rights should help to change outworn policies. Self-determination should not be abandoned. By raising the consciousness of women and men about the violations of women's rights, they will be in a position to be authentically self-determining (Wetzel, 1986).

Analysis of Workplace Oppression

The Committee for Asian Women (1988) has developed a framework for the analysis of the triple oppressions that affect women workers. They include the State (Government), Capital (Management) which may exploit all workers for their own purposes, and Male Domination (Patriarchy) which is specific to women, although certainly shaping the lives of men as well. The Government has a wider meaning than just the group of people who govern a country. A range of other measures utilized by the Government operate in conjunction with the leadership to control the populace. Every country has a ruling class, an elite, that has power and generally a large share of the wealth as well. Whether an industrial elite that owns the nation's industry, or an agricultural elite that owns the land, they certainly want to perpetuate their station. Control is achieved in two forms, by consent or by coercion. The former method utilizes parliamentary democracy, bureaucracy, and the judiciary system to create the image that its citizens have choices. The choices are often limited to those set by the state itself. Objections to their rule may be met by severe repression, ridicule, or more covert actions. The more blatant method, control by coercion, is utilized by dictatorships and military regimes. They have no hesitation in employing the state machinery, such as the military or police, to suppress those who oppose their rule.

The Government also has a range of other institutions or machinery. The media (newspapers, radio, and television) are key instruments which propagate state ideas and agendas, and where its effectiveness in influencing their policies and control is most visible. This is obviously true in overtly repressive regimes. Though less likely to be recognized, it also can be true of democracies and republics where a few elite own the network and newspaper chains that dominate the country. For women workers, the images of women's roles in society are very much shaped by how the media portrays women. The educational system is another mechanism of possible repression, as are the various religious, cultural, and other traditional institutions. Even the notion of the "family" is used extensively to dictate and shape women's lives whenever the leadership feels a need to do so.

Management works closely with the state in the oppression of women workers. Operating to derive maximum profit negatively affects the working conditions of women. Costs are minimized by whatever means, including paying women low wages and working them long hours under poor conditions. The workers are forced to fight management just to improve their lives. Subtle methods are also used by Management to control the women in their employ. For example, they play up the notion that women are only providing supplementary wages to the family, thus deserving less. Women are viewed as weaker and more submissive, and thus more easily manipulated. Temporary contract conditions, little or no benefits, promotion discrimination, and no access to skilled training and better jobs are only a few of the common methods used against them. Sexual harassment is not unusual, and some factories go so far as to organize beauty contests to exploit women as sexual objects, undermining them as serious workers.

Patriarchy, the third oppression, is the reality of male domination in women's lives at all levels of society. Since men are the decision-makers in the government, they dominate ownership of land, business, and industry. At home, fathers, husbands and often brothers are the family decision-makers. Thus, patriarchy in society ultimately means that women have little of substance to say about their lives. Women are socialized to support the myth that men are more capable and that women's main responsibility is to bear children and maintain the household. Throughout the world, women who work outside the home, as we have seen, carry a double burden.

Male domination has an economic base regardless of the political base of the country. The caretaking and housework that women do goes unpaid everywhere, and men are not only reluctant to do without their unpaid labor, but in most cases demand it.

Thus, the Government, Management and Patriarchy are all interrelated. The lives of women workers in and outside of the home are controlled in all environments. It is not uncommon to hear that women are called "to perform their national duty" whenever there is an economic boom or industrialization takes place. In times of recession, however, it is "the woman's responsibility to stay home and look after the children. It is the husband's job to bring the money home." The state similarly controls their reproduction, openly or manipulatively mandating one or two children in times of over-population, and "women's patriotic duty" to have children during periods of under-population. Yet, parental leave, child care, and flexible work schedules with benefits are points of contention in the workplace. When organizing women workers, then, all three aspects of oppression (Government, Management, and Patriarchy) must be kept in mind.

Women workers in Asia identify four major reasons that inhibit them from being active participants in organizing efforts. The insights are generalizable to women everywhere:

1. Their social background influences them. Most are not aware of their rights or existing labor laws. Poverty makes them accept their oppression;

2. Their inhibitions are culturally based. They are encouraged to be quiet, gentle and subservient. This attitude is pervasive even in the workplace where they remain quiet and try to withstand their intolerable working conditions without reacting;

3. They experience fear in three different forms: Fear of management when they have fear of losing their jobs, being dismissed, or even censured as activists who pose a real threat to employers concerning working women's livelihoods. Fear of government, because management is always backed up by the government and its political system. Women's demands for better working conditions go unheeded, or even punished by labor departments, police, or the military. And finally, fear of society, which often stigmatizes women who speak out. Active women workers have to contend with family, friends, and a community that finds it difficult to accept. In some societies, women have to seek permission from the men in their families in order even to participate in outside activities.

4. Married women workers find it difficult to be active because they have to bear the burdens of child care, housework, and work outside the home.

In addition to these obstacles, management and authorities prevent women from organizing by bribing them (offering them promotions and other benefits that would discredit them and cause divisiveness should they accept), transfers, fabricated negative reports, hired hoodlums to abuse and harass them, slurs on their character, court actions, threats to close down the factory should it become organized, labeling organizers as communists in capitalist countries, and refusal to negotiate with women (Choi Wan and Shun Hing, 1985). (See Committee for Asian Women in the *Person-Environment Program Models* section of this chapter for a discussion of organizing strategies based on their threefold premises.)

ANTI-DISCRIMINATION POLICY ANALYSIS: EMPLOYMENT

Article 11: Employment
Article 11 requires governments to take all appropriate measures to
eliminate discrimination against women in employment. It is desirable
to discuss both the current situation and the way in which it has changed
over time (Convention, 1980).

Pertinent Questions for Analysis: Employment (IWRAW, 1988)

- What provisions exist to eliminate discrimination against women in
  employment?
- What percentage of the total workforce is women? Of the total
  workforce between ages 15–24? Ages 25–44? Ages 45 and older?
- Are there professions which, by law or custom, tend to be filled
  predominantly by, or closed to, women? What are they?
- Are women, by law, entitled to receive equal pay for equal work or
  work of the same value as men? What percentage of men's wages do
  women receive? What ways are available to challenge discrimination
  in pay? Have these been successfully used?
- Is work done by women in the home counted as part of the work done
  in the labor force?
- Is unpaid agricultural work counted as part of the country's gross
  national product?
- What is the retirement age of men and women? Do men and women
  contribute the same amounts towards their pensions?
- Do wives benefit from pension plans held by their husbands, and vice
  versa?
- Do women, in law and practice, have the same rights as men
  to: old age or pension benefits? disability benefits? job training?
  promotions? retirement? paid annual leave or vacation? any other
  employment-related benefit?
- What are the provisions for paternity and maternity leave?
- Do women have the right to maternity leave without loss of employment, seniority or social allowances? Is maternity leave paid? If so,
  by whom? What penalties exist for violations? Are they enforced?
- Is dismissal of women on the grounds of pregnancy, maternity leave,
  or marital status prohibited by law or policy? Is it done in practice?
- How are women's safety and health, including reproductive health,

protected in the workplace? Do these laws and practices discriminate against women?

* What types of child care are available for working women? Does government support, financially or otherwise, child care arrangements? Is child care adequate?
* What percentage of employers provide child care? What percentage of children 0–3 are in child care? Ages 3–6? How are school age children cared for when mothers who work longer than the school day?
* Are nursing breaks for breast-feeding mothers required by law? In practice, are they provided?

Forward-Looking Strategies: Employment (1985)

Estimates and projections of the International Labour Office indicate that women's presence in the labor force will increase steadily to the year 2000, surpassing that of men at that time. The type of work available to the majority of them, as well as the rewards, will continue to be low, unless profound and extensive changes are made. Their employment is likely to be concentrated in areas requiring lower skills, lower wages, and minimum job security. Therefore, they will continue to receive a lesser share of the world's income and assets. Yet, women increasingly have sole responsibility for the economic support of the world's children. (In some countries, this is already true of more than one-third of the children.) *Forward-Looking Strategies*, then, must be progressive, designed to support effectively women's roles and responsibilities. They must be equitable, with specific measures to prevent discrimination and exploitation of their economic contribution at both national and international levels.

Legislative Measures

Employment policies should be consistent with economic and social policies which promote full employment that is productive and freely chosen. If governments are to attain their national goals, they should recognize the importance of and full utilization of women's potential for self-reliance. To this end, legislation should be enacted, and programs should be formulated and implemented to provide women's organizations, cooperatives, trade unions, and professional associations with access to credit and other financial assistance, in addition to training and extension services. Measures based on legislation and trade union action should be taken to ensure equity in all jobs and to avoid exploitative trends in relation to part-time work, as well as the tendency towards the feminization of part-time, temporary, and seasonal work (a peripheral or marginal labor market), or those increasing numbers in the informal economy.

The impositions of sanctions, dismissal on the grounds of marital status, pregnancy or maternity leave should be prohibited. Measures also should be taken to facilitate the return to the labor market of women who have left for family reasons, and to guarantee their right to return to work following maternity leave. Women should be given opportunities in accordance with the protective legislation of each country, especially in the labor market, in the context of measures to stimulate economic development and to promote employment growth, as well as to ensure the right to organize.

Governments should also devote special attention to the broader and more equitable access and inclusion of women in management, a significant factor in the development and realization of human rights. Policies should provide the means to mobilize public awareness, political support, and institutional and financial resources to enable women to obtain managerial positions and other jobs involving more skills and responsibility in all sectors of the economy. These measures should include the promotion of women's occupational mobility, focusing on the lower and middle levels of the workforce where the majority of women work, with particular attention to fields previously regarded as male preserves. (See *Forward-Looking Strategies* in Chapter 5 regarding education and training.)

Easing High Unemployment

High unemployment levels that persist in many countries require that governments strengthen their efforts to cope with the issue by providing more job opportunities for women. Women generally account for a disproportionate share of total unemployment. Due to their limited qualifications, geographical mobility, and other barriers, women's prospects for alternative jobs are also limited. General policies designed to reduce unemployment or to create [living wage] jobs are often of greater assistance to men than to women. Specific measures should be taken, therefore, to permit women to benefit equally from national policies. Measures, such as training, should also be taken to alleviate the consequences of unemployment for women in declining sectors and occupations, in order to facilitate the transition.

Cottage Industries

Governments should recognize the importance to national industrial development of improving the conditions and structure of the informal sector, the role of women in it, and the allocation of resources and training. Traditional craft and cottage industries, and small industrial efforts of women should be supported with credits, training facilities, marketing opportunities, and technical guidance. Producers' cooperatives also should be supported, and women should be encouraged to establish, manage, and own small enterprises.

The grass-roots participation of women should be supported in energy-related needs assessment, technology and conservation, management, and maintenance efforts. For example, stoves should be improved and disseminated to reduce the drudgery involved in the collection of fuel by women. (See Chapter 8 for a discussion of rural women and economic development in agriculture and industry.)

Easing Women's Work Burden

In order that the views of women may be incorporated in governmental activities, consultative mechanisms should be established, together with supportive ties to women's grassroots organizations. These might include self-help community development and mutual aid societies. The paid, and particularly the unpaid contributions of women to all aspects and sectors of development, should be recognized. Concrete steps should be taken to quantify, measure, and reflect these contributions in national accounts, economic statistics, and the gross national product. They remain unremunerated in relevant fields such as agriculture, food production, reproduction, and household activities.

The international economic situation, the debt crisis, poverty, continued population growth, rising divorce rates, increasing migration, and the growing incidence of female-headed households have all impeded the effective participation of women in development. Social adjustments to ease women's burden of child and household care must accompany the actual expansion of their employment, and recognition of the fact that they constitute a significant proportion of producers.

PERSON-ENVIRONMENT PROGRAM MODELS: EMPLOYMENT

Annapurna Women's Center/Credit Union – *Bombay, India*

Bombay's Annapurna Women's Center (Annapurna Mahila Mandal) is named for the Goddess of Food. As folklore tells it, Annapurna is a woman who successfully takes charge of her household when her husband deserts her, while providing for the whole world. She represents an organized, socially aware, economically independent, and self-reliant woman. The namesake reflects the image and character of the organization that came into being in 1975. A grassroots enterprise, this "family" of initially illiterate women who lived in poverty now are respected for their economic independence. With the leadership of the founders, a staunch trade unionist, Prema Purao, and her late husband, Dada Purao, who was Secretary of the All India Bank Employees Union, 25,000 women over the years have been taught the tools of entrepreneurship. The first group of women had been cooking meals for men who came to Bombay to work, but did not have the wherewithal to prepare their food. Before Annapurna, they each worked alone, vulnerable to those who took advantage of their isolation and need.

Because the women had no collateral and were rejected by bankers, they had to resort to moneylenders (who were also their grocers) when the women were asked to extend credit to their customers. They were badly exploited due to illiteracy, often even unaware of the extent of their debt. Such indebtedness took an even greater toll when they were forced to have sexual relations with their grocers as a stipulation for ensuring a continuation of supplies. Through organized efforts they learned how to overcome their fiscal slavery by banding together as a group of women who are accountable to each other. Rather than banks being asked to provide loans to individuals, the group guarantees the repayment. The banks have responded with low interest loans. Not only are the women's fiscal problems solved, but each woman is able to break out of her isolated individual existence, relating supportively to other women who are doing similar work.

As the program has developed, vocational training has expanded to advanced catering education, tailoring, and nursing hostel and telecommunications service management. The women are given instruction in literacy, basic functional education, tutorials in English, mathematics, and accounting. With the help of audio-visual aids, awareness classes are conducted for area and women workers on a weekly basis. The topics covered have included religious literature, the economy, political awareness, sati (the burning of widows), dowry, bride-price, and other current issues. Seminars on health, legal aid, and violence against women in the family are also conducted (Prema Purao, 1989).

Grameen Bank/Credit Union – *Dhaka, Bangladesh*

The Grameen Bank was founded in 1976 by Muhammad Yunus, a professor of economics who was teaching at Chittagong University in a rural village of Bangladesh where more than half of the people are landless. (Grameen in English means rural or village.) The Bank was initiated with five objectives: (1) to extend banking facilities to poor women and men; (2) to eliminate the exploitation of money-lenders; (3) to create opportunities for self-employment for the vast unutilized and under-utilized labor resource; (4) to bring the disadvantaged people within the folds of some organizational format which they can understand, operate, and in which they can find socio-political and economic strength through mutual support; and (5) to reverse the age-old vicious cycle of "low income, low savings, low investment, low income" into an expanding system of "low income, credit, investment, more income, more credit, more investment, more income" (Yunus, 1982, 11).

Women who are abandoned or divorced in Bangladesh are in a particularly untenable situation; they have no means of livelihood, and their parents will not welcome them back. Struck by the severe situation of the women, the founder initially made personal commercial bank loans and became a grantor to the region for women's income-generating projects. Seventy-seven percent of the loans now go to women. Despite the fact that no one involved had banking experience, the enterprise has been so successful that it has been replicated in Malaysia, India, and Malaui. Some United States banks are investigating expansion of the ideas to their country as well. Women as a group are the "collateral" that guarantees each loan.

The Grameen Bank, however, is much more than an ordinary public bank. It provides women grantees services which enhance their well-being, health, and productivity. Services are based on the principle that poor women should have equal opportunities, but its own existence also depends on a productive clientele. Banking becomes a way of achieving human rights and dignity without losing sight of the goal that the poor should receive what is rightly theirs already.

The organization conducts Training Trainers Programs called "Social Economic Development for Landless Women and Children." Women who show evidence of leadership when they are trained by the bank, create centers in their villages in which to teach other women. The training includes knowledge about child survival, helping the women involved to pass on the lessons of unity and discipline that they have learned. There is evidence that their daughters and sons will not pass on the subservient condition of women to another generation (Jannat Quanine, 1989).

Committee for Asian Women – *Kowloon, Hong Kong*

The Committee for Asian Women is an ecumenical, Christian sponsored coordinating program in support of women workers in twelve regions of Asia. Based in Hong Kong, the program was initiated in 1980 in response to industrialization and the economic exploitation of women workers. Urbanization for the women of Asia proved to be even more consciousness-raising than the UN Decade. The focus of the program is conscientization and support. Through small group seminars women share experiences across countries, exchanging ideas and resource materials. The coordinating body works to overcome language barriers and to tailor information to local needs.

Unheard of in the beginning, women workers now go on strike, though organizing is often grounds for dismissal. They are becoming a political force even though in countries like Bangkok and Korea only male workers are allowed to negotiate, and trade unions are pro-management and male-oriented. The situation is volatile. Research reveals that fifty percent of female factory workers remain single, not necessarily by choice in cultures that do not support single women. Their working conditions are poor, their shifts rotate weekly to keep them from organizing, and they have little chance to meet men. The women support their rural families, but no one supports them, emotionally or financially. A major goal of the organization, therefore, is to help the women to organize to find dignity in themselves.

The Committee for Asian Women works with local and national women workers groups; at labor centers other than trade unions where legal advisors, organizers (many of whom are social workers), and alternatives to trade unions are located; and with women's non-governmental organizations and women's church groups. They publish and disseminate a newsletter in three languages (Chinese, Korean, and English). In order to reach the largest number, they try to make their publications simple enough to understand even when one has only a beginning level of language literacy. Interestingly, though words like feminist and patriarchy are considered too "loaded" to be used, "male domination" is universally accepted as a concept to be changed (Loh Cheng Kooi, 1989). The following strategies and visions for organizing women workers were conceptualized by the Committee on Asian Women.

Women Workers' Organizing Strategies and Visions

All three oppressions of women workers, described above in this chapter (Government, Management, and Patriarchy) should be handled simultaneously. They are of equal importance. Three specific areas need to be considered in focusing on these oppressions; they are Content, Strategy, and Vision.

Content: When women engage in struggles against the exploitation of

Management, they must also be engaged in the eradication of gender oppression. The approach must be holistic and integrated. For example, if a training course is being planned, the content of the training materials should be examined to ensure that stereotypical ideas about women are not being propagated. Care also should be taken to guard against one aspect of oppression being subsumed by another, or one being assumed to be of greater importance than another.

Strategy: A united front must be taken, linking the struggles of women with other movements, while at the same time maintaining an autonomy. Women organizers need to be flexible in their work, whether concerned with small groups, national, or international alliances. The major issue is how to develop a strategy and build alliances with other movements, yet not have the issues of women workers overshadowed. It is the organizers' responsibility to prioritize and create balance. While building linkages is recognized as important, one must be wary of how linkages are built. Maintaining identity as women workers is essential, even though part of a trade union movement, a political party, or social movement.

Vision: Before planning strategies, the vision of what the organizers' want must be very clear. For example, if their vision is merely for better paid workers, then the struggle is within Management for better pay. If their vision is equal rights with men in the present system, they must be clear about what is meant. Are they talking about equal rights in terms of voting, equal pay within the system, or are they talking about creating a different society altogether? If they are envisioning an equal society, then they must be certain that their vision is congruent with their demands. Changes must be built from the ground up as part of an overall movement. For example, if the trade union movement is hierarchical and male-dominated, then they need to participate and start questioning the workstyle of their employers. Visions determine how far one's demands go and what the future will hold (Loh Cheng Kooi, 1988).

Norwegian Housewives' Association – *Oslo, Norway*

The Norwegian Housewives' Association, founded in 1915, is one of the country's largest women's organizations. Internationally oriented, its membership has conducted projects in developing countries since 1975. High on the Association's agenda is the right to negotiate payment and relief for those with heavy nursing and caretaking commitments. They are a visible political pressure group, making their views known at local, national and international political levels. The organization has programs serving 35,000 children, and 2000 study groups to encourage their membership to greater awareness. Their overarching purpose is to promote the goals of the *Forward-Looking Strategies*, particularly by achieving recognition for the unpaid work that is generally carried out in the home and community by women, to the point where it is included in the gross national product statistical reports everywhere in the world. To accomplish their mission and to stimulate working in the home and community, they propose: (1) Equal responsibility of husband and wife for the entire income and property; (2) Equality between husband and wife, and between one and two income families in tax and pension systems; (3) Economic equality between families caring for their own children and those using the services of government-sponsored kindergartens and institutions; (4) Compensation for loss of the ability to work during illness of the housewife; (5) Adequate assistance to cover the expense of caring for handicapped or elderly members of the family; and (6) Provision of nursing care in the home by family members is a social service and should be paid as such (Ingunn Birkeland, 1987; 1988).

Indicators of Economic Well-Being (Dixon, 1980)

Ruth Dixon's assessment of the impact of development projects on women suggests that studies use five measures as indicators of economic well-being. While her work was designed for developing countries, the indicators below can be utilized when congruent with the concerns of women in industrialized nations.

Income (in cash, kind, or trade in relation to cost of living)
Household income can be measured according to amount and how secure it is (such as the extent of seasonal fluctuation, short-term employment, and long-term prospects.) Who earns the income in proportion to the total is critical to understanding the domestic economy. In countries such as Africa, for example, women are expected to provide for themselves and their children's subsistence, while men's earnings go to larger cash outlays. Who receives direct economic returns to their labor, and who engages in unpaid labor should be noted. Do women who contribute to surplus production have direct access to and control over earnings, or are their husbands paid for their wife's labor? Who pays for which expenses, and do special projects increase women's unpaid labor, while not increasing their paid labor?

Access to Credit
Has the project affected the supply and cost of credit or loans available

to participating households? Are both female and male family members eligible? Are women-headed households eligible? Are collateral requirements such that women can afford them?

Land and Water
The amount and quality (productivity) of legally owned land is assessed, as well as the amount and quality of land available for use, such as leasing, share-cropping, and tenancy. The security of the land and water use rights are also measured. The issue here is the equitable distribution of resources between the landless, or nearly so, and landed classes. It is crucial to note if the project expands or contracts women's legal or traditional rights to land ownership. For example, does a scheme designed to secure tenant rights address what happens to wives of tenant farmers (or recognize women as farmers themselves)? Are women granted land of their own, legally recognized as joint owners, or with rights equal with their husbands? Are titles granted to men only, undermining the women's inheritance rights, as well as current access? Does the project reduce men's landlessness as male heads of households, but not female heads?

Technology and Technical Assistance
Access to technology and technical assistance increases productivity and the potential for higher economic returns. Their quality, appropriateness to local conditions, and frequency of use is important to assess. Which households and which household members, have the greatest access to labor-saving technology, thus permitting them to reduce their energy and time, while increasing productivity? What are the distributional effects of the introduction of new technology? Who is bypassed and who benefits? Do planners considered the development of technology for domestic use as important as technology for the production of surplus in agriculture and industry?

Other Assets in Relation to Debts
What are the ownership or use rights of buildings and other capital goods such as animals and household goods? What are the amount of savings and debts? How are assets distributed within the household? Who owns them, uses them, has the right to sell or trade them, to give them away, or to bequeath them? What independent assets do women control? Does the project improve or undermine their ability to accumulate assets?

7 A World Health Mandate

> By health I mean the power to live a full, adult, living, breathing life
> in close contact with . . . the earth and the wonders thereof – the sea
> – the sun.
>
> Katherine Mansfield (1888–1923)

Primary health care is neither easily accessible for the majority of the
world's people, nor are there services on which to depend. Despite the
fact that the World Health Organization proposed a goal of "Health for
All by the Year 2000," which virtually every provider of health care in
the world espoused, the closer we come to the target date, global statistics
and trends do not give much cause for hope. Malnutrition is increasing,
rather than decreasing throughout the world, safe water is not available to
seventy-two percent of the lowest income countries, and the mortality rates
are staggering in many African, Asian, and Latin American nations.

Even in relatively well off countries like the United States, health
conditions are shocking. Poverty affects more and more women and their
children; they rank eighteenth in infant mortality among industrialized
nations; and homelessness is a way of life for an estimated two million U. S.
citizens each year. Single women with children are the fastest-growing
segment of the homeless population, with single women representing ten
to fourteen percent of the total homeless population. The seven hundred
thousand homeless children are twice as likely to develop chronic illnesses,
mental health problems, and to fail in school (McGinley, 1987; National
Association of Social Workers, 1989).

Health and Mental Health

The health of women and their low status are intricately intertwined. Any
serious attempt to improve their well-being must deal with those ways in
which their health is affected negatively by social customs and cultural
traditions. The women of the world too often lack even the knowledge
and conviction that they are human beings, that their lesser status is not "as
natural and unchangeable as the fact that they are female." No matter which
way these women look, there is reinforcement for the perception they have

of themselves as being of little importance and value. It is not surprising, therefore, that women everywhere are likely to suffer from depression and anxiety, the world's leading mental health problems (Lyons, 1984). This is as true in North America and Europe as it is in developing countries (Viswanathan and Wetzel, 1992).

In Bangladesh, Women for Women, an organization of scholarly action-oriented researchers, published a comprehensive study of health and mental health for their country's end of the Decade of Women. They point out the interaction of psycho-sociocultural issues and the many ways in which society affects the health of every member of the family, particularly its more vulnerable groups (Huq, Johan, and Begun, 1985). Physical health and mental health are inseparable concepts. The authors define mental health as "more than the absence of disease. It implies a feeling of well-being and an ability to function in full capacity, physically, intellectually and emotionally" (48). The women of Bangladesh, like the women of the west, were found to be mentally ill at a 2:1 ratio as compared with men. They are in a lower status in almost all aspects of life, including social, economic, educational, and political life. Comparing these findings with studies concerning the mental health of woman all over the world, the researchers concluded that depression is by far the largest category affecting all women. There are no socially acceptable outlets for their unhappiness, and the prognosis depends on how well they can "fight back the challenges of social conflicts . . . " (65).

The Bangladesh researchers underscore the importance of including the sociocultural environment and the gamut of economic activity, as well as unpaid work in the home, when assessing women's health and mental health conditions. Too often, they note, female health is perceived solely in terms of reproductive health and "good muscular body and perennial energy for hard work," congruent with roles conceived by the world view of male dominated societies. Any symptoms that do not impede sexual and home maintenance activities, they report, are ignored (Huq, Johan, and Begun, 1985; Wetzel, 1987). (See Chapter 8 for a comprehensive discussion of mental health and rural women, much of which is pertinent to women from urban areas of the world.)

Reproductive Control

The World Health Organization reported in 1987 that 900,000 women die every year because of preventable pregnancy related causes, 200,000 of them following unsafe, non-clinical abortions. Many of the dead are exhausted women, worn out from eight to ten pregnancies, who are unable to feed their children adequately. Ninety-nine percent of the deaths take place in developing countries; maternal mortality is the single most neglected health problem in the third world. The extremist foreign aid abortion policy of the United States, ironically announced at the 1984 World Population Conference in Mexico City, has caused untold harm to millions of the world's women. Foreign funding was denied to any reproductive health organization that addresses abortion except to discourage even safe, legal abortions. Referrals are forbidden even if no U.S. funds were used to make them. Over eight hundred programs in eighty countries have suffered. Women's health services have either had to go without funding, or are bound to withhold information from their clients. The result is that women have been subject to unsafe methods and unhealthy babies. One hundred to 200 infants out of every 1000 babies born alive have died in their first year of life. But the tragedy does not end there.

For every mortality statistic, there are ten to fifteen mothers and babies who suffer long-term physical, mental, and psychological damage because of complications during pregnancy and childbirth. (The Bush administration and Supreme Court extended these policies to U.S. citizens in 1991.) Failure to inform a woman about all of her reproductive health options not only violates medical ethics, but prior to 1991 would have been considered illegal in the United States. Efforts are being made to revive the former leadership of the U.S. in the area of humane domestic and international support of the reproductive health of women (McGinley, 1988; Teltsch, 1988; International Planned Parenthood Federation, 1989). However one feels personally about the abortion issue, the facts concerning the lives of women must not be forgotten or dismissed.

Women's world-wide disadvantaged social position is reflected in a range of related health problems. Reproductive freedom means giving women not only the choice not to have children, but also the choice of when to have them, free from economic constraints, social prejudices, or state control. Sterilization abuse, as practiced on poor women in Puerto Rico, on Native American reservations, in China and throughout the developing world is as great a deprivation of reproductive freedom as is the denial of abortion or safe contraceptive methods. The growing prevalence of female infanticide is shocking in countries where girls are viewed as a drain on the family, and in no position to bring honor to them, to ensure continued lineage, and be economically productive. The perception of women as inferior, and the reality of their demeaned position perpetuates the likelihood that they will continue to be rejected, even to the point of death, despite the fact that governments are overtly opposed to such extreme practices.

Malnutrition

Sex bias in favor of boys and men in some countries extends to the allocation of protein and the family food supply, resulting in a higher incidence of malnutrition among girls and women. The World Health Organization suggests that about half of all women and two-thirds of pregnant women in developing countries (excluding China) suffer from nutritional anemia. Anemia, also common among poor women in relatively developed countries, is caused by inadequate nutrition, arising from poverty and from food allocation disparities. It is complicated by intestinal parasites and malaria. Malnutrition combined with frequent pregnancies can lead to a maternal depletion syndrome that results in high rates of death in pregnancy and childbirth. Death rates are exceptionally high for adolescents who are childbearing because of the physical and mental immaturity of the young mothers, combined with their lack of education. The risks are even greater when they are single, even when one takes into consideration the risks of all forms of violence with which many wives contend. Single women are not necessarily less likely to escape abuse from men in their lives.

Drug and Alcohol Abuse

Sexism, racism, poverty, and cultural expectations add to the stigma of women's health and mental health problems. For example, in the United States drug and alcohol abuse, whether her own or a partner's, have devastating effects on women. They are linked to almost three-fourths of sexual abuse cases, including rape and incest, half of spouse abuse, and approximately one-quarter of child abuse cases. Drugs and alcohol are related to teen pregnancy, violence and suicide, as well as sexually transmitted diseases, AIDS being the most recent example. While the particulars may vary with the culture, they affect women regardless of ethnicity, religion, sexual preference, economic class, or community (Women's Action Alliance, 1988).

AIDS and Human Rights

The human rights of people with AIDS (acquired immunodeficiency syndrome) merits special attention due to the environment of fear, threat, and the discrimination that has been called the "third epidemic." Persons in the grip of poverty are much less able to be cognizant of infringements on their rights and possibilities for redress, and they often live in fear of retaliation should they take exception. Forced detention, isolation, separation from families, rejection, breaches of confidentiality, denial of educational resources and peer support, denial of housing, health care, employment, insurance, social security, and the stigmatization of health care workers are some of the miscarriages of justices invading the international community (Mann, 1988). Women throughout the world who are threatened with AIDS or who already are infected with the HIV virus commonly suffer in ways seldom addressed. They lose any reproductive freedom that they have, are subject to violence and forced sexual intercourse (without contraceptive safeguards) by their infected partners, have little or no rights to abortion, and cannot get pre or post-natal care.

By 1988, in New York City alone there were 70,000 infected babies orphaned, most often the children of women of color. AIDS has been the city's leading cause of death among women aged 25 to 34 for a number of years. By 1990, it was rapidly rising nationally as a leading killer among women aged 15 to 44. Yet, many doctors and hospitals refuse to treat or operate on women who are suspected of being infected (Rodriguez, 1988; Lambert, 1990). Even so, there is little effort to raise the public's awareness of the rights of women in regard to their freedom to deny sexual intercourse to their husbands. In most countries, including most states in the U.S., the law does not even consider rape by a husband to be a crime. An expert speaking to the UN on behalf of human rights and AIDS lamented that "women all over the world are just waiting to die" because they have no rights to their bodies or the behavior of their husbands. Still, he contended that his organization "would not presume to tell others what to do" (Klouda, 1988). (See Chapter 6 for discussion of *The Paradox of Self-Determination and Oppression.*)

Caretaking

The United Nations (1988) reports that women do most of the caretaking in the world, leading to their greater dependency, and imposing great constraints on them and on their chances to avail themselves of job opportunities. The unequal female caring ratio also shows that changes in age structure penalize women. The elderly represent a growing share of the total population. Already more numerous in more developed countries, they will fast become so in developing nations in the 21st century. Women lose as life long unpaid or poorly paid caregivers, and as people who often nurture, but live without nurturance themselves. Since health care systems largely focus on the male model of acute care, women's very different health needs are less likely to be met. This is especially true if one is poor (Older Women's League, 1988). (See Chapter 10 for a discussion of women with physical and mental disabilities.)

Chronic Fatigue and Workload

Less than half of the world's people have access to safe water. In most developing countries women have the responsibility of providing it, walking long distances for several hours a day, carrying heavy loads of water home. Although they are the main providers and consumers of water, they are seldom consulted when water supply projects are initiated.

It is easy to see why so many women suffer from overwork and exhaustion throughout their lives. This is true of rural and urban women in developing countries where they must spend long hours gathering firewood for fuel, as well as supplies of water, then cooking and cleaning, and caring for children and husbands. They also devote many hours to agricultural labor in rural areas, just as they do in more developed countries. Chronic fatigue is common in industrial societies as well, where wage-earning women with children also have the double burden of a job outside the home and within it. Their fatigue is constant and debilitating, contributing to their ill health (International Planned Parenthood Federation, 1985).

Pesticide Poisoning

Throughout the world, women are exposed to hazardous chemicals, common pesticides that have been found to cause long-term chronic effects, including sterility in females and males, birth defects, nerve damage, paralysis, and poisoning of children and adults. In rural areas in developing countries, women often work directly with pesticides. In other regions of the world, their contact is indirect, but no less dangerous. In their roles as housewives they are exposed to the dangers of pesticide residue, contamination of ground water, and chemical waste disposal. Less likely to be recognized is the internal threat to their bodies through sexual intercourse. (A man who has handled pesticides normally touches himself when urinating. The transferred poison then penetrates the vagina of his wife.) Yet, despite women's extended contact, little evidence exists of educational attempts to teach women about potential pesticide hazards. Only men are given instruction, amd that is inadequate. Pesticides in countries like Africa are even sold without warning labels side by side with food in grocery stores (Anstey, 1986). Aware of the dangers for women in African nations, Anstey (1988) developed a graphic manual for distribution across cultures. Because of the many sects and disparate languages spoken in Africa, as well as high rates of illiteracy among women, multiple translations from English were not practical. Instead, simple pictures clearly convey the messages that are so important to the health of these rural women and their families.

Mobilizing an International Health Care Movement

Primary health care must become a social movement, a movement in which people from all walks of life are involved as active partners in achieving their right for health care, not just passive recipients of so-called benefits. The major ways in which female activists work to promote women's health include consciousness-raising and education, creating new knowledge, providing alternative services, and influencing public policy. These methods are successful in developing collective leadership which encompasses all levels of society. Such leadership is enabling and empowering, building self-confidence founded on the inherent strength and ability of the people.

One of the more crucial functions of such leadership is to raise awareness and concern for the issues of equity and social justice in society as a whole. There can be no health equity unless the societies in which we live are aware of the social injustices within them. Partnerships and new alliances must be built in support of universal health (Barrow, 1988).

Women have traditionally been the key agents of health care within the family and the community. They provide an estimated ninety-five percent of all informal care, far exceeding that of the formal health sector. Most health decisions are made by women; they have the main responsibility for maintaining standards of hygiene; they determine diet; they care for children, the sick, and the elderly; and they transmit knowledge and attitudes on health care issues. Women's access to health care information and resources, then, is an important determinant of their own health, that of their families, and the entire community. Local women's organizations are a natural entry point for such community-based programming. Women can play an important role in community health by teaching their neighbors about sound health and nutrition practices, and by providing physical and psychological support to other women during pregnancy and childbirth. Health education and action programs to eradicate diseases and for the dissemination of appropriate technology are also excellent vehicles for women's expertise (International Planned Parenthood Federation, 1989).

Health education campaigns should focus on promoting those actions which people can undertake for themselves, and those actions that have the greatest impact at the least cost. This should not be interpreted as permission to exploit women as voluntary or underpaid workers. Health care deserves respectful remuneration. Without it programs suffer from worker turnover and service deterioration, and the health of women who do the work suffers in turn. The rationale for the program in the first place is undermined as health problems are exacerbated. It has been shown that training women as community health workers, employing them in referral services and at immunization posts can lead to dramatic results. But they will not be able to meet the challenge if efforts are not made to change negative perceptions of women and by women themselves. Ironically, they often are the first to blame themselves for poor health conditions, the inevitable psychological injustice of the oppressed.

UNICEF (1984) described a program that restored the confidence of Kenyan women, apropos of this discussion. The local health practices of the women had been stopped by bureaucrats and physicians who led the women to believe they knew nothing of worth. They often waited despondently for outside help, therefore, before addressing even simple health care tasks. Through local community organizations and in public meetings, confidence was restored in over 240 women when they were trained as community health workers. Serving a population of 120,000 people, in three year's time the experiment proved to be a phenomenal success, lowering disease and increasing healthful conditions dramatically. Positive perception and resultant action turned the tide (Wetzel, 1987).

Anti-Discrimination Policy Analysis: Health

Article 12: Health
Article 12 requires that all states agree to take all appropriate measures to provide women and men equal access to health services, including family planning (Convention, 1980).

Pertinent Questions for Analysis: Health (IWRAW, 1988)

- What health facilities and personnel are available for women? This could include hospitals, clinics, health posts, and other facilities, as well as physicians, nurses, auxiliary health personnel, family planning workers, and community agents.
- What are the major causes of female mortality and morbidity?
- What is the maternal mortality rate?
- What are the infant and child mortality rates for boys and for girls? What are the major causes of infant and child mortality and morbidity for boys and for girls?

- What is the average life expectancy for men and women?
- What are the crude birth rates and crude death rates for men and women?
- What percentage of women receive prenatal care?
- What is the average number of live births per woman?
- What is the unmet need for contraception?
- What is the prevalence of contraception, by method? What legal or cultural obstacles are there to women receiving health care services, including family planning?
- Is the husband's authorization required, either by law or in practice, before a married woman can receive health services including family planning?
- Is abortion legal? If so, under what circumstances? Is the cost of abortion covered under national insurance or social security? Can poor women receive free or subsidized abortions? If abortion is legal, how available are services in practices?
- If abortion is not legal, is it performed anyway? What statistics are available for death and/or illness due to or related to abortion? What provisions are made for care of women with incomplete abortions?
- Is female circumcision practiced? If yes, under what circumstances? Is it legal?
- What laws exist regarding violence against family members? Have they been used successfully by women?

Forward-Looking Strategies: Health (1985)

The vital role that women play as providers of health care, both inside and outside of the home, should be recognized. Basic services for the delivery of health care should be created and strengthened, with attention to levels of fertility, infant and maternal mortality, and the related needs of most vulnerable groups.

Disease Prevention

Local women's organizations should be encouraged by the government to participate in primary health care activities, including traditional medicine, with emphasis on preventive, rather than curative measures. They should devise ways to support women in taking responsibility for self-care and in promoting community care in rural and urban areas alike. But it is important that efforts not be limited to the informal sector alone.

At the governmental level, measures should be taken to control epidemic diseases, and to vaccinate all children and pregnant women against endemic local diseases and others recommended by the World Health Organization, eliminating any differences in coverage between girls and boys. (Vaccinations should preferably be given to girls before puberty in regions where rubella is prevalent.) The quality and quantity of vaccines, and their preservation, should be ensured, as well as the full and informed participation of women in chronic and communicable disease control programs.

It is important that health education be geared towards changing attitudes, values, and actions that discriminate against women and girls, and are detrimental to their health. Steps should be taken to change the attitudes, knowledge, and composition of health personnel, so that an appropriate understanding of women's health needs is ensured. A greater sharing of health care and family responsibilities by women and men should be encouraged. The formulation and planning of women's health education needs should involve them, being certain that information meant to be received by women is relevant to their health priorities, and is suitably presented. Health education should be available to the entire family, particularly through the educational system and other appropriate channels, as well as through the health care system. Public expenditures for health, education, and training, and the provision of health care and health care services for women should be increased.

Research

Assessments should be made of the actual impact of science and technology on the developments that affect women's health, income, and status. Policy formulation should include relevant findings to ensure that women benefit fully from available technologies, and that any adverse effects are minimized. Efforts should be intensified in the design and delivery of appropriate technology, and attention should be given to the best possible standards. The implications of advances in medical technology are of particular importance.

Governments should widely apply and utilize the appropriate gender-specific indicators for monitoring women's health that have been and are being developed by the World Health Organization. This will develop and sustain measures for treating low-grade ill health and for reducing high morbidity rates among women, particularly when illnesses are psychosomatic, social or cultural. [Research on terminal illnesses for which women are at high risk should be given priority. Among them are heart attacks, breast and uterine cancer, tuberculosis and AIDS.]

In order to be readily accessible and acceptable, appropriate health facilities should planned, designed, constructed and equipped. Services should be congruent with the timing and patterns of women's work, as well as with their needs and perspectives.

Control of Income

Women should have access to and control over income so as to provide themselves and their children with adequate nutrition. Activities should be promoted by governments to increase awareness of the special nutritional needs of women, providing support to ensure sufficient rest in the last trimester of pregnancy and while breast feeding. Interventions should also be promoted to reduce the prevalence of nutritional diseases such as anemia in women of all ages (particularly young women), encouraging the development and use of locally produced weaning food.

Control of Drugs

Efforts to eradicate the trafficking, marketing, and distribution of unsafe and ineffective drugs should be intensified by the international community, including educational programs to promote the proper prescription and informed use of drugs. Efforts should also be strengthened to eliminate all practices that are detrimental to the health of women and children; and to ensure that all women have access to essential drugs that are appropriate to their specific needs. Information on the appropriate use of essential drugs recommended by WHO should be made widely available to women, being certain that all imported and exported drugs are WHO certified. Ways and means of assisting women consumers through the provision of information and the creation of legislation should also be established by governments. Consumer consciousness and protection from unsafe goods, dangerous drugs, unhealthy foods, and unethical and exploitative marketing practices [such as the Nestlé Corporation's free distribution of infant formula in the first week after childbirth, effectively undermining lactation], should be guarded against. Strong and active organizations for consumer protection should be established by non-governmental organizations.

Control of Reproduction

The ability of women to control their own fertility is basic to their enjoyment of other rights. All individuals and couples have the fundamental human right to be informed and to decide freely the number and spacing of their children. Maternal and child health and family planning should be strengthened, producing relevant information and creating services. Irrespective of their population policies, government should encourage access to such services.

To ensure a free and voluntary choice, family planning information, education, and means should include all medically approved and appropriate methods. Family life and responsible parenthood education should be widely available and directed towards both men and women.

Pregnancy occurring in adolescent girls, whether married or unmarried, has adverse effects on the mortality and morbidity of both mother and child. Recognizing this, governments are urged to develop policies to encourage delay in the commencement of child bearing, making efforts to raise the age of entry into marriage in countries where this age is still quite low. Both girls and boys should receive adequate information and education.

Governments and organizations responsible for distributing and administering fertility control methods and drugs should ensure that they conform to adequate standards of quality, efficiency, and safety. Information about contraceptives should be made available to women, and incentive and disincentive programs neither coercive nor discriminatory. They should be consistent with internationally recognized human rights, as well as with changing individual and cultural values.

Women should have the same access as men to affordable preventative, curative, and rehabilitative treatment. General screening and treatment of women's common diseases, including cancer, should be conducted wherever possible, together with concerted efforts to reduce high levels of maternal and child mortality.

Professional Roles

Women's participation in professional and managerial positions in health institutions should be increased, including higher levels of medical training and training in other health-related fields. Appropriate legislation, training, and supportive action should be taken, as well as effective community involvement. Representation in local and national councils and committees is essential if they are to progress, their employment and working conditions as health personnel and workers expanded and improved at all levels. Traditional female healers and birth attendants, known as midwives in some cultures, should be more fully and constructively integrated in national health planning.

Occupational Health and Safety

The public and private sectors should enhance occupational health and safety. Health risks that endanger reproductive capabilities should cover both female and male workers, discriminating against neither. Efforts should be directed equally at the health of unborn children, pregnant and lactating women, the impact of new technologies on their health, and the harmonization of work and family responsibilities. The environmental impact of policies, programs, and projects concerning women's health and activities, including their sources of employment and income, should be assessed, and the negative effects eliminated rather than access to the jobs in question.

Provision for parental leave following birth [or adoption] of a child, and accessible child care facilities should be made for all working parents, female and male.

Environmental Safety

In the coming decades, changes in the environment will be critical to women. Their role as intermediaries between the natural environment and society with respect to agro-systems is key, as well as the provision of safe water and fuel supplies, and the closely associated problem of sanitation. This is of particular concern in areas experiencing increasing demographic pressure, whether rural or urban. Improvements could bring about reductions in morbidity and mortality, better regulation of fertility, and population control. The results will be beneficial to men, women and children, as well as to the environment. (See United Nations Population Fund for a discussion of gender role analysis in Chapter 3.)

PERSON-ENVIRONMENT PROGRAM MODELS: HEALTH

Bangladesh Women's Health Coalition – *Dhaka, Bangladesh*

Bangladesh Women's Health Coalition is an affiliate of the International Women's Health Coalition, founded in 1980, providing family planning clinics and other health services throughout the country. Because they accept no monies from the United States, they are the only non-governmental organization in Bangladesh to provide "menstrual regulation" counselling and services, a dilation and curettage procedure.

The Bangladesh Women's Health Coalition includes in its objectives an expansion of its role in promoting high quality, comprehensive care that is attentive to women's legal, social, and economic status and responsibilities. The organization encourages women to give equal attention to their daughters' health, as to their sons' (Sandra Mostafa Kabir, 1989). (See Chapter 6 for examples of women's employment programs and social empowerment, so important to their health, and Chapter 8 for a discussion of rural women, mental health, and economic development.)

Women in Development Consortium in Thailand/Friends of Women – *Bangkok, Thailand*

The Women in Development Consortium in Thailand (WIDCIT) is a joint project of Thailand's Chulalong Korn, Thammasat and Khon Kaen Universities, and York University in Canada. The following five-day training program, conducted by Friends of Women, was organized for disadvantaged factory women of Thailand. Their health needs assessment studies indicate that it is essential to stimulate women to focus on themselves, their situation, needs and aspirations, to encourage them to play an active role in the public sphere, to contribute to society, and to be given recognition. A participatory, non-hierarchical group dynamics approach is taken; the facilitators train the trainers, and everyone then trains the trainees. All trainers must attend all sessions, so that everyone learns all of the information shared, both formal and informal.

Train the Trainers Program
First Day: participants share their family life backgrounds, talking about such things as their childhood experiences, sex discrimination by parents, and what caused them to migrate from a rural to an urban area to become factory workers. They speak of their adjustments to workplace conditions. (The women work on a weekly shift rotation basis that alienates them from one another. They are unable to form relationships. Even when ill, they are not allowed to slow down. There is no time to plan, to go to school, or to upgrade themselves. If they must miss work, they have to find a replacement and pay them themselves. Friends of Women, in fact, provide the funds so that they can meet their obligations while undergoing training.) The trainees at this stage generally are not conscious of their health needs in relation to their work.

Second Day: The focus is on occupational health issues. Medical doctors are brought in to discuss women's bodies. They teach the participants about the function of their organs and the interactional impact of chemicals and working conditions on each organ (for example, the effects of prolonged standing and bending over, poisoned air, and unceasing noise). Discussions also address traditional beliefs that are unfounded, making a distinction between superstition and viable folk healing.

Third Day: Discussion centers on economic problems of the workers, using a micro approach. Participants are asked to analyze their income and expenses, figuring out how they spend their money. Different colors of paper are used for different denominations. As they categorize expenses and earning, the outcome is very visible. The recorder graphs the information to further clarify their experience. By the afternoon of the third day, their consciousness is beginning to be raised. They talk about their poor health conditions, their stress related to shift work, the fact that they are underpaid, and the realization that double time would not be a valid solution, since they are already overworked. Their exhaustion, in fact, is often the trigger to their enlightenment. They come to the conclusion that both individual and collective efforts are needed.

Fourth Day: The fourth session, focusing on laws and politics, is conducted by labor lawyers. The women learn what is required to improve living and working conditions. A feminist educator discusses labor protection standards, labor protection, and labor relations laws. They learn that different levels of law must be addressed. Many employers' "laws," for example, are negotiable because they are arbitrary and even against national laws. It is also important to distinguish between old and modern labor laws since they are often in conflict, having contradictory provisions. In such cases, a judge's interpretations may be arbitrary. For example, according to law, collective bargaining in Thailand need not be labor union initiated, as it is in some other countries. Any group can engage in bargaining provided one-fifth of the workers are represented. Still, organizing is very difficult because of the shift system and the fact that contracts are of only three months' duration; nor can social security operate with such uncertainty. The discussion of politics is also on two levels. Participation in factory politics (collective bargaining) is encouraged, as is participation on the national level. Advocating for changes in social security laws, for example, requires a national campaign. Women can encourage political parties to pay attention to female labor and associated necessities, such as child care. The trainers educate the permanent migrant workers who may not have changed their domicile (a home registration prerequisite) to do so, in order to be able to vote.

Fifth Day: The final day of the workshop integrates all that went before in the previous four days. A recorder draws representations of the information on the board, leading the group from step to step. They move from personal to social problems, and then to economic and political concerns, charting the connections between them. Analyzing solutions together, discussing pros and cons, issues are addressed at two levels, the individual and the collective. For example, they discuss the possibility of working more for more money versus receiving more money for fewer working hours. (In Thailand, an employer can force a person to work overtime. While this does not hold true in all countries, there is often implicit pressure to do so.) (Malee Pruekpongsawalee, 1989).

Inter-African Committee/On Traditional Health Practices – *Addis Ababa, Ethiopia*

The Inter-African Committee (IAC) on Traditional Practices Affecting the Health of Women and Children has offices in Addis Ababa, Ethiopia and Geneva, Switzerland. Their newsletter is an outstanding example of communication that is both substantive and supportive. It provides an exchange of information about experiences gained in the African women's campaign against harmful traditional practices. The issues are delicate ones that are subject to cultural taboos, causing feelings of isolation and fear in the women involved. The newsletter is their voice, offering encouragement and ideas to enrich the activities of African women, letting them know that they are not alone in their struggle. Typical content includes articles are included that report on seminars on female circumcision; traditional practices, such as decorative scarring of the body; accepted beatings by husbands, polygamy, and isolating and unhealthy birth delivery practices; the need for safe motherhood; adolescent marriage and pregnancy that is encouraged to the detriment of young girls; eating taboos in some countries whereby girls and women are restricted in the food they eat; and the inferior status of widows. Many of these issues are common to all African women, but are not limited to them by any means (IAC Newsletter, September 1988).

Helping Hand/Elder Housing – *Hong Kong*

Helping Hand of Hong Kong is a voluntary social service organization that began in 1978 when a small group of people, many of whom were disk jockeys who were instrumental in publicizing the situation, responded to what was then a little recognized problem, the plight of elderly single people who were homeless. (They lived in "cage housing," a shocking notion, until we stop and think that many homeless in the west do not even have a cage to live in.) Initially a housing project for elderly men, the program today serves women and men in over eight temporary housing areas and four permanent sheltered housing estates. Designed as self-care units, they are planning housing for the frail elderly who need health and other caretaking services. Their efforts have motivated the government to provide permanent public housing for single elders.

Funding is one of the most impressive aspects of Helping Hand. Proposals for capital costs are most easily financed, for donors are given visible credit for furniture and equipment. Maintenance, however, is a more difficult challenge, but one that has been met through an annual Cookie Campaign that is timed to coincide with Chinese New Year festivities. Cookie companies are asked to donate the 90,000 eight-inch diameter chocolate chip cookies. They are packaged in bright red cardboard envelopes with gold Chinese characters and the Helping Hand logo. A perforated tab serves as a raffle ticket which is an added incentive for purchasing this 20 Hong Kong dollar cookie. Local dignitaries (such as senators, sports and entertainment figures) support the project by autographing the envelopes and thus raising the price of these collector's items. The campaign has become so popular that people in the public eye sometimes ask to have their pictures taken while signing their names before television and newspaper photographers (Cynthia Hui, 1989).

United Nations Population Fund – *New York, New York, USA*

The Technical and Evaluation Division of the United Nations Population Fund (UNFPA) has identified the following emerging needs and issues in population communication and education, focusing on women's concerns: (1) Research techniques to enhance participation of women in population activities; (2) Involvement of women as health educators or communication specialists in the design of service delivery; (3) Encouragement of women to use clinic services and of clinic outreach workers to take into account women's needs; (4) Language used in family planning giving adequate respect to women's dignity, to be non-sexist, and to be sensitive to cultural and religious differences; (5) Approaches to adolescent females, taking rural and urban differences into account, responsibility in sexual behavior, and the importance of young girls planning their first pregnancies in accordance with opportunities for education and future employment; (6) Empowerment of newly married women to resist pressure from inlaws and friends to have the first child as soon as possible after marriage; instead, delaying the first pregnancy; (7) Implications of AIDS in regard to women should be taught in population education and communication programs; (8) Encouragement of women to design communication and education programs to support one another in taking control of their bodies and health, especially in fertility management; (9) Education of men to understand women's rights in the context of the Universal Declaration of Human Rights; and (10) Communication with men as individuals and as a group in male-dominated organized cultural, religious, and employment institutions.

Further, the UNFPA underscores the need for sex-segregated data, comparisons between women and men, and gender role analyses in all population and development studies, within the context of each country, each project within it, and the objectives of the project (Mallica Vajrathon, 1989).

Indicators of Physical Well-being (Dixon, 1980)

Ruth Dixon's assessment of the impact of development projects on women has identified the following six indicators of physical well-being:

Access to Food, Water, and Fuel

Particular attention must be paid to the sexual division of labor in agriculture, as well as other arenas. The same is true of cultural norms in the home in regard to food. Often girls and women eat only what is left, and with restrictions as to their diet at that. Food programs in schools favor boys since girls are more likely to be kept at home. Project planners must understand fully the role of girls and women in food production, distribution, and consumption if benefits are to be distributed equitably.

Access to and Quality of Housing

Is there adequacy of protection against the elements? What is the amount of space per person? What are the household amenities and other indicators such as cultural acceptability? Do home improvements (such as electricity) benefit one sex more than the other, or one household more than another? Are there negative aspects that might affect females more than males (such as crowding due to immigration for employment), or insufficient temporary shelter for migrant workers? Do women-headed households qualify for low cost loans for housing, and are these women included in relevant training programs? Given that most women spend more hours per day in the home than men do, any positive or negative changes are likely to affect them more intensely. Are the design and location of housing units appropriate for their needs?

Environmental Quality
This component of physical well-being is assessed, among other indicators, by the existence of sanitary facilities, the adequacy of drainage, the degree of air and water contamination, and the prevalence of environmentally-based diseases, as measured in the home, the workplace, and in the community. The relationship of persons to their physical environment is determined in part by the sexual division of labor, and by cultural norms that determine the nature and location of various patterns of daily or seasonal activity. Shifts in sexual division of labor may have unintended consequences; even when a positive improvement, attention must be paid to the stresses of change. Successful agricultural projects in traditional purdah-observing societies, for example, may lead to women and girls withdrawing from the labor force to stay at home in seclusion, the more highly valued practice. Though they can afford to do so, with darkness and inactivity, the incidence of vitamin D deficiency and associated diseases (even obesity) increases significantly. [So, too, do vision problems.]

Access to Medical Care
Are preventative and curative health care and family planning information and services accessible? Preference is often given to the more highly valued male members of the family. Women's access is sometimes constrained as well by cultural restrictions on contact between males and females. Projects designed to deliver health services must have a clear women's component, with special efforts made to train female medical practitioners to reach female clientele in an environment sensitive to their concerns. Without them, women will reject the program, or suffer needlessly when they are desperate to seek help.

Personal Safety
Personal safety is a central concern, though seldom discussed in the evaluation literature. This indicator is measured by the degree of exposure to, and protection from, personal violence or accident and injury. The protection of girls of marriageable age is of particular concern in societies which place high value on female chastity as a kin group symbol of honor. Training projects, for example, should not expose women to sexual harassment or walking long distances. Safe places to spend the night and safe transportation that is not controlled by men would solve such problems.

Rest and Leisure
Rest and leisure, seldom considered for women, is measured by the intensity (energy) and extensiveness (time) of labor required, and by the

number of hours available to household members to eat, sleep, and relax. Daily, weekly, and seasonal fluctuations are important, as are differences in age, sex, household composition, class, landholding status, and occupation. Research indicates that women have far less time for rest and leisure than men do. They are often the first to rise in the morning, and the last to go to sleep at night. It is important that new projects do not add to their already heavy burden. Expanded activities and technologies too often do just the opposite, with little or no compensating gains. The intensity and extensiveness of labor inputs of all household members should be assessed before undertaking new projects. Female workloads must be reduced. If they are not reduced, they should be undertaken only in exchange for some other valued resource, from the perspective of the women involved, and with appropriate social supports (Ruth Dixon, 1980).

Violetta Clean/Chemical Dependency – *West Berlin, Germany*

In the region formerly called West Germany, women who abuse drugs either go to jail for four years, or they can choose twelve to eighteen months of therapy. Violetta Clean, a home for women who have alcohol and other drug problems, is one of their options. The participants (called "Violettas") receive counseling and group therapy that help them to get in touch with the traumas that have affected their lives. (As many as 70 percent have been sexually abused.) The young women lack self-esteem and are encouraged to recognize their strengths, despite their substance abuse problems. Each woman is supported in the development of her own unique identity, which inherently includes responsibility as a prerequisite for healthy maturity. When the women reach a point in their recovery when they can begin to venture into the world, they are assigned to Cafe and Treff fur Frauen (Extra Dry), a women's cafe owned by Violetta Clean which features health food, coffee, and tea. The women work in pairs, cooking and baking for the cafe twice weekly in four daily shifts of six hours each. Others work in groups of two or three, cleaning the restaurant and waiting on tables under the direction of a facilitator. When they are ready to begin to work alone, they do so for two to four hours. All tips go to the maintenance of Violetta Clean, and the women decide together how the money will be spent (Margit Huperz, 1988).

Alcoholism Center for Women (ACW)/Ethnic and Lesbian Services – *Los Angeles, California, USA*

The Alcoholism Center for Women provides one of the largest and most comprehensive recovery programs for women in the United States. Serving women who are at high risk for alcoholism, ACW focuses on prevention as well as treatment. Special programs are designed for Latina and Black women, lesbians, incest and battering survivors, and adult children of alcoholics. These groups represent at least 25 percent of women who drink and up to 50 percent of all women with a drinking problem. Lapis, a program of prevention and community services, develops stress management skills and the enhancement of self-esteem through strategies that integrate ethnicity, culture and sexual orientation. One of the very few programs of its kind in the world, it is specifically designed for Latina and Black lesbians (Kathryn Robyn, 1990).

GADE (Group for the Support of Ethnic Development) – *Oaxaca, Oaxaca, Mexico*

The Regional Research Group of Oaxaco (Grupo de Estudios Regionales de Oaxaca) has conducted participative social action research on the subject of midwifery in two indigenous and two peasant communities in rural Mexico. They defined indigenous women in terms of their history (length of time in the area), geographical location, relationship to the land, customs, and their administrative and political structure. The peasants are Mestizos who are part white and part Indian; they actually make up 80–90 percent of the Mexican population.

The project incorporates western and popular medicine (herbal and other alternative cures). The information collected has been disseminated to the women, as well as to health authorities who train midwives. Prior to the investigation, much of their curriculum contained misinformation. The researchers have developed a video and a book on the subject as well. Of particular importance was the first opportunity for some of the indigenous and peasant women to socialize across communities when they were brought together in 1987 for the first time, thus broadening their world view and experience (Paula Sesia-Lewis, Virginia Alejandre, and Maria Christina Galente, 1989).

8 Rural Women, Mental Health and Economic Development

> I suppose the pleasure of country life lies really in the eternally renewed evidences of the determination to live.
>
> Vita Sackville-West, *Country Notes*, 1940

Even though the United Nations has recognized the higher rates of mental illness among women throughout the world (Women's International Network, 1985), the reality was virtually ignored by the recorders of the Decade of Women. The *Forward-Looking Strategies* do not mention the subject. I have chosen to incorporate mental health concerns into this chapter on rural women because they are most vulnerable, and because most of the world's women live in rural areas. The content is based on cross-cultural research conducted at Forum '85, the non-governmental component of the final United Nations Decade of Women meeting in Africa (Wetzel, 1987). This section deviates slightly from the format of other chapters in that the entire chapter is organized around the identified negative barriers and positive catalysts for human development and mental health. They are described in Chapter 1 as person-environment dimensions of Aloneness, Connectedness, Action, and Perception, and are the concepts on which the programs detailed in each chapter are based. Much of the discussion is also pertinent to urban women, many of whom are emigrating from rural areas, and are projected as a majority population in the early 21st century.

THE ALONENESS CONTINUUM

To be alone in the world in a negative sense is both a physical and a psychological reality. Women are alone when they have no family, close love relationship, friends, or community resources. They also may be emotionally alone and painfully lonely when people in their lives are unsupportive and uncaring, when they have sole responsibility for their families, are without external help, and have nowhere to turn. Women's need for aloneness in a positive sense is generally overlooked, although it is fundamental to the process of psychic growth, to individuation – the process of becoming fully authentic – role free, without facade, and transcending social and cultural constraints. Regardless of the culture, each woman must recognize that she is a unique individual, never before and never again to be duplicated. Her personal qualities, like those of others, should be honored and respected. The culture, of course, will influence the degree of positive aloneness needed.

Women in Isolation

The fact of living in a rural community impacts on the autonomy of women. Studies indicate, for example, that rural women are less likely than their urban counterparts to know about contraceptive methods. A survey in the Yemen Arab Republic showed the most striking difference, with a 74–18 percent awareness differential. The geography – mountains, rivers, rugged terrain, and long distances – tend to isolate rural women, making family planning education less likely (Population Reports, 1985). When they cannot feed and care for their growing families, women blame themselves, experience guilt, self-reproach and depression, since they do not understand the larger causal forces. In a health services survey by the Zimbabwe Women's Bureau, the women spoke of the characteristic problems of geographical isolation:

> We don't have a clinic in our area. During the rainy season children can even die in the house because the clinic is too far away and there is a river between our homes and the clinic which is difficult to cross. (McCalman, 1981, 13)

The sense of isolation and sole burden of responsibility weighs heavily on the shoulders of many other of the world's women. According to the last "special government study" conducted by the United States Bureau of Census in 1978, one out of three families is headed by women. Since that time, the figures have escalated markedly. The International Labour Office reports a conservative estimate of three out of every ten households headed by women in developing countries, notably in Africa. The lives of these women are particularly difficult, usually living below the poverty line, not unlike women alone in the United States.

Like their rural North American counterparts, African women are alone for an array of reasons. One, because their husbands have emigrated to urban areas, sometimes staying in touch, but seldom to be relied upon as they develop new relationships. While the rural women must become the sole family providers, they lack legal status to make necessary decisions. Two, women alone may be widows of husbands who die earlier in life from natural causes and from warfare. Surviving wives have few options to improve their conditions. Alone, they lose their rights to the land and are not recognized as a group who would receive special consideration. Three, divorcees are in a marginal position in their family system with or without dependent children. Discriminatory practices often exclude them from sharing any part of their former husbands' property. Divorcee-headed households are spreading in Africa because of rejection by the family of origin. Four, single mothers are a significantly growing phenomenon. In Botswana, for example, eighty percent of all unmarried women above age twenty-five have children. Just as many women in the western hemisphere are choosing not to marry, so it is in African countries. The reasons they give are somewhat similar – to retain freedom, and to avoid waiting on and supporting their husbands on their small salaries. Stress among rural poor mothers is compounded by the dual role of nurturer and provider, roles reflecting women's lot throughout the world (Youssef and Hetler, 1985).

In the United States, of the 20.6 million people living alone, sixty percent are women age fourteen and over. At least nine million of them are single mothers; one million of these mothers are children themselves. Statistics indicate a growing trend toward single motherhood among white women who, contrary to conventional wisdom, represent the majority of single mothers. Black women have an eighty-five per capita count, but their numbers are diminishing (Children's Defense Fund, 1986). Pregnant, single adolescent girls in the U.S. are ten times more likely to suicide than are other teenage girls according to the U.S. Bureau of Census in 1978. With more accepting mores, their mental health would now be less at risk were it not for the spectre of poverty.

THE CONNECTEDNESS CONTINUUM

Connectedness as a central theme is more obvious to theorists in its negative dimension and to the women of the world on the positive side. Psychological theories concerning depression abound which translate connectedness as dysfunctional dependence. Whether a state, trait, or developmental phase, the message is clear: "Outgrow it." The female experience, however, is couched in relationship, interdependence, empathic understanding, mutual nurturance, and informal support systems. A number of feminist theorists since the 1970s have argued that these positive relational aspects of women's development should become models for our alienated world (Miller, 1976; Chodorow, 1978; Gilligan, 1982).

The connectedness continuum is not only an individual possibility; connectedness can be conceptualized at the societal level as well. The massive movement towards women's support groups, social reform and ideological revolution throughout the world has not been matched since the mid-1800s in the United States. British and U.S. historians have called their women's club movement of greater social significance than any former two hundred year period (White, 1904; O'Neill, 1969). The promise continues to hold true for the women of the world as history begins to repeat itself on an international scale. Clearly, this time the women of the developing world are leading the way.

Social Cohesion and Religion

Social cohesion as a negative societal characteristic was introduced by Murphy, Wittkower and Chance in 1967 in an international cross-cultural inquiry into the symptomatology of psychotic depression. It was found that the degree to which a community member shares values, beliefs, and norms (the degree of social cohesion) is directly related to anger and the level of depression. The less cohesive the community, the freer persons are likely to be to pursue their private ends and hence be free of depression. Guilt feelings, self-depreciation, and depression were strongly related to traditional religious involvement.

Contemporary research is corroborative. According to a comprehensive international study concerning the progress of women during the UN Decade of Women, the "liberalization of the law to provide equal rights for women is slowest in countries in which traditional social and religious practices have strictly enforced women's subordinate status . . . " (Sivard, 1985, 32). Customary practice prevails even when these countries have sex-equality provisions in their constitutions. Nawal El Saadawi, former practicing psychiatrist, writer, and feminist Egyptian activist, spoke to the issue at the Nairobi conference in 1985:

Whenever you go to the roots of anything it is political . . . Health is linked to the government, religions, politics, and the economics of poverty . . . Fundamentalists throughout the world are using God to hide inequalities and economics. Jews, Hindus, Moslems, and Christians are funded by their government leaders, and women are the first victims. These sects distort their religions. They don't teach what is in the holy books. They just want to maintain male power.

El Saadawi used the Koran as an example of such distortions. "The Koran prohibits polygamy," she said, "yet, Islamics want to institutionalize the practice."

Global Connectedness

Recognition that global connectedness in regard to mental health is essential to understanding human beings and their conditions has been with us for over six decades. Even so, western logic and values that focus on cure and ignore prevention have dominated the world mental health scene. The importance of a world view, reinforced by the 1948 International Congress on Mental Health with its theme of World Citizenship, did nothing to dispel the trend (World Federation of Mental Health, 1948). Ethnocentric biases have resulted in unfortunate misdiagnoses and treatment (Lin, 1984). Until the 1970s, the World Health Organization uncritically promoted the western system, a system that did little to reach the rural poor. Today, there is general recognition of the need for a global vision which seeks to understand interacting international and indigenous forces, whether social, cultural, economic, or political. Still, ISIS (the International Women's and Communication Service) tells us,

> Three-quarters of Third World doctors work in cities where three-quarters of the health budget is spent. But three-quarters of the people and three-quarters of the ill-health is in rural areas. (ISIS, 1983, 147)

Non-Governmental Collectives

Clubs and cooperatives which connect people have proven to be the most successful vehicles of the World Food Programme (1985). It was created in Rome, Italy for the purpose of development assistance for the world's poorest women in developing countries. Goals include improving their nutrition, providing educational opportunities for women and girls, creating opportunities to earn money, to build self-reliance, and to help meet women's basic needs. Approaching these goals can ensure the prevention of depression.

In most rural communities in Africa, collectivism is an important element in women's social, religious, economic, and cultural activities.

In twenty-four African villages, for example, they are engaged in the World Health Organization's Women in Health Development program. Primary health care is delivered through a system of self-reliant health cooperatives which work for rural development. The problems of drinking water provision, day care, gardening, and road construction are addressed as entry level topics, with the primary agenda of all-round physical, mental, and social development.

In Bangladesh, the more educated women are sharing their skills with rural women and girls, focusing on literacy, citizenship, economics, and health (Bangladesh Federation of University Women, 1985). But local efforts cannot hope to address the staggering needs throughout the world. The Committee on the Status of Women in India has concluded that their primary health service is ill-equipped to provide curative care. Women in Bangladesh and India, unlike the rest of the world, have constantly higher death rates as compared to men up to the age of fifty. Health and mental health services have not reached women; and those in rural areas are at a particular disadvantage. It has been concluded that services must include resocializing women and their families to get help at earlier stages of illness and to dispel the prevalent myths of "women's resistance to disease." Others suggest plugging services into women's group activities and income-generating projects where they can get group support and encouragement (Murthy, 1985).

What is true of girls and young women is true for the elderly. In the U.S., eighty percent of rural elderly women live in poverty, as do eighty-seven percent of rural elderly women in countries like Kenya. Their need for relationship and support is critical, as is their need for health care, both physical and mental. The importance of intergenerational connectedness is underscored in Kenya by the fact that older women are the traditional birth attendants, delivering eighty percent of the children. If they were made aware of primary health care practices and the psychological needs of the women they serve, the health and mental health of rural women and their children would be enhanced (Kenya NGO Organizing Committee for Forum '85).

THE ACTION CONTINUUM

Multiple Responsibilities and Economic Action

The multiple responsibilities of rural women throughout the world only differ by degree. In most countries, they work long hours within the home and community, providing agricultural and maintenance services to their families without pay, insuring that they will be the poorest of the poor. Lacking access to resources which would enable them to be self-sustaining, they often work outside the home where they continue to be exploited. (See Chapters 6 and 7 for discussions about women's employment and health conditions.)

Speakers at the Forum '85 session on *Development Alternatives for Women of a New Era* (DAWN), underscored the reality of women's universal economic condition. From Asian, African, and Latin American nations, they emphasized a salient reality summarized by a Sri Lankan:

> The more women work, the poorer they are. The White Economy is the money economy, not the world economy.

Women, they said, paid the cost of their countries' deficits. When husbands migrate to urban areas and families cannot afford to hire agricultural labor, the women must compensate for losses by intensifying their unpaid labor (Sivard, 1985). Chronic exhaustion is not unusual. In a personal interview a Sudanese social worker reported:

> Women whose husbands migrate work around the clock. So do the others really. They have very little rest and are very stressed. No one helps them. They tend the garden, care for the children, walk many miles twice a day for water, and gather fuel wood. They cook and clean and try to earn money. When they get depressed, people say it is the occult and ostracize them.

Cultural Action

Inequality is increasing throughout the world, with government after government pressing for domestication of women (called "housewification)," attempting to turn the clock back to a time of purely subservient service on the part of women. In a workshop on the *Needs of Rural Women* by the International Alliance of Women, the importance of breaking down old destructive traditions was emphasized, as it was in a *Women and Health* session by the National Nurses of Kenya. They, too, reported that chronic exhaustion leading to depression was common among rural women who represented eighty percent of their patients. Fifty percent of females hospitalized for psychiatric problems were between the ages of fifteen and thirty-five; most are unemployed housewives. Married women rearing children were at highest risk. A psychiatrist detailed the leading contributing causes of mental illness in Kenyan women as "emotional deprivation" in married women, lack of self-image, and self-effacement. Other causes included more than three children born less than three years apart, and lack of civil rights, such as legal defense and property inheritance entitlement. Personal and social well-being clearly are inextricably linked. These findings echo U.S. and British research on women (Wetzel, 1984). Mental health, the participants agreed, must be promoted in the community. But as a Kenyan social worker reported, "Too often psychiatrists just house the mentally ill, giving them drugs and releasing them. Patients then don't think they need to do anything about their problem." The issue is not confined to Kenya; it is universal.

UN Action

Violence, another factor that impacts on mental health, is on the rise against women worldwide. The United Nations Division for Economic and Social Information (1985) included in the official conference agenda which was endorsed by the Decade of Women, the need for governments to "undertake effective measures to provide shelter, support, and reorientation services for abused women and children" (7). They also called for recognition of the vital role of women as health care providers both in and out of the home. Social service priorities focus on adequate child care and education for working parents to reduce the double burden of women. The need for men and society as a whole to share responsibility for reproduction and child rearing is documented. There is special concern for women in rural areas due to the deteriorating conditions.

THE PERCEPTION CONTINUUM

Most theories of depression cite perception or cognition as one of the most important characteristics regarding both prevention and cure, as well as growth and development. How one views the world, the self, and the future are well-tested attitudes. Negativity is correlated with depression and positive ideation fosters well-being. But what of the realities of the lives of the world's women that have been described? Research also tells us that vulnerability to depression increases when positive ideation conflicts with negative reality. Although negative perception certainly reflects contact with women's reality, the development of positive aspects of aloneness, connectedness, and action make possible the realization of positive self-perception. The implications are great for combatting women's hopeless, helpless, and worthless feelings that usher in depression (Wetzel, 1984). Still, it is not enough to place the responsibility solely on women.

Changing Social Perception

Women's contributions and needs must be attended to very seriously. Their health, both physical and mental, cannot be viewed in isolation from wider considerations, according to the Director General of the World Health Organization. "Employment [beyond subsistence], education, social status, the freedom to plan their families, equitable access to economic resources and political power" are all essential factors (Mahler, 1985,1). The reality is that women blame themselves for their condition. A Nigerian children's television executive told the author:

> Mental health is a tremendous problem in Nigeria. Women are in fear of their husbands, of not having a home, of not being able to feed their children. They are depressed and anxious and think it is because they are bad.

A social worker from Kenya described the situation in her country:

> A woman I see is so depressed she cannot think of anything good about herself or her life. She thinks she is worthless and everyone says she is. Her situation is so bad, it seems true. I feel so alone and don't know if I'm doing the right thing for her.

The impact of such women on the mental health of this social worker reminds us of the common human need for perceived effectiveness that all people share.

Changing Cultural Blindness Concerning the Human Rights of Women

At the Association of Women in Psychology (1985b) workshop, a woman from The Netherlands described how perception clouds entire mental health systems:

What they don't see doesn't exist. They don't see sexual violence or incest, and when lesbians are depressed, it is because they are lesbians. They don't see them.

Up country, in the more isolated rural Kenyan areas, "Women may be sexually assaulted while on the way to the well, but they are ignored because men don't perceive it as a problem," according to two Nairobi outreach workers. They reported that these rural women have many mental health problems that also are ignored. "There are many female street people. If they are crazy they go to the garbage. It is not acceptable for anyone but the police to help them."

Changing perceptions of women is as essential in later life as in earlier years. A study of depressed elderly farm women in Switzerland is exemplary (d'Epinay, 1985). In a complex analysis of their life histories and their "meaning and value systems," their high rate of depression was explained by a cognitive theory of culture shock. The culture shock theory considers depression to be a way out of the conflict between traditional values and normal human needs. These rural women became aware of the widespread demand to accede to a life of suffering and subservience by their husbands, the church, and the community, in short, to view themselves as inferior beings. Psychologically wounded by their shocking realization, they become depressed to numb their psychic pain.

The International Federation on Ageing reports that "aged women suffer significantly more than men in rural areas" (22). The phenomenon of the feminization of old age in rural communities is a striking reality on a global scale, according to the American Association for International Aging. In their report to Congress they argue that "Rural development should be seen as a key to the overall problem of the aging" throughout the world, as it is the key to integrated and balanced national progress in largely agricultural economies (Select Committee on Aging, 1985, 43). The care of the elderly, they recommend, should go beyond disease orientation to take into account the interdependence of the mental, social, spiritual, and environmental factors. The ability to cope is correlated highly with their sense of self-esteem, self-image, and well-being (Peace, 1981).

There is no country or region on the face of the earth in which women experience equality (Sivard, 1985). Might it be that the governments of each nation are threatened by the unity of the women of the world, preferring women to be isolated, unconnected to one another, their actions limited to obedience and self-effacing perceptions? The free and poorly paid services of women would prevail, reason enough for the renewed universal thrust toward female domestication. But more important, nations may be threatened because women's identification with women on a global scale means that their support for killing one another's children is less likely. A statement made by a black woman from the United States at the spontaneous closing Unity Session at Forum '85 captured the essence of women's universal message when she declared," We are not fighting to oppress and dominate, but to heal and liberate." Not only would mental health be assured for women, but equality, development, and peace, and employment, health, and education could be real possibilities for all. It may seem like a fantasy, but most women who attended the Nairobi conference came away believers.

ANTI-DISCRIMINATION POLICY ANALYSIS: RURAL WOMEN

Article 14: Rural Women
Article 14 acknowledges the special problems faced by rural women and the significant roles that they play in the economic survival of their families and communities, including their work in the non-monetized sectors of the economy (Convention, 1980).

Pertinent Questions for Analysis: Rural Women (IWRAW, 1988)

- What special programs, if any, have been developed to meet the needs of rural women?
- How does the mortality rate of rural women compare to that of urban women? The maternal mortality rate? Life expectancy? Nutritional status? Percent receiving prenatal care? Family planning services?
- What are the infant mortality rates in rural compared to urban areas?
- Do rural women have access to social security programs?
- In rural areas, are married, widowed, divorced, non-married, and childless women treated differently from each other?
- How does the availability of health services, including family planning, in rural areas compare to those in urban areas?
- What percentage of rural girls and women are enrolled in primary, secondary, and university level education? How do these percentages compare with urban enrollment?
- What percentages of rural women ages 15–24 are illiterate? Ages 25–44? How do these percentages compare with urban ones?
- What type of work is generally done by rural women (including cooking, cleaning, water carrying, child care, marketing, etc.)?

- Can women hold title to land?
- What percentage of agricultural work in rural areas is done by women? Is it counted in the economic statistics (such as GNP) of the country?
- Does the state recognize the right of rural women to organize self-help groups and to participate in cooperatives and other economic or development programs as individuals? Or is this right restricted to family membership?
- Are there women's self-help groups or cooperatives in rural areas? Describe briefly.
- What community activities do rural women participate in? Are there any religious or cultural traditions which keep women from participating?
- What percentage of agricultural credit and loans in rural areas are actually given to women?
- Can women use rural marketing facilities to sell their goods? What percent of these facilities are used by women?
- Are agricultural extension services designed to reach women directly?

The *Forward-Looking Strategies* section below focuses on the economic aspects of the well-being of rural women. Even the Decade of Women had not yet learned that the internal world is inextricably linked to the external environment, and can be equally resistant to change. Economic and political development are absolute necessities, but they are not sufficient in themselves. In any case, mental illness is correlated with their absence. The *Forward-Looking Strategies* detailed in all chapters, in fact, impact positively on the mental health of all women. (The *Person-Environment Program Models* section will bridge the gap in this chapter by focusing on rural women, mental health, and economics).

Forward-Looking Strategies: Rural Women and Economics (1985): Contributions of Rural Women

The 1979 World Conference on Agrarian Reform and Rural Development viewed the improvement of the vital role of women as a prerequisite for successful rural development, policy, planning, and programs. But their significant contribution to agricultural development has been more widely recognized as a result of the Decade of Women. Of particular note is women's contribution in working hours to agricultural, fishery, and forestry production and conservation, and to various parts of the food system. Still, projections indicate that poverty and landlessness among rural women will increase significantly by the year 2000. To stem this trend, governments should implement, as a matter of priority, equitable and stable investment and growth policies for rural development. This should ensure the reallocation of each country's resources which in many cases are largely derived from the rural areas, but allocated to urban development. [This recommendation should not pit the needs of rural poor women against urban poor women. Urban development has not benefitted either rural or urban women.]

In many regions of the world, women as key food producers play a central role in the development and production of agriculture and food. They participate actively in all phases of the production cycle, including conservation, storage, processing, and marketing of food and agricultural products. Their vital contribution to economic development, particularly in agriculturally based economies, should be better recognized and rewarded. Development strategies and programs, as well as projects and incentive programs in the field of food and agriculture, need to be designed in a manner that fully integrates women at all levels of planning and implementation, monitoring evaluation in all stages of the development process of a project cycle.

Governments also are urged to give priority to the development of a social infrastructure in both urban and rural areas. Examples are adequate care and education for the children of working parents, whether work is carried out at home, in the fields or in factories, to reduce the double burden of working women.

Hunger and Malnutrition

Concrete and adequate resources for the benefit of women, and others in extreme need, should be a world priority. The dramatic deterioration of food in developing [and increasingly, industrialized] countries has resulted in an alarming number of people, mostly women and children, who are exposed to hunger, malnutrition, and even starvation. The international community, particularly donor countries, should be urged to assist women by continuing and increasing financial assistance to enhance their role as food producers. Emphasis should be on providing training in food technologies, so as to alleviate the problems on their continent resulting from extended drought and severe food shortages. Emergency assistance should be increased and accelerated to alleviate the suffering of starving and dying women and children wherever it exists. Governments should involve women in the mobilization and distribution of food aid in all countries affected by drought [or floods], as well as in the fight against desertification. This includes large-scale afforestation campaigns (planting of woodlots, collective farms, and seedlings).

Monitoring, and Evaluation and Knowledge Dissemination

Monitoring and evaluation should be included in governmental initiatives, and the allocation of resources between men and women in mixed projects should be modified.

The dissemination of information to rural women through national information campaigns is important, using all available media and established women's groups. Such efforts should include the exposure of local populations to innovation and creativity through open-air films, talks, visits to areas where needs are similar, and demonstrations of scientific and technological innovations. Women farmers should participate in research and information campaigns and be involved in technical cooperation and exchange of information among developing countries. Rural women should benefit from land reform, and their customary land and inheritance rights should be protected under conditions of land shortage, land improvement, or shifts into cash-cropping. They should also have access to training in and assistance with financial management, savings, investments, and reallocation of land resources, with priority placed on production, especially of staple foods.

Participation in Appropriate Technology

Rural women should be integrated into modern technology programs that introduce new crops and improved varieties, rotation of crops, mixed farming, mixed and intercropping systems, low-cost soil fertility techniques, soil and water conservation methods and other modern improvements, such as irrigation schemes and drilling of accessible wells.

Women can be freed from time and energy-consuming tasks by utilizing appropriate food-processing technologies that will affect improvements in their health. Appropriate technologies can also increase the productivity and income of women, either directly, or by freeing them to engage in other activities. Such technologies should be designed and introduced, however, in a manner that insures women's access to the new technology and its benefits. They should not displace women from means of livelihood when alternative opportunities are not available. Appropriate labor saving devices should utilize local human and material resources and inexpensive sources of energy. Since women are the users, the design, testing, and dissemination of the technology should be appropriate to them. ("If it's not appropriate for women, it's not appropriate.") Governmental organizations can play a valuable role in this process.

Agriculture and Industrial Linkages

Industrial development problems of developing countries reflect the dependent nature of their economies and the need to promote transformation industries based on domestic agricultural production. There needs to be a special interest in the promotion of technical training of women because they are an important part of the agricultural work force. In this respect, governments should take the following recommendations into account: (1) There should be a link between agriculture and industry; (2) Steps should be taken to eliminate any obstacles to the participation of women in industry. Some of these obstacles are energy, the limited markets of some developing countries, the rural exodus, poor infrastructure, lack of technical know-how, the dependence of industries in some countries, and the lack of financial resources; (3) Steps should be taken to promote women's equitable and increased participation in industry by enabling them to have equal access to and to participate in adult education and in-service programs. Such programs should teach literacy, as well as saleable and income-generating skills, encouraging women to participate in collective organizations, including trade unions; (4) Industrial cooperation among developing countries should be promoted by creating sub-regional industries; (5) The industrialization effort of developing countries, and the integration of women in that process, should be assisted by international organizations and developed countries.

Economic Policy and Planning

Governments should recognize the potential impact of short term economic adjustment policies on women in the areas of trade and commerce. Governmental policies should promote women's full participation and integration in these areas. Alternative sources of finance and new markets should be sought to maintain and increase the participation of women in these activities. Appropriate measures should be taken to ensure that legal and administrative impediments are removed that prevent women from enjoying effective and equal access to finance and credit. In addition, positive measures should be introduced, such as loan guarantees, technical advice, and marketing development services. The positive contributions of women traders to local and national economies should also should be recognized. Policies should be adopted to assist and organize these women.

Transportation Policies and Planning

As operators and owners of means of transport, women's roles should be promoted through access to credit and other appropriate means and equal consideration with regard to the allocation of contracts. This is particularly important for women's groups and collectives, especially in rural areas. They are usually well organized, but cut off from serviceable means of transport and communication. With due regard to women as producers and consumers, measures should be formulated to increase the efficiency of land, water, and air transportation. All national and local decisions concerning transportation policies, including subsidies, pricing, choice of technology for construction and maintenance, and means of transport, should consider women' needs. Decisions should be based on consideration of the possible impact on the employment, income, and health of women.

Rural transportation planning in developing countries should aim at reducing the heavy burden on women who carry (on their backs and heads) agricultural produce, water, and wood for fuel. The depletion of forest areas on which most rural women rely for much of their income and energy needs should be prevented. Innovative programs should be initiated with the involvement of both women and men.

In exploring modes of transportation, efforts also should be made to avoid loss of income and employment for women through the introduction of costs that are too high for them. The increasing ratio of women whose income is essential for family survival should be taken into account in the choice of modes of transportation and the design of transport routes.

Concepts of Mental Health

The concept of mental health and the stigmatization of mental illness is stigmatized to the point of taboo. This is particularly likely to prevail in rural areas where women are at very high risk. Even in the more developed world where mental health is a more accepted concept, the influence of the women's movement has not yet reached large numbers of rural women. Moreover, attention to women's fundamental human needs and psychological well-being has been an uncommon consideration even among most globally-oriented feminists until very recently. It is important to think of the facilitation of mental health as educational programming, a concept that is more likely to be accepted throughout the world. Hence, the attention to mental health earlier in this chapter on rural women will be extended to the *Person-Environment Program Models* section below.

(See Chapter 6 for a detailed discussion of rural and urban women and employment.)

PERSON-ENVIRONMENT PROGRAM MODELS:
RURAL WOMEN, MENTAL HEALTH, AND ECONOMICS

Association for Women in Psychology/Mental Health Agenda-Washington, DC, USA

The Association for Women in Psychology (AWP) developed an International Feminist Mental Health Agenda for the Year 2000 on the occasion of the Decade of Women world meeting. Considered a working draft, the document is designed to increase awareness of the fundamental importance of changing attitudes of inferiority and powerlessness in efforts to promote women's equity worldwide. The report is intended as an organizing tool, a strategy in itself for promoting such equity. Women's mental health, defined as their "psychological and emotional quality of life," includes the development of social and cultural standards that reject inequality, discrimination, and the undervaluation of women as acceptable norms. Such norms are currently perpetuated in the home, schools, religious institutions and the work place, directly undermining and interfering with women's ability to experience psychological and emotional quality of life.

Because women from rural and urban areas alike are taught to accept their lot, they undervalue themselves and are put at greater risk of chronic psychological disability. To lessen or eliminate the devastating impact on their mental health, it is important not to blame them for their inability to function. Efforts should be made to avoid humiliation, degradation, and punishment that further undermines their psychological well-being. It is also essential to identify cultural environmental conditions that directly or indirectly perpetuate low self-esteem, emotional instability, depression, anxiety, feelings of powerlessness, and fear of violence. Three levels of assistance (prevention, maintenance and care, and restoration of health) are required. The following questions should be addressed:

1. What are the manifestations of stress or breakdown in your culture? Where do people experiencing chronic psychological problems go for help?

2. Who takes primary responsibility to help them? How does your culture understand and respond to mental illness?

3. Are the following considered to be symptoms of mental problems:

loss of self-esteem, emotional/mood disability, depression, feelings of powerlessness?

4. Is there a social stigma for having psychological problems?

5. What cultural attitudes, values, or expectations seem to have an effect on mental health in your culture? On women? On men?

6. What are the consequences of being temporarily or permanently disabled in your culture? For women? For men?

7. What kind of effect does poverty have on mental health in your culture? On women? On men?

8. What are the social conditions in your culture that cause one diagnostic category or one form of psychological disability to be more prevalent than another? What causes women to be more frequently identified with one category than men, and vice versa?

Each country or culture should also question its prevailing mental health model to determine to what extent it may create or perpetuate conditions that undervalue women, and therefore contribute to their disfunction. By responding to the following questions, each culture's understanding of this problem will be enhanced:

1. What is the model of the mentally healthy individual? of the mentally healthy woman? of the mentally healthy man? Do these differ, and if so, is the difference one that invalidates, removes power, or creates a sense of inferiority in one or the other?

2. Are there different child-rearing or socialization practices that may create a sense of inferiority in either sex, or create dysfunctional patterns later in life?

3. Do the educational, psychological, religious, or legal systems in your culture maintain these destructive differences?

4. What special needs exist for individuals at different developmental points in the life cycle, and how can the mental health system respond to these unique needs to prevent future dysfunction?

5. What is the prevailing model of diagnosis and treatment within your country?

6. How is the model reflected in mental health theory, education, training, and research?

7. What is considered socially deviant behavior?

8. Is there a difference between social deviance and mental illness? Are men and women disproportionately assigned to either category?

9. In what ways may the effects of chronic stress be misidentified as mental illness?

10. What support structures for women exist in your culture to enable changes toward improved psychological health?

11. Among providers, administrators, and policy-makers in your culture's mental health system, are there differences between women and men in their decision-making power and salary level?

12. What changes are needed to eliminate inequities identified in response to these questions (Association for Women in Psychology, 1985)?

Three-Phase Model of Feminist Therapy (Ballou and Gabalac, 1985)

Ballou and Gabalac's Three-Phase Model of Feminist Therapy is based on the assumption that women as a gender are oppressed, their oppression limiting their ability to improve their social and economic conditions, and impacting negatively upon their psychological development and status. Therapeutic interventions intended to assist women in attaining and maintaining mental health, therefore, must also address the power system environment in which they live. Feminism can provide insight into the ways that women have learned to accept their devalued status, self-defeating, and limited options, and to produce self-denying behaviors (Ballou and Gabalac, 1985, 79).

The Three-Phase Model of Feminist Therapy includes harmful adaptation, corrective action, and health maintenance, described as follows:

Harmful Adaptation is "the process whereby women learn to accept dependency and to practice self-negating behavior." The five stages of harmful adaptation are humiliation, inculcation, retribution, conversion, and conscription. These stages are representative of the power system's dynamics and their effect on women. Women actually experience the dynamic and its psychological impact. Social constraints and other external forces become, in effect, individual consciousness. The *Effects of Oppression* table reveals the behavior and feelings of women as they experience each phase of harmful adaptation (Ballou and Gabalac, 1985, 82).

Corrective Action is "the process of replacing harmful adaptation with positive self-concept." Intervention involves both the undoing of the damage of harmful adaptation, and a confrontation with the attitudes and practices in the environment that are destructive to women.

Health Maintenance is "the process of mobilizing feminist resources to change the environment of all women and to encourage women's growth

The Effects of Oppression

Harmful Adaptation	Experience of	Behavior / Feeling
Humiliation:	Being overpowered, exhausted, defeated, unable	Doubt, fear, self-hate, rage / shame, submission, or withdrawal
Inculcation:	Being taught "correct" behavior (behavior that won't be punished); being instructed in survival; being presented contaminated data	Reception of power system ideals, demands; anxiety / fear about ability to perform to standard; must obey rules; must secure protection and escape punishment; conflict between need to learn correct behavior and loss of self
Retribution:	Being threatened with loss of rewards; punishment if correct behavior is not practiced; repressing or punishing opposing data and actions	Resignation; compliance with power systems' values and demands; anxiety / depression; self-hate; helplessness; hidden tension
Conversion:	Accepting power system values and goals as own; accepting own state of dependency as good; distorted perception	Rejection or denial; repression of own goals, values, and experience contrary to power system values, as bad, relief / hope, acceptance of inferior status and constrained nature; identification with aggressor, or reaction formation
Conscription:	Serving as power system spokesperson and harmful adaptation trainer; justifying dependency as only natural and virtuous state for women; being complicitous with power systems	Apologetic, self-denying behavior is used to ingratiate self to "superiors;" denial of health and worth of all non-dependent women; self-righteous presentation of power systems' values; feelings of anger, depression, self-hate for failure to reach sublimation and repression of independent self, wishes, and visions; rigid denial of any values contrary to power systems'

Corrective Action and Health Maintenance*

Harmful Adaptation	Corrective Action	Health Maintenance
Humiliation: Self-shame, overwhelmed by other's strength	Separation: Self discovery, study of harmful adaptation environment	Recognition: Pride in celebration of womanhood
Inculcation: Invalidation of own experience, acceptance of others' values	Validation: Validation of own thoughts and feelings even if incongruent with power systems' values, developing woman's identity	Expression: Sharing of own experience and perceptions
Retribution: Isolation from women and compliance with power systems' expectations under threat of reprisal	Association: Finding acceptance in company of women with diverse values and experiences	Cooperation: Development of interdependent working relationships with women
Conversion: Denial of self-responsibility, entrusting care of self to others' strength	Authorization: Acceptance of responsibility for self; building own strength, woman's identity, articulate own goals	Identification: Acknowledgement of bond of responsibility between all women, pooling of strengths
Conscription: Presentation of subordinate roles, inferior status as only proper choice for women	Negotiation: Interaction with power systems on own behalf to meet needs, goals; active resistance to harm, withdrawal if necessary	Confrontation: Alliance with other women to work for change in systems or creating alternatives

*Tables excerpted from Nancy W. Gabalac and Mary Ballou with David Kelley, *A Feminist Position on Mental Health*, 1985. Courtesy of Charles C. Thomas, Publisher, Springfield, Illinois.

and development." The *Corrective Action* and the *Health Maintenance* phases are interrelated (Ballou and Gabalac, 1985, 99).

Appropriate Technology Association – *Northeast Province, Thailand*

A group of male engineers who are engaged in research on rural technological development have included an experienced female social work educator as the chair of their team. She also acts as an advisor on person-related and social issues. (The men had found that their technological knowledge lacked important "people dimensions" that impinged on the successful outcome of their projects.) The team's research includes indigenous technology with villagers, evaluation of new methods, and dissemination of information. The social implications regarding the women of this rural province proved to be important to the development of the village. The social worker's skills helped them to be aware of the women's lack of esteem, personal pride in their work, and confidence in themselves. Changing their negative self-perception was as critical to success as learning how to adapt to marketing needs and to improving the quality of their home made products. The women had been weaving reams of cloth that were not only of poor quality, but had no market. Their predictable failures only added to their already low opinion of themselves. As a result of their new training, they have developed original mulberry dyes, have quality controls, and have learned how to do marketing research for crafts and food production. They have become part of a regional network, cooperating with the transfer and exchange of appropriate technologies for women in other Asian countries . Their newfound confidence has even lead to their development of water pumps, sorely needed due to lack of water in the northern part of the country (Chalermasri Dhamabutra, 1989).

International Planned Parenthood Federation/Mental Health – *London, England*

The action proposals for mental health enhancement detailed below have been adapted from the International Planned Parenthood Federation's (IPPF) proposals for the enhancement of physical health, which of course remain valid: Women's self-help groups face certain limitations, such as the small-scale nature of their activities, their lack of knowledge of mental health strategies and techniques, their lack of experience in leadership skills and financial management, and their lack of resources. The following IPPF proposals for action indicate ways in which women's organizations, whether local, national, or international, can participate more effectively in programs to improve their well-being.

Grassroots Self-Help Groups
At the local level, grassroots self-help groups should identify community mental health needs, as well as the resources (people, equipment, funds) already available in the community to meet these needs. Next, the actions needed to enable women's groups to participate in meeting local mental health needs (training, fund raising, project planning) should be identified. The local mental health needs identified should then be communicated to the formal mental health system, in order to make the delivery of mental health services more appropriate and responsive. Peer support will need to be provided for women adopting new health care practices that also foster mental health (such as nutritional diets, child care practices, women's support groups, and family planning).

Regional and National Women's Organizations
Regional and national women's organizations must listen to the needs of grass-roots organizations. It is their role to channel this information to governments. Activities should be developed that meet identified community needs, and complement the activities of self-help groups. Such groups should be kept informed about available outside resources and how to obtain them. Training programs can be conducted to enable women's self-help groups to increase their understanding of the essential elements in primary mental health care, to develop their skills, and to share experiences in solving local problems. Accordingly, local bodies also can be influenced by regional and national organizations to divert greater resources to projects and activities which will directly affect women's mental health and which support women's self-help organizations.

International Women's Non-Governmental Organizations
At the international level, women's non-governmental organizations can collect and disseminate information to both governments and women's organizations on women's mental health and the role of women's organizations in primary mental health care. The flow of resources to women's mental and physical health and development projects can be stimulated, and international plans can be translated into activities that reflect national priorities and concerns. International women's organizations should take an advocacy role in promoting issues and programs which relate to women's mental health and in which women's self-help groups could appropriately participate (Blakey, 1985).

9 Equality, the Family, and the Law

Being a mother is a noble status, right? Right. So why does it change when you put "unwed" or "welfare" in front of it?

Florynce R. Kennedy, "Institutionalized Oppression vs the Female," in *Sisterhood is Powerful*, Robin Morgan, Ed., 1970

Limitations on the rights of women cannot be adequately challenged without due process and equality of access and resources. The law is one of the many instruments that women can utilize in their efforts to gain justice in an unjust society. But laws that are not founded on reality are more likely to be abusive. Major parts of our lives are dominated by assumptions which are based on tradition and the notions of bygone eras which no longer hold within them the ring of truth. Outworn assumptions weigh heavily on each of us, and on humanity as a whole. Unless we find the courage and integrity to tap our own raw experience, rather than ready made preparations, we fall victim to a crime that is never taken up in a book of law – the crime of thoughtlessness. This was the message of Clara Wichmann, a Dutch lawyer and women's advocate of the early 1900s (van Walsum, 1989). It remains the challenge of the world of women and their families as we approach the 21st century.

Equality of relationships between women and men is fundamental to achievement of even basic human rights. But equality does not ensure equity. Equal units of service results in unequal consequences, and fair opportunity is not only imperfectly carried out in the world, but within the family, and across different families. The extent to which natural capacities develop and reach fruition is affected by all kinds of class attitudes and social conditions. (For purposes of this discussion, the notion of class is extended beyond economics to encompass ethnicity, gender, and other divisional hierarchies.) Equality is the choice of the advantaged, while the disadvantaged recipient places priority on equity. The former hopes to retain the relative advantages under prevailing conditions, while the latter seeks distributive justice. The concept of distributive justice is particularly relevant to those who serve the least advantaged, the historical domain of social workers (Rawls, 1971; Lewis, 1982). As social workers or others in allied fields dominated (numerically speaking) by women, or as the least advantaged, women have a stake in this conceptual framework. When thought through, its application can be as useful in revealing old injustices, as it is in advancing justice. (Rawls' application to gender issues is my own.)

Distributive Justice

Utilizing social contract theory, John Rawls (1971) developed a set of reasonable value aspirations that are appropriate to the concepts of equality and equity between women and men. The desired values are liberty and opportunity, income and wealth, health and educated intelligence, and self-respect. With the addition of meaningful work (presumably associated with income and wealth, or perhaps self-respect) and mutually support-ive relationships (an unrecognized value of great importance), Rawls' conceptualization may be useful to women and social justice. Although he does not address gender issues, justice, by definition, is conceived as fairness, the first virtue of social institutions. No matter how efficient or well-arranged laws and institutions may be, they must be reformed or abolished if they are unjust. What is just and unjust, however, hinges on the principles assigned as basic rights and duties for determining the proper distribution of benefits and burdens.

The effects of justice are profound and pervasive; and they are present from birth. Institutions, starting with the family, favor "certain beginnings" over others who are born into different positions. The female's position uni-versally is subservient to the male's, though certainly in varying degrees. Their expectations of life are determined by laws and the political system, as well as by social and economic circumstances. These especially deep inequalities are not only pervasive, they cannot be justified on the basis of merit or deservedness. It is these inequalities to which Rawls' principles of social justice for institutions must be concerned.

Rawls' first principle contends simply that each person is to have an equal right to the total system of basic liberties compatible with a similar system of liberty for all. His second principle is more complex because it deals with the reality of unavoidable social and economic inequalities. Such inequalities are to be arranged so that they are to the greatest benefit of the least advantaged. This is consistent with the "just savings" principle, "an understanding between generations to carry out their fair share of the burden of realizing and preserving society" (289). Also, social and economic opportunity should be "attached to offices and positions open to all under conditions of fair equality of opportunity" (302). If we apply these principles to the family, "offices and positions" can be translated as "head of the household." The willingness to even make the effort to negotiate family leadership is itself dependent upon congenial family and social circumstances. A class system that relegates groups of people to different stations in life can be generalized to gender hierarchies within families which create caste systems of males and females. Societies and families alike tend to be divided into separate biological populations, discouraging openness and diversity. What is more, they are permeated by genetic policies, more or less explicit, and seldom to the advantage of women who are the less fortunate. By accepting a hierarchical principle of difference, everyone is duped into viewing the ostensibly "greater abilities" of those who dominate as "a social asset to be used for the common advantage" (107).

Perhaps it is such skewed thinking that has perpetuated the myth of females not being concerned with social justice, a myth that is so pervasive that feminists have been moved to develop theories of relation and caring to explain women's behavior (Gilligan, 1982). It seldom occurs to anyone to question the social injustice of male behavior, except to say that their principles are based on law. Perception is a powerful phenomenon.

Even in a well-ordered society that satisfies Rawls' two principles of social justice, the family can be a barrier to equal opportunity because the shaping of a female child's aspirations varies among families, as it does between individuals in them. Girls, so ultimately, women, come to accept consciously their internalized inferiority, passed on to them by their families and culture, sometimes unconsciously, and sometimes with intention. The fact that many women collude in their own oppression, then, must not be taken as an excuse for injustice.

Affective ties, according to Rawls, should be characterized by a concern for the realization of one another's interests, and a sense of justice on behalf of each. This aspect of social justice is seldom part of women's experience. An equitable division of labor between women and men could make it a reality. A just social union, according to Rawls' principles, will require that both parties willingly participate in meaningful work within and outside of the home as they are so inclined. If such justice is to be realized, non-governmental organizations must keep pressure on insensitive governments concerning the rights and roles of women.

The assumptions that male development planners make about women in society are powerful because they are seldom stated. It is believed to be "natural" that women's place is in the home, regardless of whether or not they are employed. It is assumed that the tasks they are expected to perform are universal, based on the biological imperatives of sex. Bearing and rearing children, their most important role, defines their entire lives. Since it is assumed as well that men control families, it is deemed just as "natural" that they are the heads of them (Rogers, 1984). In governmental policy and law throughout the world, families are called "female-headed" only when men do not live in them.

Domestication of Women

On every continent, there is a movement on the part of the media, political, economic, educational, and religious institutions to revive flagging traditional views that women should stay at home. This has been termed the "domestication" or "housewification" of women. In new atmospheres of competition in Asia, for example, the old official line that women should share equally in building socialism, has been muted. Instead, employers, local officials, and journalists have openly stated what others persist in believing privately, that women are better suited for housework and should be "liberated" from outside jobs. Many employers, forced for the first time to make a profit, are refusing to hire women, arguing that they cannot afford maternity benefits. Factories are firing two women for every man, and families in rural areas are withdrawing teenage girls from school on the grounds that only sons need to be educated. This is a startling about face in a society where nearly seventy percent of women work outside the home (Associated Press, 1989). Similar stories have been reported in many countries, including the United States where journalists in recent years have made a point of featuring stories about women who have reached higher levels of management, but have chosen to stay at home. A leading homemakers' magazine, *Good Housekeeping*, has built an advertising campaign on the idea of the "new traditionalist," the educated woman who is proud and content to stay at home to care for her home and family. All of this is happening, ironically, at the same time that the government is demanding that poor women, largely single mothers who are caring for their children, work outside the home as a requirement for welfare assistance.

United Nations Initiatives

The importance of sharing domestic and parental responsibilities has been addressed by the United Nations over the past two decades in a number of documents and resolutions. To that end, necessary public actions have been identified by the *Expert Group Meeting on Social Support Measures for the Advancement of Women*, held in Vienna, Austria (Rao, 1988). The group recognizes that women are already sharing in the process of societal development, and there must be a redistribution of tasks. They emphasize that the concept of equity is more appropriate than the term equality, since equality does not exist in the basic process of reproduction. Given that the reproductive function itself cannot be shared, they contend that there should be criteria for an equitable distribution of those tasks remaining. Equity could pertain to the father and society through the demonstration and fulfilling of joint responsibilities, assuming a larger portion of domestic tasks, providing health services, and making flexible work arrangements which take account of the mother's needs at this time. As detailed below, the family, the community, and the government are key players in the implementation of social support development on behalf of women's advancement.

The Family

The family is conceptualized in many ways throughout the world. The nuclear family, characterized by a man and woman usually joined in socially recognized union, and their children, is the type best known to the western world. There are many offshoots of this model in contemporary society which together actually outnumber the traditional minority. They include single parent families (generally adult women and children) and non-traditional co-habiting couples of the same or opposite sex who form consensual unions (Kendall, 1988). Groups of individuals, usually single women who otherwise would be living alone, are bonding together to form quasi-extended families for mutual support.

The more traditional extended family, long the norm in many developing countries, consists of two or more nuclear families affiliated through parent-child relationships, sometimes extending for four generations. (In the west they tend to be the relatives of husbands and wives.) The polygynous family remains significant in some Arab, African, and Asian cultures, with between two and four wives permitted, based on the religious doctrine. There are, of course, many nuances that deviate on the family theme regardless of its defining characteristics (Kendall, 1988; Rao, 1988). In 1988 and 1989, ECOSOC, the United Nations committee concerned with issues of economic and social development, focused attention on a definition of "family" on which all countries would agree. The effort was highly controversial. Only The Netherlands wanted to define the family as a flexible concept that would include other than the traditional nuclear and extended family constellations. Hence, a compromise was made leaving the term, family, undefined. Participating nations did agree, however, that the problems of families deserved a special international year in which to address the issues before them.

The urban and rural experience is more distinctively different for women than are indigenous national characteristics of other countries. Rural women throughout the world have much more in common than they have with their countrymen and women. The same hold true for urban women who are most likely to come in contact with the arts, ideas, and goods of other nations. Most women today live in poor rural families, a fact that will prevail until the turn of the 21st century when projections indicate that the urban population will surpass it, if only by a margin. Urban women, however, like their migrant rural sisters, are not any better off socially or economically. Social supports have diminished as urbanization has lead to the breakup of the extended family in many countries. The world of poor urban women is likely to be harsh and unrelenting. (See Chapter 6 for a discussion of urban and rural women and employment opportunities, and Chapter 8 concerning the psychology and economics of rural women, much of which is relevant to rural migrants to urban areas.)

Despite diverse life styles ranging from simple hunting communities to nations that are highly industrialized, all societies assign roles for social organization on the basis of gender, age, and various other considerations. In all societies, the housewife role is denigrated due to its perceived lack of economic value. With development, the status and worth of women has worsened. The first point of intervention, then, is within the family itself. Education and socialization are essential to building the kind of self-esteem and sense of worth that is needed. It is important to sensitize parents to the negative impact of preferential treatment of males in the family. It is equally important to change discriminatory practices towards females throughout their life cycle, including those relating to food, health, education, and property.

While laws and policies are necessary, they are not sufficient. The informal role of the family can make a real difference, emphasizing a productive and not just reproductive image of girls. Religious values can be a rich source of support if the original scriptures are used as references. Most advocate an equal partnership between women and men, as opposed to those that are reinterpreted to render women inferior. Research also indicates that establishing a bond with at least one other significant person is important to the development of children, as it is to the mental health of women and men. The problem of a single support is obvious; one is at risk of losing a lifeline. Hence, people in the community are essential to women's well-being, as well as to their advancement (Wetzel, 1984; Rao, 1988).

The Community

The ideal of equal partnership between women and men in the family cannot be achieved without the community. The Group for Social Support Measures for the Advancement of Women calls bonds in the community "we-consciousness," a way of thinking that is more developed in the eastern world. With a growing number of women working outside the home, the need for community child care facilities has substantially increased. Measures are also needed for the care of the elderly who are isolated because of urban migration of their families, and others who are not covered by social security. Women are at risk in each category. Supports must include access to simple technology to ease domestic burdens and to improve productivity.

Community studies reveal that women's mutual support organizations are highly successful even when informal and relatively unorganized. It is women, after all, who know how things work in a community. To overlook this reality by seeing them as exclusively domestic and maternal does not do them justice, and shortchanges the community in the process. This is true of elderly as well younger women. Those who are concerned with the worldwide increasing longevity of elders, and the economic burden of taking care of them, overlook the fact that many are still productive members of society. They, too, are engaged in entrepreneurial activities, utilizing the skills and talents developed over the years. One such project was initiated by elders in Bogata, Columbia who established a commercial bakery. Thousands of destitute elderly, most of whom are women, are employed in their successful enterprise.

Community self-help educational programs can strengthen women's problem,-solving capacity, equiping them with coping skills to deal more effectively with the environment. Special efforts should be made to engage adult women who have not completed school or were deprived of going altogether. A sense of inferiority, feelings of powerlessness and resignation defeats their motivation to get involved in anything. Learning to read and write can change their self-image and expand their horizons to include the larger community. The investment will come full circle. (See Chapter 5 and Chapter 8 for further discussion of women's educational projects.)

The Government

However successful, problem-oriented, and narrowly focused programs may be, without the government as a strong advocate and resource they will not prevail. The issues of equality and equity for women cannot be treated in isolation from their other pressing problems. Governments must recognize the interdependence of poverty, unemployment, poor health, lack of education, and low quality and high density housing. Comprehensive social welfare programs must be implemented that keep the goals put forth in mind. Social support measures which can promote attitudes towards sharing of responsibilities within the family and also lighten the burden of housework are fundamental values to be integrated in such programs (Rao, 1988).

Mass media in all its many forms can play a very supportive role in changing stereotyped images of women which inhibit their advancement. Because recreational components can easily be built into modern forms of communication such as radio, television, film, video, plays, music, dance, and print media, there is an intrinsic appeal that motivates people's interest. Countries with unique art forms, often the traditional domain of women, can promote existing aspects of their roles in a positive, creative manner. It is customary in some rural areas for neighborhoods to participate actively in radio and television, a particularly important field in those with high illiteracy rates. The practice would also serve women well in industrial areas (Rao, 1988).

The problems, policies, and laws involved in reconciling the needs of family and working life are not unique to any country. All governments can develop regulatory policies that make integration of these two spheres of life less stressful. By way of example, Stoiber (1989), an expert on European policy analysis, suggests the following four criteria against which family "leave entitlements" should be evaluated: (1) Do the policies provide an adequate level of protection for maternal and child health? (2) Do they promote long and short-term economic security for women? (3) Do they support, or at least not impede, occupational mobility and advancement for women? (4) Do they impose excessive burdens on employers, require a high level of public sector expenditure, or have other distorting effects on the economy?

Concerned with measuring the progress a society makes in advancing the cause of Singapore's women to equal status with men, Kum (1980) uses indicators which she calls Legal and Social Indexes. The Legal Index encompasses Political and Civil Rights, Marriage Laws, Capacity (Legal Existence) of Married Women, and Maintenance and Property Rights (Economic Dependence). The Social Index includes Education and Employment (and the correlation between the two), Women as Home-makers (attendant resources, such as creches, day care, and on-site medical care), and Family Planning (including maternal and child health services).

It requires concerted action on separate fronts to elevate women from the low social status they have held for so long. The laws must be reformed to remove those components that are discriminatory, providing opportunities for financial independence and control over her own reproduction. At the same time, laws should support equal child care and home management responsibilities of men and women.

It is clear that writing new laws and developing new policies will not be enough to change gender inequality. Nor will providing access to education, technology, and employment be adequate. Family structures, the decisions made within them, and women's access to technology are all connected in an interdependent global economy. Understanding the cultural, economic, and political context of access, then, is the real key to equality of opportunity and equity (Bourque and Warren, 1987; 1989).

The collapse of a range of totalitarian dictatorships in Eastern Europe, the Soviet Union, Africa and South America gave rise to emerging democracies in the early 1990s. The experience gave rise, too, to awareness that democracy also has many faces. It became increasingly clear that people power, the ideological roots of liberal democracy, erodes in the absence of economic democracy. "Pure capitalism," devoid of an economic rights ethic, can be destructive to those who are unable to survive in the world's so-called free marketplace due to inherent systemic inequities. The women of the world, individually and collectively, head the list. Supply side economics, blind to their restricted opportunities, also ignores their largely unpaid and underpaid work. By way of contrast, produce-controlled economics would reward them fairly for their important contributions to society. Increasingly, women are advocating capitalist inspired social democracy which they view as a melding of popular and economic, produce-controlled democracy. In its absence, democracy for women, while certainly an improvement over totalitarianism, will nonetheless perpetuate their poverty and oppression.

Poverty

Throughout the world, the largest poverty groups are female-headed households, which are estimated to represent one-third of all households. The second largest is the elderly, a greater proportion of whom are women. By the age of eighty-five, there are twice as many women as there are men. (Recall that eighty percent of the elderly poor are women.) Together, these young and elderly women make up over seventy percent of the poor in most countries. There is no doubt that poverty has rapidly become feminized on a global scale (Seager and Olson, 1986; Goldberg and Kremen, 1991).

Available statistics repeat the theme: 78 percent of all people living in poverty in the U.S. are single women and their children; they are the fastest growing group of homeless. In Australia, the proportion of single women in poverty is 75 percent. In Canada, 60 percent of all women over 65 are poor, and in Chile, 29 percent of women-headed households fall into the lowest income bracket. The reasons for women being poor are directly associated with their domestic responsibilities, lack of affordable child care so that they can work outside the home, and their being ghettoized into low-paying jobs when they do. In agricultural economies, women are often denied land ownership, credit, and money. Worldwide, women are dependent on men, therefore, for access to the formal economy's resources and rewards; when men are absent, they are cut off.

Recessions and other economic crises strike earliest and hardest at those with the least income, namely women and children. The poorer the family, the larger the proportion of income spent on the necessities of life, such as food, fuel, and health care. Any decline in income threatens their very survival. Their numbers are on the rise because families headed by single women are rapidly increasing everywhere due to divorce and migration when men seek seasonal or permanent work away from home (Seager and Olson, 1986). In some countries, it is young women who are migrating to cities, sending their meager pay home to husbands, fathers, and children in the care of their grandmothers. As cheap laborers for multinationals, these migrant urban women are also locked into poverty. (See Chapter 3 regarding international sex industries and Chapter 6 for a discussion of employment and women.)

Violence Against Women: Battering and Rape

Violence against women stems, in large measure, from their inferior position. It is difficult to get accurate data on battering because, like rape, it is seriously under-reported due to women's fear and sense of futility. In some countries, these crimes go unreported because they are not even acknowledged. The statistics that are available hint at the magnitude of the ever-increasing problem. Seventy percent of all crimes reported to the police in Peru are of women beaten by their partners. In just one year in Brazil, 772 women were killed by their husbands, considered to be non-criminal honor killings until 1991 (Brooke, 1991). In Japan, wife beating is the second most frequent cause of divorces initiated by women. And in the United States, the Federal Bureau of Investigation has estimated that one woman is beaten every eighteen seconds. Indeed, violence towards wives is one of the major reasons that many women everywhere choose to be single. (That is not to deny that single women experience violence.)

Rape, a violent act to establish power over a woman, is most often committed in the home. Women of all ages and appearances, from infancy through old age, are equally likely to be victims. The U.S. Federal Bureau of Investigation reports that a woman is raped every six minutes, and one out of every ten women will be raped in her lifetime (Holtzman, 1989). One study reveals that 90 percent of gang rapes, 83 percent of pair rapes, and 58 percent of single rapes are premeditated. In most cultures rape is either condoned or legitimized by ignoring it. (Pornography, it has been said, is the theory, and rape the practice.) As discussed in Chapter 3 in connection with the ethos of trafficking, raping of wives by husbands is not viewed as a crime in most regions of the world, including most states in the U.S. When the act is severely punished, as in Muslim countries, it is because it is viewed as an affront to the possessing male, not to the female victim who is ostracized. This motive is played out in times of war when men rape and plunder to establish dominance over opposing military forces (Seager and Olson, 1986).

The legal system itself is part of the problem. Institutional rape by prison guards and police, orderlies in mental hospitals, and guards and other authorities in refugee camps serve to remind women of their powerlessness in the system. It is an increasingly common occurrence. Battered women's shelters and rape crisis centers have been created by women organizing locally throughout the world, often in the face of opposition and harassment, usually without the support of the legal system or local and national governments. It is feminist lawyers and other women activists who are addressing the issues (Seager and Olson, 1986). Violence against women is an international problem, not restricted to any income group. While violence against children has had some visibility, women have remained relatively hidden. Even they are prone to internalize the concept that husbands have rights to their bodies, thus tolerating their violence. Neither legal protections nor social services in most societies are sufficient (Skrobanek, 1988; Padhye, 1988).

In extremely repressive countries, such as in South Africa, women active in the shelter movement choose not to encourage battered women to use the law because they believe that it is an illegitimate system. It is particularly dangerous for black African women to seek help from the police. They are likely to be sent back to their "homelands," rather than being given aid (NiCarthy, 1987). "Homelands" is a euphemism for resettlement camps and populations of women, children, and the elderly (who also tend to be women). They are areas that were established by the government as part of its policy of apartheid. Because there is little or no employment in the homelands, able-bodied men usually work and live in South Africa, leaving those who are unable to work in the homelands (Fiske, 1989).

Most research on sexual violence is concerned with the treatment of victims or offenders, rather than with prevention. Preventive strategies currently being used focus on victim control or offender control. The technique used for control related to victims involves educating women about a variety of safety precautions and situations to avoid. Controlling the activities of women to prevent sexual assault is the traditional approach that has been used for generations. It has been far more likely to contribute to their oppression. Not only are they restricted in dress, behavior, and mobility, but there is a tendency to assume that women who do not comply with such avoidance actions have caused, if not contributed to, their assaults. The responsibility for the attacks are thus shifted from the assailants to the victims.

Sexual offender control techniques rely on three strategies: deterrence, incapacitation, and rehabilitation. Deterrence has been attempted through early detection, tracking, treatment, or arrests and convictions of boys thought likely to become rapists. Incarceration of rapists is intended to incapacitate them by isolating them from the rest of society. A rehabilitation through offender treatment programs is designed to lower recidivism, although success rates vary. A combination of these last two methods have been tried primarily in Europe where several countries have offered the choice of castration or chemotherapy to reduce testosterone levels in career rapists and child molesters. With estimates that women's risk ranges from one in three for spouse abuse, one in five for child molestation (mostly related to girls), and one in eight for rape, it is more likely that the prevention of sexual violence must address the problem as fairly normative behavior in men, rooted in current social structures. Targeting isolated groups does not address the pervasive reality. A social order is needed in which men do not learn to be sexually violent toward women (Sparks and Bar On, 1985).

Dowry Murders

Historically, dowry, called "stridhan," was a gift of cash or kind, usually gold ornaments, given to a woman in India at the time of marriage. It was to provide her with a measure of economic security in case of emergency. Similar systems prevailed in France, Portugal, Spain, Italy, on the continent and in Europe. Another largely although not totally, obsolete practice was that of bride-price, wherein the bridegroom's family offered a price to get a suitable bride for their sons of marriageable age. Today, the dowry system among Hindu families in India is no longer a small nest egg for her protection. Instead, it has become an occasion when some men even kill their wives for failing to deliver on demand material goods from their fathers as a continuing dowry payment (Bhowmik, 1988). A modern phenomenon, these murders are not to be confused with sati, in which people have forced women to suicide on their husband's cremation pyres. Unlike dowry murders, sati was never widespread; it is not a common occurrence today, although it still exists.

Dowry murders are a vicious urban, middle-class competition for status and luxury goods, at the expense of daughters. The demands of in-laws, which sometimes escalate after marriage, leaves newly married daughters virtual hostages against payments by their parents. The young women are harassed by the in-laws with whom they must live, and are neglected by their own parents if they complain. Both families collude in the murders; one to find a new more lucrative hostage; the other to be free from harassment and expense (Papanek, 1989). Legislation against dowry has been enacted, but it has not solved the problem. It must be backed by social education which creates social awareness regarding the need for a new social order that respects the equal rights of women and men, rejecting male dominance (Bhowmik, 1988).

Veiling of Women

There is a resurgence of veiling practices in Muslim countries, even where there had been no such tradition before. While some defend the practice as a deterrent to sexual harassment, most agree that the veil is an enforced abridgement of women's rights, existing for the benefit of men. The practice of seclusion is related, whereby women are confined to their house or family compound as a symbol of male wealth and high status (Seager and Olson, 1986).

Veiling, called purdah, is a Persian word which refers to "the conceal-ment of women and the separation of the worlds of women." It is a major aspect of purdah, according to Jeffrey who conducted a sociological study of the practice when it was still possible to do so (1979, 3). Purdah, she points out, is not just a Muslim tradition based on the Islamic religion. It is also common among Hindu women, though not identical. Purdah has its parallels over the Middle East, the Mediterranean and the Indian sub-continent. Sexual apartheid, the seclusion of women can be only partially explained by Islamic doctrine. South Asia and Eurasia from India through the Middle East, the Balkans, and even parts of northwestern Europe to the Iberian peninsula report this sharp separation and differentiation between the spheres of women and men. Such seclusion is coupled with the twin notions of "honor and shame," with women the locus of family repute. Their vulnerability to men necessitates constant vigilance over their virtue.

The keystone to the maintenance of purdah is the asymmetry between the sexes and economic powerlessness of women. There is more than forced compliance and complaining obedience, however, to explain the perpetuation of the custom. Internalization of the important elements of the ideological status quo among women is evident, reinforcing its stability. Men prevent women from organizing, overtly and covertly, because they have the power to punish those who transgress the bounds of acceptable behavior. The potential power of men within the family to repudiate their wives, leaving them abandoned and impoverished, is as strong as any physical fear. Moreover, men on the outside harass women who have had no opportunity to learn how to interact, competently and confidently, with the world of men. Though individual women are not isolated from one another within households, women in different households are. They are indirectly in competition with each other for scarce resources, available only through their men. Finally, their energy levels may be low due to restricted exercise in the confines of their homes, plus long work hours in the household. Elderly women, after long years of socialization, are often as conservative as most of the men.

Since the time of Jeffrey's study, the small modifications being asked for have been blocked by fundamentalist governments. Most women who take exception to their conditions only argue that the customs impact negatively on their ability to perform their domestic duties. Too many children, for example, take time away from household chores; wearing the burqua (a totally concealing garment from head to toe) makes it difficult to get around; and lack of education and purdah makes them feel stupid in relation to men and even other women because they are not worldly-wise. Raised in a devaluing environment, these women have little concept of self-esteem. They, like their men, view shame, embarrassment, and dependent behavior in women as positive female attributes. They look upon women who do not reflect them as disgraceful. But it is not unknown for some men, more aware of the changes in the outside world, to take the part of younger women who are unsatisfied with the old customs. The power of such men can make a difference. Bonds of affection also link women whose interests might otherwise be in conflict.

PART I

Anti-Discrimination Policy Analysis: Social and Economic Equality

Article 13: Social and Economic Benefits
Article 13 seeks to ensure that women have equal access to family benefits, to loans and credit, and to the enjoyment of all aspects of recreational and cultural life (Convention, 1980).

Pertinent Questions for Analysis: Social and Economic Equality (IWRAW, 1988)

* Do women, particularly married women, have access to loans, mortgages, and other forms of financial credit? If not, what are the constraints?
* Do they need the consent of their husbands or another male to obtain credit?
* Do married women, in their own right or as mothers, have access on their own to family benefits such as: children's allowances, housing allowances, public housing, health insurance or coverage, or other government subsidies or allowances?
* Do unmarried and married women have the same access to benefits?
* What legal or cultural obstacles are there to the full participation of women in recreational activities, sports, and other aspects of cultural life?

Forward-Looking Strategies: Social and Economic Equality (1985)

Increasing Participation and Resources
The enhancement of women's equal participation in development and peace requires the creation of human resources, recognition by society of the need to improve women's status, and the participation of everyone in the restructuring of society. In particular, it involves building a participatory human infrastructure that will permit the mobilization of women at all levels and within different spheres and sectors. In order to achieve optimum development of human and material resources, women's strengths and capabilities must be fully acknowledged and valued. This includes their great contribution to the welfare of families and to the development of society. Men, women, and society as a whole must share this responsibility if the goals and objectives of the Decade are to be attained. It also requires

that women play a central role as intellectuals, policy and decision-makers, planners, and contributors and beneficiaries of development.

If there is continued slow growth [or recessions] in the world economy, it is feared that there inevitably will be even more negative implications for women. As a result of diminished resources, action to combat women's low position may be postponed. Of particular concern are efforts to counteract their high rates of illiteracy, low levels of education, discrimination in employment, their unrecognized contribution to the economy, and their special health needs [both physical and mental]. The attainment of the goals and objectives of the Decade is possible if a pattern of development is established promoting fair and equitable growth on the basis of justice and equality in international economic relations. There could be a significant improvement in the status of women, at the same time enhancing their effective contribution to development and peace. Such a pattern of development has its own internal dynamics that would facilitate in turn an equitable distribution of resources. It is conducive to promoting sustained, endogenous development, which will reduce dependence. It is important that efforts of this kind to promote the economic and social status of women are grounded on the principles of a new international economic order. These principles include self-reliance, both collective and individual, and the activation of indigenous human and material resources. In the long term, the restructuring of the world economy is to the benefit of all people in all countries.

PART II

Anti-Discrimination Policy Analysis: Equality before the Law

Article 15: Equality before the Law
Article 15 commits states to take all appropriate measures to accord women equality with men under the law (Convention, 1980).

Pertinent Questions for Analysis: Equality before the Law (IWRAW, 1988)

- Are women treated equally in courts?
- Can women sue and be sued in their own name?
- Can female attorneys represent clients in court?
- Can women serve on juries?

- Can women serve as witnesses? Does their testimony carry the same weight as that of men?
- Do women have the right to make contracts in their own name (including credit, real estate, and commercial transactions)?
- Do women have the right to administer property without interference or consent by a male, regardless of whether they acquire it during marriage, bring it into marriage, or are unmarried?
- Can women be executors or administrators of estates?
- Has the country outlawed, by judicial decision or statute, contracts that restrict women's legal capacity?
- Do women have the right to choose the place where they live? Do traditions or customs restrict women from exercising this right?

Forward-Looking Strategies: Equality before the Law (1985)

Legislating Equality
In most countries, the inequality of women to a very large extent stems from mass poverty and the general backwardness of the majority of the world's population. Their condition is caused by underdevelopment, the outcome of imperialism, colonialism, neo-colonialism, apartheid, racism, racial discrimination, and of unjust economic relations. The unfavorable status of women in many relatively developed and developing countries is aggravated further by de facto (actual) discrimination on the grounds of sex. Such discrimination has been justified on the basis of psychological differences, rather than on larger social, economic, political, and cultural factors. While there is no physiological basis for regarding the family and household as essentially the domain of women, for devaluating domestic work, and for regarding the capacities of women as inferior to those of men, the belief that such a basis exists perpetuates inequality. The structural and attitudinal changes necessary to eliminate it are inhibited.

In order to promote the equality of women and men, governments should ensure both sexes equality before the law, the provision of facilities for equality, and educational opportunities and training, health services, equality in conditions and opportunities of employment, including remuneration, and adequate social security. They should recognize and undertake measures to implement the right of women and men to employment on equal conditions, regardless of marital status, and their equal access to the whole range of economic activities. [To achieve equity, even greater attention must be paid to gender imbalances.]

A major obstacle to the full participation of women is the sharp contrast between legislative changes which address de jure (indirect) discrimination, and effective implementation of these changes. De facto and de jure discrimination often persist despite legislative action, particularly in reference to marital and family status. Also, because of the socio-economic inequalities which determine women's knowledge of and access to the law, the law as a recourse does not automatically benefit women equally. Their ability to exercise their full legal rights without fear of recrimination or intimidation is also uneven. The available recourse to justice and the achievement of expected results in regard to changes in laws have been hampered in many instances by the lack or inadequacy of the dissemination of information on women's rights.

Political Commitment and Reform

On the basis of human dignity, political commitment must be strengthened to establish, modify, expand, or enforce a comprehensive legal base for the equality of women and men. Legislative changes are most effective when made within a supportive framework which simultaneously promotes changes in the economic, social, political, and cultural spheres – then social transformation is more likely to be realized. If true equality [and equity] are to become a reality for women, a major strategy must be the sharing of power on equal terms with men.

All laws should be reviewed by law reform committees comprised of equal representation of women and men from governmental and non-governmental organizations. This will serve as a monitoring device, as well as a view to determining research-related activities, amendments, and new legislative measures.

Training Legal Personnel

Appropriate forms of in-service training and retraining should be designed as actions necessary to ensure that the judiciary and all paralegal personnel are fully aware of the importance of women achieving their rights. Such efforts are congruent with internationally agreed instruments, constitutions and laws.

PART III

Anti-Discrimination Policy Analysis: Marriage and Family Law

Article 16: Marriage and Family Law
Article 16 seeks to eliminate discrimination against women within marriage
and the family (Convention, 1980)

Pertinent Questions for Analysis: Marriage and Family Law (IWRAW, 1988)

- Are family relations governed by civil law, religious laws, customary laws, or a combination of these? Please explain.
- Do women have the same right as men to choose a spouse?
- Do women have the right to enter into marriage only with their free and full consent? If so, how is the right enforced?
- How are betrothals made? Do traditional customs apply? If so, what are they and how do they affect women's choice in marriage?
- Is there a minimum age at marriage for males and females? What is it? Is it enforced? If so, how? Is child marriage a matter of custom in particular areas or among particular groups? Is it legally recognized?
- Is the age of majority different for males and females?
- Is registration of marriages and divorces required by law?
- Is it customary or legal to pay a bride price or dowry? If yes, what is its effect on marriage?
- Do women and men have the same rights and responsibilities during marriage? If not, how do these differ, both in law and in practice?
- Is polygyny (one man having more than one wife) permitted by law? Is it done in practice? What percentage of marriages are polygynous?
- In polygynous marriages, what are the rights and responsibilities of husbands towards wives and wives towards husbands?
- What are the rights and responsibilities of men and women living in union (i.e., living together but not legally married) towards each other and towards their children?
- Do women have the right to decide freely and responsibly the number and spacing of their children? Do they have access, without having to ask anyone's permission, to information and services for family planning?

- What is the law and practice concerning abuse of wives or live-in companions?
- Do women have the same rights as men, regardless of their marital status, to make decisions about the upbringing of their children?
- Do women have the same rights as men in matters of guardianship, wardship, trusteeship, and adoption of children?
- Do married women have an equal voice with their husbands in the management and disposition of property acquired during marriage?
- Do women have the same rights as men to choose a name, profession, occupation?
- Do women have the same rights as men to own, acquire, manage and dispose of property?
- Is divorce available to men and women on the same grounds? Is divorce by "renunciation" done in law or practice? Are divorces registered?
- Who generally retains custody of children after divorce? After death of a husband? Do the practical results in custody matters differ from the law as written?
- Are divorced husbands [or wives] required to pay child support? Are child support orders enforced?
- What are the legal obligations to pay maintenance to a divorced husband or wife?
- How is property among former spouses divided after divorce? Is a woman's work in the home, or her unpaid agricultural labor, counted as contribution towards the value of the property?
- Legally and in practice, what are the rights and obligations of widows? In what way, if any, do they differ from the rights and obligations of widowers?
- Do widows and daughters of a deceased parent have a legal right to inherit land and other property if there is no will? Can a widow or daughter receive property under a will?
- Do male and female children receive equal inheritances by law if there is not will?
- Is the levriate (widows having to marry the deceased husband's brother) practiced by groups?
- What percentage of households are headed by a female? What percentage of poor households are headed by a poor female?

Forward-Looking Strategies: Marriage and Family Law (1985)

As is evident from the review and appraisal of the Decade of Women, despite the fact that in some countries and in some areas women have made significant advances, overall progress has been modest. Women's consciousness and expectations have been raised, but it is important that this momentum not be lost, regardless of the poor performance of the world economy. New challenges are being presented, requiring new perspectives, strategies and measures, as a result of changes occurring in the family, in women's roles, and in relationships between women and men. It is necessary to build alliances and solidarity groups across sex lines if structural obstacles to the advancement of women are to be overcome.

Overcoming Resistance

There is a deeply-rooted resistance among the world's conservative elements to the attitudinal changes necessary for a total ban on discriminatory practices against women at the family, local, national, and international levels. In some countries, discriminatory legislative provisions still exist in the social, economic, and political spheres. These include civil, penal, and commercial codes and certain administrative rules and regulations. In some instances, civil codes have not yet been studied adequately to determine action for repealing those laws that discriminate against women. Nor are they ready to determine, on the basis of equality, the legal capacity and status of women, particularly married women, in terms of nationality, inheritance, ownership and control of property, freedom of movement, and the custody and nationality of children. Civil codes, especially those pertaining to family law, should be revised to eliminate existing discriminatory practices, including wherever women are considered as minors.

Legal Rights of Married and Single Women

In order to grant them equal rights and duties, the legal capacity of married women should be reviewed. Marriage agreements should be based on freedom of choice and mutual understanding and respect. The equal participation and valuation of both partners should be paid careful attention. The value of housework, then, must be considered an equivalent financial contribution.

As an aspect of their equality and freedom under the law, the right of all women should be guaranteed (especially those who are married) to independently own, administer, sell or buy property. Both partners should be granted equally the right to divorce, and under the same conditions. Custody of children should be decided in a non-discriminatory manner, with full awareness of the importance of both parents in the maintenance, rearing, and socialization of children. Women should not have to forfeit their right to custody of their children, or any other benefits, simply because they initiate a divorce. Legal or other appropriate provisions should be made to eliminate discrimination against single mothers and their children, without prejudice to the religious and cultural traditions of countries, and taking into consideration the de facto situations.

Consideration of Married Couples

Governments are urged to consider the special needs of the growing number of couples who are employed in public service, particularly the foreign service. Consideration should be given to the couple's desire to be assigned to the same duty station in order to reconcile family and professional duties.

PERSON-ENVIRONMENT PROGRAM MODELS:
EQUALITY, THE FAMILY, AND THE LAW

Clara Wichmann Institute/Feminist Lawyers' Research Center –
Amsterdam, The Netherlands

The Clara Wichmann Institute, a research center for women and the law, was founded in 1987. Three voluntary organizations made up of feminist lawyers and legal academics in Amsterdam merged to share ideas, build expertise, and develop and implement new legal strategies on behalf of women. The Institute represents virtually hundreds of women lawyers who now have shared staff support, office space, and facilities that include a documentation center.

The oldest of the three participating organizations, the Association for Women and Law, founded in 1980, had over 200 members within a decade. It is divided into five law groups that specialize in labor, family, health, social security, and criminal law regarding sexual violence. They include in their work migrant women's issues, old age pensions, women and economic independence, and the redistribution of paid and unpaid labor. In regularly scheduled plenaries the members share expertise, lecturing on and discussing new developments on current legal issues, and in smaller group meetings opinions are formulated concerning legal positions on women's issues, writing commentary on pending legislation, letters to the bar or magistrate, and development of articles.

One of the participating organizations is made up of feminist lawyers and Women's Studies faculty at a number of Dutch universities. The two fields joined forces in 1984 to found the legal journal, *Nemisis*, a theoretical periodical about women and the law which had 1600 subscribers by 1989. The journal has received acclaim for the quality of its articles which provide both technical legal information and a forum for discussion of moral dilemmas that can make law a two-edged sword, particularly when addressing the concerns of women (Sarah van Walsum, 1989).

Another participating organization is a fund-raising component, roughly translated as "The Test-Case Fund for Law and Women." Backed by hundreds of donors, the Fund provides financial backing for low-income women who are prepared to go to court on issues of essential importance to women in general. The Fund also helps find experienced lawyers, and makes certain that the cases are well covered by the media, thus informing women at large of the legal resources available to them.

Women's Vigilance Committee/Violence Against Women – *Bombay, India*

Founded in New Delhi in 1977 in reaction to bride-burning dowry deaths, the Bombay branch of the Women's Vigilance Committee (Mahila Dakshata Samati) officially opened its doors in 1983. The grassroots members who work with the organization, however, had been active in the field of women's liberation long before. They felt that they would be more effective if they worked in a coordinated manner, rather than individually. The Samati, as they call themselves, make decisions by consensus, and remains unaligned with political parties and ideologies. Instead, they focus on what they consider to be a transcendent goal, the emancipation of women from social and legal chains. Their activities include running family guidance clinics, educating the public in a variety of ways, training counselors, and arranging public meetings designed particularly to involve and inform women from the poorest sections of society.

The Family Guidance Clinic is essentially geared to conflict resolution between family members, generally but not always, husbands and wives. Their primary clients are usually women, but the counselors make a point of listening to the spouse as well. They talk with both parties, meet in their homes, and speak with relatives. In order to accomplish reconciliation, the Samati places conditions on the husband, making it clear that violence is out of the question, warning that they will take the case to court if he is not in compliance. When legal aid is needed, they make arrangements with free service centers, as well as well-known advocates when appropriate. In some cases they approach police authorities, registering complaints and following up when necessary. There are occasions, in fact, when they provide police protection themselves. Their services extend to the courts and hospitals where they also act as advocates for women who are abused. The Samati's work on behalf of women's rights has extended to the government in reaction to fascist "blackshirts," a fundamentalist Hindu group that is claiming superiority and using Nazi tactics against women, demanding that they "know their place" (Sudha Varde, 1989).

Women for Women/Legal Rights – *Dhaka, Bangladesh*

Women for Women, an organization of feminist scholars in Dhaka, has published a series of pamphlets to inform women in Bangladesh about their rights. Two of them concern their legal rights in marriage and divorce; one is devoted to the situation of Muslim women, and the other to Hindu women. The author, Barrister-at-Law Rabia Bhuiyan, is the Minister for Women's Affairs and Social Welfare. Although there are many law books and other legal literature on Muslim law, they are written for lawyers, law students, and academicians. Women for Women's materials, instead, are written in such a way that they are readily accessible to all women and other lay members of society. Women need to know their legal rights concerning marriage, dower, divorce, and maintenance and custody of children. In the case of disputes arising over these issues, they need to know what remedies are available to them and where to find them.

The purpose of the work is also to create awareness among women and to inform them about their basic marital rights, so that they may feel more confident about their legal status in the family. The women are then more likely to seek legal redress should any of their rights be violated. In the case of Hindu women, marriage is an indissoluble union. There are many nuances of the law, though, that are important to their well-being and that of their children. In 1983, for example, a Cruelty to Women (Deterrent) Punishment Ordinance was enacted (Bhuiyan, 1989). Women for Women's materials are distributed in both Bengali and English.

Consciousness-Raising Street Theater for Women's Emancipation/Stree Mukti Sanghatana
– *Bombay, India*

Stree Mukti has directed its efforts towards the advancement of women and their rights by creating awareness in the society about women's issues. Using the performing arts as promotional mediums they believe in involving males (husbands, brothers and sons) as well as females of all ages. Convinced that every social movement needs a definite ideological base, as well as a tangible program, their message is consistent and clear, capturing the imagination of the people. Through their street play, "No Dowry, Please," their aim is to dispel the "gloom that has settled over Indian womanhood" in the form of dowry. They insist that it is not enough to proclaim the end of the legal dowry system. Rather, every young man and woman, as well as their parents, must give serious thought to the institution of marriage. Prior to the writing of the play, Stree Mukti conducted a series of discussions in various colleges for an entire year. The play was based on the ideology that emerged from those discussions. Written materials, posters, and slide shows supplement their performances for further reinforcement. The initial production has been followed by a sequel, "We Will Smash the Prison," also about the dowry issue, and "A Girl is Born," a popular play about the plight of single mothers. Wherever Stree Mukti performs, they mobilize members of the audience to get involved in their organization. Rural audiences have proven to be the most responsive of all (Sharda Sathe, 1989).

Stone Center for Development Services and Studies/Sexual Violence – *Wellesley, Massachusetts, USA*

The Stone Center in Wellesley, Massachusetts has developed a social change approach to the primary prevention of sexual violence toward women. Their perception of the task of a prevention movement is the deinstitutionalization of sexual violence. In contrast, the principle of respect for persons must be institutionalized. They note two types of political action needed, both of which must take place at the state and community levels: legal action to codify law and policy, and social action to change social patterns and practices. This requires mobilizing institutions to support and effect social change. The summary below illustrates the activities in each political action arena.

Legal and Social Action
Legal Action includes the identification of current laws and policies that

support violence against women; the creation of new law and agency policy that reflects respect for women as persons; and the enforcement of women's control of their bodies.

Social Action includes the identification of current norms that support violence against women; the creation of new norms that reflect respect for women as persons; and the enforcement of women's control of their bodies.

These guidelines form the bedrock of social justice. Enforcement means gaining institutional support for women to protect one another, and expanding their ability to define their own needs for full participation in society. The goals are:

To pursue social justice: Educational materials and counseling must include content that makes it clear that the prevention of sexual violence is a social justice goal, not crime prevention. Programs should be developed that teach self-respect, respect between women, and respect between women and men.

To reject violence as normative: The process of teaching girls and women how to integrate sexual violence as an expectable reality in their lives must be rejected, just as we must stop denying that it is evidence of systemic woman-hating. Women are not, in fact, respected and protected as a norm. They must recognize this and be supported in their efforts to join with other women in challenging violence against them as a given.

To help women to be active and expressive: Women and girls must be taught that they are active people whose wants, needs, and feelings can be priorities; and that they can and should express and act upon them. They must be taught to actively take care of themselves, to make decisions about their own lives and safety for their own sakes. This is a fundamental change from women's socialization. The fact that it is still a subject of public debate reflects the fact that it is not yet normative, even under duress. Programs that also build a sense of community responsibility, based on respect for persons and the promotion of social change goals, are also needed. Women in communities can lead actions to redress violation of their self-respect as women. They can do this by supporting one another; actively intervening in community problems before dangerous situations get out of control; insisting on respect for all women; insisting that violence against women and women's safety be priorities on public agendas; actively disseminating information among women regarding actions to stop violence; supporting women's anger at injustice; creating support networks in communities; making it clear that women want to end harassment and the constant threat of violence and want the freedom to be anywhere without fear (Sparks and Bar On, 1985, 6)

To promote men's understanding and change: Programs are needed for boys and men that emphasize treating women as autonomous people, changing stereotypical perspectives of women that dehumanize and devalue them. The view of men as dominant, as aggressive competitors with one another, and as persons who denigrate women either publicly or privately must be rejected. Clear curricula must be developed that teach girls and boys what patriarchy is, the extent to which it exists, the ethical issues regarding violence, and how patriarchy combined with violence influences the lives of women by restricting and controlling them.

Teaching must employ a structural analysis of the problem of violence, rather than a communications approach. That is not to say, of course, that teaching does not communicate. It is only to emphasize that there is a danger in reducing a systemic social problem to an individual communications issue. The communications model naively assumes that if the person just communicated clearly, all would be well (for example, the notion that rape occurs because of a simple misunderstanding between two people who are equally to blame for not having given the correct cues). Besides being oversimplified to the point of absurdity, this leads to yet another variation of blaming the victim.

To refine therapeutic strategies for offenders: Rather than focusing on aversive techniques to change behavior, another way of modeling institutional violence, work with offenders should be evaluated in terms of promoting respect for women as autonomous persons.

To foster mutual responsibility and caretaking: On the community level, programs should emphasize the mutual responsibility of all people for one another, whether within the home or outside, even when strangers are involved. Neighborhood programs can foster respect and caring for one another by building accountability on a personal and a neighborhood level, and by helping everyone to feel empowered to act. As the primary setting for social action, the community must emphasize the political nature of prevention work. It is political because it affects both the personal and the societal levels of the power relationship between women and men (Sparks and Bar On, 1985).

Battered Women's Action Group – *Cape Town, South Africa*

In most countries, grassroots women who organized shelters have educated social workers and other professional women about the political realities of battering. An example of how one social worker can motivate others to do more appropriate professional work can be found in Cape Town. Practicing social work there since 1975, Merlyn Lawrence observed that her colleagues approached the problem of battering by doing marital counseling. Women were referred to police who viewed the problem as a private domestic affair, forcing the women to return to dangerous homes. There was little factual information available to either the professional community or to women-at-large, and resources were scarce. When research revealed the high incidence of violence encountered by the clients of all Cape Town professionals, Lawrence recommended a move away from the psychopathological approach which focuses on the individual, to viewing women-battering within its broader social context. With such an approach, the grassroots community, the professional community, and the agents of social control were targeted for change, assisting them with preventive and treatment measures. Her recommendations called for education and training, large scale community awareness and involvement, the establishment of refuges, twenty-four hour crisis hotlines, and further research focusing on improving services and implementing new ones. Guidelines were also drawn up for professionals.

Finally, Lawrence developed the Battered Women's Action Group (BWGA), a coordinating body founded in 1984 at a meeting of several health, religious, welfare, and community organizations. In just one year, BWGA met regularly to educate each other about battering and to share information about their organizations; drew up a dossier of information on resources, bibliographies and literature, distributing them among members, as well as public and professional groups. They gave thirty presentations and workshops to over 1000 people; wrote articles for various newsletters, magazines and newspapers; and were involved in radio and television broadcasts. They also served as a back-up to Rape Crisis, who they influenced to include services to battered women, assisting them with a phone-in weekend which launched their counseling service; and raised funds and negotiated for a shelter for battered women which was opened by Rape Crisis. The organization has evolved to become part of the anti-apartheid movement and the United Women's Congress. The latter group campaigned against sex abuse, produced a pamphlet, and conducted mental health workshops on sex abuse of prison detainees and other governmental oppression (Merlyn Lawrence, 1987).

Mexican Human Rights Academy – *Mexico City, Mexico*

The Mexican Human Rights Academy (Academia Mexicana de Derechos Humanos – AMDH) is the only community organization that I have encountered that specifically translates women's issues as human rights issues. AMDH was founded in 1984 to promote teaching, research and public awareness of human rights in Mexico and throughout Latin America. Their Technical Office has added to those responsibilities the development and supervision of training trainers, documentation, the human rights defense network, publications and communications, and institutional and international relations. Legal cases have come to their attention as well. Discussion, colloquia and public presentations held in cooperation with several of the country's major academic centers and public institutions have focused on the relationship between the State and the exercise of civil and political rights in Latin America. The rights of women, ethnic minorities, youth and refugees have been included. In continuous dialogue with the public sector, more favorable conditions have been forged for implementing concrete programs.

AMDH has found that consciousness-raising has resulted in a more sophisticated female grassroots citizenry. They are concentrating their efforts, therefore, on health care professionals who lag behind, as well as the heads of their organizations. A 66-hour course, conducted by Lucero Gonzales, Director of the Women's Program, was designed to teach social workers and nurses about existing legislation, as well as that which needs to be changed in behalf of women. A participative consciousness-raising format is utilized, focusing on "Women, Our Bodies, and Human Rights," with particular attention to confronting violence (Mariclaire Acosta, 1989).

Women's Legal Guidance – *Villa el Salvadore, Peru*

Women's Legal Guidance (Orientacion Legal a la Mujer) is in Villa el Salvadore, one of the poorest shantytowns of Lima. These women are residents who are legal advisors trained by an activist organization, Manuela Ramos. They were recruited from a number of sectors by the Federacion Popular de Mujeres de Villa el Salvadore, a large consortium which coordinates dozens of women's programs in the community. The women say they are motivated to combat chauvinism for equality of opportunity. (In contrast, there are no men's organizations.) "Villa" is famous because it has always been self-managing. Even when it was just a squatters' plot, everything was done by the people. Their community pride is visibly impressive. All social improvements (for example, roads, schools, and medical posts) were accomplished by women, built by their hands. Water and electricity in the area were non-existent until the women marched for them. "We have solidarity in our veins." Other burroughs are now following their example of how women can organize for social change.

Ninety percent of the cases that come to the attention of the Legal Guidance Center are women abused by their husbands. Others are in need of child support, or legalizing documents, such as birth, divorce, and marriage certificates. The advisors try to resolve legal matters in lieu of court. If they cannot do so, they notify Manuela Ramos who arrange for legal services. Manuela Ramos also provides on site weekly five hour meetings, as well as being on call for emergencies. The following procedures are taken by two shifts of four women each who are on duty throughout the week:

Procedure in Case of Abuse

1. Personally report the case to the police.
2. Take the abused woman for a medical examination.
3. Call the woman's husband in for a meeting.
4. Negotiate a signed agreement from both parties not to fight for one or two months. (This is 80 percent successful.)
5. If the woman returns because violence hasn't stopped, the case is taken to Manuel Ramos for court action.

The legal advisors follow up by asking neighbors about the situation because a battered woman may be afraid to report her husband. The solidarity and vigilance of the women tends to inhibit his violence toward her. Monitoring the cases includes educating neighbors to support battered women and teaching them their rights. When professional lawyers do have to come to town, the legal advisors accompany them in talks with the husbands, since they are more familiar with the cases (Susana Goldos and Frescia Carrasco, 1989; Abelina Catpo G., Carmen Nakasato, Maria Luz Casas Y., and Irene Buendia, 1989).

10 Women at Risk/ Women in Action

> Women and revolution! What tragic, unsung epics of courage lie silent in the world's history!
>
> Yang Ping, "Fragment from a Lost Diary" (1908–)

The United Nations *Forward-Looking Strategies* (1985) highlight the fact that there are populations of women whose vulnerabilities are compounded by particular characteristics of age, socio-economic condition, political pressures, minority status, geography, circumstances, and combinations of these factors. Many of the issues have been discussed in earlier chapters to greater and lesser degrees, but all deserve special attention because of their seriousness. The problems vary widely from country to country, as do the diverse groups of women involved. While strategies will need to be shaped to fit these multiplicities, all require fundamental changes in the economic situation of women which produces deprivation, and all require upgrading women's low status which accounts for their extreme vulnerability to poverty. Emergency assistance measures should be taken at the individual and group level. At the same time, broader efforts should be directed towards the reallocation of resources and decision-making power, and towards the elimination of inequality and injustice.

But social development efforts have proven to be inadequate in the absence of personal development. It is important to recognize and build on the coping skills of women already developed as basic strategies for survival and on their personal sense of self-worth. Strengthening the capabilities of their organizations also should be a first priority, so as to provide them with physical, financial, and human resources, in addition to education and training. The aspirations of women-at-risk must be revitalized in order to eliminate chronic despair that is so characteristic of their daily lives.

A basic strategy for the improvement of women's condition is the identification of needs through gender-specific data gathering. Economic indicators should highlight situations which are sensitive to extreme poverty and oppression. Spatial, socio-economic, and longitudinal characteristics also should be sought to better formulate and implement policies, programs, and projects. Monitoring should be intensified at local, regional, national, and international levels.

PERSON-ENVIRONMENT PROGRAM MODELS: A GLOBAL ZEITGEIST

Successful women's programs around the globe have much in common. There is something called a zeitgeist in the air . . . a trend of thought and feeling . . . the spirit of the age. The women of the world may not know there is a women's movement; they may never have heard of the UN Decade of Women; in many countries, there is little acknowledgement of the dynamic international feminist movement that exists. Still, successful programs everywhere share the following characteristics that incorporate all four dimensions of human growth and well-being: Connectedness, Aloneness, Action, and Perception.

- consciousness-raising regarding gender roles, and the importance and worth of every female as a fundamental right, recognizing their work as important work to be respected and counted on an equitable basis;
- forming interdisciplinary professional partnerships with poor women, training trainers to serve their own communities, with professional women providing resources and supervision;
- addressing the fundamental right of every woman to live without fear and domination, whether in the home or society; to be treated with respect; to be educated; and to be paid equitably for their work;
- sharing of home maintenance and child care with men on an equal basis; in short, restructuring the family and society from a human rights, social justice perspective;
- teaching fundamental rights regarding health needs, both mental and physical, including the individual and mutual need for nurturance, freedom from exhaustion, and participation in decision-making, within and outside the home;
- teaching women that both personal development and action, and collective social development and action are essential if their lives are going to change for the better;
- teaching women about their existing rights, how to execute legal and political critical analyses and development of legislation and policies, always beginning with their personal experience, generalizing it to

national and international policies, so that the connection becomes
real;

- engaging in participative social action research, culminating in
  participative psychosocial programming, they have adopted Friere's
  (1978) conscientization model, even when they never heard of him;
- developing credit unions, and coupling personal development with
  social/economic development of women, never ignoring either end
  of the spectrum.

Note that the emphasis may be different, but that all activities are
action-oriented in a positive sense, reducing negative activity; they intrinsically change self-perception and the perception of others from negative
to positive; they move from isolated, alienated aloneness to positive
aloneness, a sense of self; they decrease controlling connectedness and
increase supportive relationships. In the process, the profile of women is
changing. This is the global zeitgeist, the spirit of the age. This could be
the zeitgeist in all communities . . . the spirit reflected in a commitment
to women. Their well-being is our well-being, whatever one's gender,
ethnicity, age, or position in society. The problems of women are the
problems of the world. Their profile is our mirror image. Their solutions
are our own.

SPECIAL POPULATIONS AT RISK

Comprehensive efforts at multiple levels are needed to overcome barriers
to cooperation on behalf of the myriad problems of women in general, and
special at-risk populations of women in particular. To that end, the basic
strategies and measures for implementation found in the *Forward-Looking
Strategies* and related materials incorporated in *The World of Women: In
Pursuit of Human Rights* should be taken seriously. Among them are
technical cooperation, training, and advisory services; institutional coordination, research and policy analysis; participation of women in activities
and decision-making; and widespread information dissemination. The following summaries excerpted from the *Forward-Looking Strategies (1985)*
bring to the surface some of the most vulnerable groups of women.

Women and Children under Apartheid

Direct inhumane practices such as massacres and detention, mass population removal, separation from families, and immobilization in reservations

are perpetrated on women and children under apartheid in South Africa and other racist minority regimes. Considered the most oppressed group, they are subject to detrimental labor migrant system laws which relegate them to homelands where they suffer disproportionately from poverty, ill health, and illiteracy. Full international assistance, therefore, should be given to them. Their basic needs should be identified, including those in refugee camps, and they should be provided with adequate legal, humanitarian, medical, and material assistance, in addition to education, training, and employment.

Apartheid is institutionalized and experienced in day-to-day political, legal, social, and cultural life, creating enormous barriers to advancement, equality, and peace. Women, as well as their governments, must strengthen their commitment to the eradication of apartheid, supporting their struggling sisters by keeping informed, disseminating information widely, and building awareness in their countries about the situation. Individuals and women's groups can organize national solidarity and support committees as a means of educating the public about the brutal oppression of women and children under apartheid. [Althoug conditions are improving with the weakening of apartheid since the Decade of Women, they still prevail.

Women and Children in Areas Affected by Armed Conflict

Serious threats are imposed by armed conflicts and emergency situations on the lives of women and children, causing constant fear, danger of displacement, destruction, devastation, physical abuse, social and family disruption, and abandonment. These threats may result in complete denial of access to adequate health and educational services, loss of job opportunities, and general worsening of material conditions. Many have been struggling for decades for the survival of their families and their people. They are vulnerable to imprisonment, torture, reprisals, and other oppressive practices, as well as from internal discrimination in employment, health care, and education.

Women in Areas Affected by Drought

During the Decade of Women, the phenomenon of drought and desertification escalated until it affected several countries, rather than a few localities. The result has been that the conditions of people who are affected by famine and far-reaching deterioration of the environment, have been miserable. The lives of women and children, whose situations are already precarious, are particularly wretched. In addition to emergency measures, concerted efforts need to be taken to promote programs and productive activities between countries concerned to combat the problem. Measures should be taken to ensure that women's contribution to production is taken into account. They should be involved more closely in the design, implementation, and evaluation of the programs planned, with ample access to the means of production, processing, and preservation techniques.

Urban Poor Women

Urbanization has been a major socio-economic trend over the past few decades, and is expected to accelerate at such a rate that by the year 2000 about half of the world's women will be living in urban areas. The number of urban women in developing countries could nearly double by that time, with a considerable increase in the number of poor women among them. In order to deal effectively with the reality, governments should organize comprehensive programs that emphasize economic activities, eliminate discrimination, and provide supportive services. Examples are adequate child-care facilities and workplace canteens to enable women to gain access to economic, social, and educational opportunities on an equal basis with men. Particular attention should be given to the informal (private) sector, since it is a major source of employment for a considerable number of urban poor women.

Elderly Women

The International Plan of Action on Aging adopted by the World Assembly on Aging in 1982 recognizes a number of specific areas of concern to elderly women, in addition to those that impact on all elders. Women's longer life expectancy throughout most of the world results in their economic need and isolation, whether unmarried or widowed. This is particularly true for women who have spent their lives in unpaid and unrecognized work in the home, with little or no access to a pension. When women do have incomes, they are generally lower than men's, partly because their former employment status has been interrupted by maternity and family responsibilities. Efforts should be made, therefore, to provide social insurance for women in their own right. Both governments and non-governmental organizations should explore the possibilities of employing older women in productive and creative ways, encouraging their participation in social and recreational activities.

The care of elderly women should go beyond disease orientation to include their total well-being. Primary health care and other efforts to provide health services, suitable accommodation, and housing should be directed at enabling women to lead meaningful lives as long as possible, in their own homes, families, and communities. Preparation should not start in old age. Rather, women should be prepared, psychologically and socially, early in life, to face the consequences of longer life expectancy. More research is needed concerning the health problems of aging women, including premature aging due to a lifetime of stress, excessive workload, malnutrition, and repeated pregnancy. Aging is a real challenge for women. Instead of perpetuating the social consequences of stereotyping them, they should be helped to [recognize their strengths], to cope in creative ways with new opportunities. The media can be of great service, assisting by presenting positive images of women, particularly emphasizing the respect due them because of their past and continuing contributions to society.

Young Women

Young women should be assisted to develop their potential, protected from abuse and exploitation. Girls and boys should be given equal access to health, education, and employment, as well as accepting equal responsibilities for parenthood, in order to equip them for adult life. With particular attention to socially and economically disadvantaged young women, urgent attention should be paid to educational and vocational training in all occupational fields. Young women and girls who are self-employed should be assisted in the organization of cooperatives and on-going training programs in order to improve their skills in production, marketing, and managing techniques. Special retraining programs for teenage mothers and girls who have dropped out of school should be developed to equip them to enter productive employment.

Steps should be taken to eliminate exploitative treatment of young women. Governments should recognize and enforce their right to be free from sexual violence, sexual harassment, and sexual exploitation. Authorities should be aware that many young women are victims of incest and sexual abuse in the family. Young women should be educated to assert their rights, and prevention programs should be developed to eliminate such abuse, by education, by improving the status of women, and by appropriate action against offenders. The elimination of sexual harassment and exploitation should be given attention, particularly in domestic service where it is most prevalent. Homeless young women are most vulnerable to sexual exploitation. Governments have an obligation to provide safe housing for these women who because of unemployment and low incomes have difficulty obtaining housing.

By the year 2000, over eight percent of both urban and rural populations in developing countries will be females between the ages of fifteen and twenty-four. The majority of them will be out of school in search of jobs. When employed, if they continue to be sexually and economically exploited, working long hours, they will continue to experience stress, poor health, low nutritional levels, and unplanned, repeated pregnancies. Too few face the fact that the lives of young and middle-aged women write the scenario for their later years. Neither young women, nor the world, can afford to perpetuate these realities.

Abused Women

Throughout the world, gender-specific violence in and outside of the family, is increasing. Governments should affirm the dignity of women as a priority, intensifying their efforts to strengthen or establish services for victims of violence through the provision of shelter, support, and legal services, among others. Public awareness of such violence as a societal problem should be increased, establishing policies and legislative measures to investigate its causes and prevent and eliminate it. Degrading images and representations of women in society should not be condoned. Finally, governments should encourage the development of educational and re-educational measures for offenders.

Destitute Women

Destitution, an extreme form of poverty, effects increasingly larger segments of the population in both developing and developed countries. Homelessness is but one outcome of this population, in which vast numbers of women are increasing most rapidly. To have any impact on the problem, the *Forward-Looking Strategies* must be implemented. Governments should ensure that the special needs and concerns of these women are given priority in all programming and policy-making.

Women Victims of Trafficking and Involuntary Prostitution

Forced prostitution is caused by women's dependence on men, and the economic degradation that alienates women's labor through rapid urbanization and migration. Resulting underemployment and unemployment leads to this form of slavery imposed on women by procurers. Social and political pressures produce refugees and missing persons which often include vulnerable groups of women who are victimized by procurers. Pornography, sex tourism, and prostitution reduce women to mere marketable sexual commodities. International measures to deal with the exploitation of women as prostitutes and to combat trafficking in women should be given urgent consideration. Resources should be provided for both the prevention of prostitution and assistance in the professional, personal, and social reintegration of prostitutes. Government efforts should be directed towards providing economic opportunities, including training, employment, and self-employment, in cooperation with non-governmental organizations. Health facilities should be provided for women and children, as well as strict enforcement at all levels to stem the rising tide of violence, drug abuse, and crime that is related to prostitution. These complex, serious issues call for increased internationally coordinated efforts by police agencies.

Women Deprived of their Traditional Means of Livelihood

Deprivation of traditional means of livelihood is directly linked to excess-ive and inappropriate exploitation of land by transnational corporations, as well as natural and man-made disasters. Poor women have already been pushed into marginal environments due to droughts, floods, hurricanes, and other forms of environmental hazards, such as erosion, desertification, and deforestation. Drought-afflicted, arid and semi-arid areas are particularly affected, as well as urban slums and squatter settlements. Other factors that deprive women of their livelihood include critically low levels of water supplies, shortage of fuel, over-utilization of grazing and arable lands, and population density. National and international measures should be taken to strengthen the ecosystem, controlling environmental degradation through national conservation strategies aimed at incorporating women's development programs, among them irrigation and tree planting, as well as orientation in the area of agriculture. Women should constitute a substantial part of the wage-earning labor force for these programs.

Women who are Sole Supporters of their Families

A larger number of women, as compared with men, are the sole supporters of families, and their numbers are increasing. Owing to the particular social, economic, and legal difficulties that they face, many are among the poorest people. They are concentrated in urban informal labor markets, and they constitute large numbers of the rural unemployed and marginally employed. When they have little economic, social, and moral support, they face serious difficulties in supporting themselves, much less raising their children alone. The repercussions for society are serious, relative to the quality, character, productivity, and human resource capabilities of its present and future citizenry.

A large portion of the relevant legislation, regulations, and household surveys confine the role of supporter and head of household to men. This underlying assumption hinders women's access to credit, loans, and material and non-material resources. If they are to have equal access, changes are needed in these areas. The term "head of household" should be eliminated, introducing others that are comprehensive enough to reflect women's role appropriately in documents, so as to guarantee their rights. Special attention should be given to the needs of women in the provision of social services. Governments should ensure that women with sole responsibility for their families receive a level of income and social support sufficient to make them economically independent and to participate effectively in society. To this end, the assumptions that underlie policies and research utilized in policy development and legislation that confines the role of supporter or head of household to men should be eliminated. Quality child care should be available to women to assist them in discharging their domestic responsibilities and to enable them to participate in and benefit from education, training programs, and employment. Unwed fathers should be made to assist in the maintenance and education of their children [as should married and divorced fathers].

Women with Physical and Mental Disabilities

Women constitute a significant number of the estimated 500 million people who are disabled as a consequence of mental, physical, and sensory impairment. Many factors contribute to their rising numbers, among them war and other forms of violence, poverty, hunger, nutritional deficiencies, epidemics, and work-related accidents. The recognition of their human dignity, human rights, and full participation in society is still limited. Because women have domestic and other responsibilities, they experience compounded difficulties. Their particular problems need to be appreciated more fully, providing them with community-based occupational and social rehabilitation, support services to help them with domestic duties, and opportunities for their participation in all aspects of life. The rights of women who are intellectually disabled should be respected, including obtaining health information and advice, as well as the right to consent to or refuse medical treatment [particularly when interventions reflect a range of opinions]. The rights of intellectually disabled minors should also be protected.

Women in Detention and Subject to Penal Law

The field of crime prevention and criminal justice recognizes that the system's equal treatment of women is a major area of concern everywhere in the world, and in some countries, the disproportionate number of indigenous women who are imprisoned. Some improvements have been made in the area of socio-economic and cultural conditions, but more need to be made. The increasing trend of more women in detention over more than a decade is expected to continue, a fact that has hidden repercussions. Women who are incarcerated are exposed to various forms of physical violence, sexual and moral harassment. Their conditions are often below acceptable hygienic standards, and their children are deprived of maternal care. The design and implementation of fair and equal treatment should take into account concrete measures at national and international levels.

Refugee and Displaced Women and Children

The protection and assistance of refugees and displaced persons is recognized by the international community. In many cases, such women are exposed to a variety of difficult situations affecting their physical and legal protection, as well as their psychological and material well-being. Specialized and enlarged assistance is called for in cases of physical disability, physical safety, emotional stress, and socio-psychological effects of separation or death in the family, in addition to changes in women's roles. Limitations are often found in their environmental confinement, including lack of adequate food, shelter, health care, and social services. What is more, the potential and capacities of refugee and displaced women should be recognized and enhanced. [It is they, after all, who are keeping their families intact.]

The root causes of the flow of refugees should be identified, as well as durable solutions. Until they are recognized, the lasting solution to the problems of refugee and displaced women and their children will not be found. Durable solutions in the immediate future, on the other hand, will lead to their voluntary return to their homes under honorable and safe conditions, and fully integrated in the economic, social, and cultural life of their countries of origin. As an expression of global solidarity and burden sharing, until this is achieved the international community should continue to provide relief assistance, as well as launching special relief programs. In so doing, the special needs of refugee women and children in countries of first asylum should be taken into account. Accordingly, similar relief and programming should be provide for returnees, offering them legal, educational, social, humanitarian, and moral assistance, as well as opportunities for their voluntary repatriation, return, or settlement.

Migrant Women

Over the years, women have been increasingly involved in all forms of migration – rural-rural, rural-urban, and international movements of a temporary, seasonal, or permanent nature. In addition to their lack of adequate education, skills, and resources, they may be separated from their families, facing severe adjustment problems due to differences in religion, language, nationality, and socialization. International migrants often experience openly expressed hostility and prejudice, including violation of their human rights in host countries. United Nations conventions and declarations should be implemented to deal with these realities, with an expanded view to the anticipated increase in the scope of the problem. Women are subject to double discrimination due to their gender. They should be given special attention, particularly with respect to protection and maintenance of family unity, employment opportunities and equal pay, equal work conditions, health care, and racial and other forms of discrimination. Benefits should be provided in accordance with the existing social security rights in the host country. If they are to be allowed to integrate themselves in their adopted country at levels that are appropriate to their potential, the second generation of migrant women also require attention, especially with regard to education and professional training. Loss of cultural values of their countries of origin should be avoided in the process [keeping in mind those that perpetuate their oppression].

Minority and Indigenous Women

Already oppressed by gender discrimination, minority and indigenous women are doubly disadvantaged due to prejudicial attitudes towards their ethnicity, color, descent, and national origin. They have been subjected historically to domination, suffering dispossession, dispersal, and economic deprivation. Measures should be taken by their governments to respect, preserve, and promote all of their human rights, their dignity, ethnic, religious, cultural, and linguistic identity, as well as their full participation in societal change. Specific measures should be taken to assist them in fulfilling family and parental responsibilities, such as addressing dietary deficiencies, high levels of infant and maternal mortality and other health problems, as well as lack of education, housing, and child care. Vocational, technical, professional, and other training should be provided. Only then can these women secure employment or participate in income-generating activities and projects, and secure adequate wages, occupational health and safety, in addition to their other rights as workers. As far as possible, access to these services should be in the language of the women concerned.

Women who belong to minority or indigenous populations should be consulted and allowed to participate fully in the development and implementation of programs which affect them. Governments should be involved and committed to the United Nations doctrines which are concerned with racial and minority discrimination, emphasizing the distinctive role of women in sustaining the identity of their people.

THE "SEVEN SINS" OF DEVELOPMENT

The year 1989 provided UNICEF with an occasion to summarize that which has been learned over the years about social development and its failures. It was the tenth anniversary of the International Year of the Child, and an opportunity for analysis of the United Nations Decade of Women's progress towards the year 2000 regarding the *Forward-Looking Strategies*. It was also the year in which the strategies for the last development decade of the twentieth century were being formulated by the world's governments. The harsh lessons which make the difference between success and failure are summarized below. UNICEF calls them development's "seven sins."

1. Development without Infrastructure

In recent years, international development efforts have yielded a range of techniques and strategies which could markedly accelerate development in the years ahead. By way of example, in the field of health, cost-effective techniques are now available from immunization to oral rehydration therapy, and from new seed varieties to new hand pumps. Advancement is of little use, however, without reliable delivery mechanisms for informing and supporting people in their use. The backbone of a health infrastructure is made up of properly trained staff and informed people. (Because it is women who are most likely to be concerned with the dissemination and utilization of such knowledge, they should be central to all educational efforts.)

2. Development without Participation

If development is to be sustained, it ultimately depends on the enhancement of people's own capacities to improve their lives, and to take control over their own destinies. Research indicates that there is an absolutely crucial distinction between the kind of assistance that enables and involves, and the kind that alienates and disenfranchises. External providers, therefore, must learn how to take a supporting role. The success or failure of development efforts, whether in agriculture, industry, water supply, or housing schemes, depend on which side of a sometimes subtle line assistance falls.

3. Development without Women

Whether or not one approves of sex role divisions of labor, the women of the world are almost entirely responsible for the physical and mental development of the next generation. In the developing world, they are responsible for producing and marketing most of its crops, and they carry the main responsibility for food preparation, homemaking, water and fuel, and nutrition and health care. Yet, most development assistance efforts, most education and training, technology and inputs, and investments and loans, continue to go to men. From a human rights perspective, such bias is fundamentally congruent with the existing inequities and injustices that women endure. Practically speaking, it is grossly inefficient, costing development efforts dearly. We know that family size, child health, and the use of available government resources are directly linked to female education. The possibilities are only beginning to be explored for women's increased productivity and incomes through credit, training, and technology. Among the most productive, yet most ignored, of all investments is that of safe motherhood and labor saving devices of particular relevance to women. [Developers have also begun to recognize the importance of working with women at the personal development level, particularly in relation to perception of themselves and recognition of themselves as people of worth and strength who are entitled to respect, opportunity, and equitable treatment. Aloneness that is reflected in autonomy, uniqueness, and intrinsic personal worth; connectedness in terms of universal truths about women, supportive relationships, and networking; and action in their own behalf come into play in the process. Thus, the developmental dimensions detailed in *The World of Women: In Pursuit of Human Rights* are recognized, however indirectly, as necessary prerequisites of social development.]

4.   Development without Environment

It was just a little over a decade ago that it was widely thought that environmental problems were a function of affluence in the industrialized world. Today, the world is painfully aware that is not so. The deforestation of land, erosion of soil, and silting of lakes and rivers are directly related to the new propensity to drought and flood in developing countries. Industrial disasters, too, reflect the fact that the environment is a critical issue for all regions. Rising concern over the depletion of the ozone layer, global warming, and the unknown consequences of the destruction of the world's forests should have made this fact clear long ago. No matter what the development initiative, the environment ought to be part of planning forethought, not the afterthought.

5.   Development without the Poor

Historically, development has been confined too often to showcase examples and pilot projects that show what can be done. Now the emphasis must shift to *doing* it. We must apply the knowledge we already have on a scale that is commensurate with the need. Called "going to scale," this means that we must reach all people, not just a percentage of them. The fact is that the problems of malnutrition, poor growth, frequent ill health, child and maternal mortality, illiteracy, and low productivity are concentrated among the *poorest* third of the families of the developing world. The same holds true for families in many of the so-called developed nations. UNICEF contends that the greatest challenge in social development is the challenge of meeting the needs of the very poorest people.

Even the most serious attempts to shift priorities in favor of the poor have often failed to reach substantial numbers of the very poorest groups. (These programs have included primary schools, adult literacy campaigns, rural clinics, and supplementary feeding programs.) The reasons for failure are complex. Among them are lack of pressure to sustain efforts, representation of the poor in decision-making, and the inversion of spending pyramids, so that the majority of resources available for development are devoted to action which benefits the poorest. Given that women are disproportionately represented among the poor, their absence again takes its toll.

6.   Development without the Achievable

Experts in the various disciplines of development are rightly taking credit for much of the data base available today. They must also take the blame, however, for the failure to implement that knowledge on a significant scale. This is true partly because research and development has focused on small-scale and pilot projects where the ratio of real resources to problems is artificially high. Because reports are made without addressing priorities or step-by-step implementation, many well-formed plans remain on the shelf, which the experts lament is because of a lack of political will. The task of development experts over the coming decades must be revised. They must shape today's knowledge into plans which are capable of attracting whatever political will *is* available, while using persuasive means to increase it. Given the fierce competition for resources in every country of the world, the challenge is the molding of available knowledge into achievable, large scale, low cost, high impact, and politically attractive plans. [The call to applied fields such as social work is loud and clear.]

7. Development without Mobilization

In the decade ahead, the task of development is putting today's knowledge at the disposal of the majority. For example, immunization facilities will not be used if parents do not know why, when, and where their children are to be vaccinated. For too long the dissemination of essential development knowledge, particularly regarding health and nutrition, has been left to health services which have had neither the time, training, or outreach mechanisms to do the job. Meanwhile, there is an unprecedented capacity, thanks to the communications revolution, to share state-of-the-art knowledge with the world. School systems reach three-quarters of the developing world's population; radio reaches a majority of homes; and tens of thousands of non-governmental organizations, including women's programs, are working in the poorest communities. In relatively developed regions of the world, the principles still hold, and access to media is even greater, extending to television. By mobilizing the social capacities of the people, the major threats to their life and health can be reduced or eradicated. They include vaccine-preventable diseases, diarrheal dehydration, acute respiratory infections, low birth weight, and maternal mortality, as well as cancer, heart disease, and AIDS. [The same capacity can be tapped to mobilize people regarding the human rights issues of women. Indeed, they are not mutually exclusive issues.]

UNICEF reminded us in 1989 that the concept of social development as a conscious discipline was only about forty years old, with efforts most of that time based on naive assumptions about the nature of the process. Today, on a firmer foundation of hard-won knowledge, techniques, strategies, and guiding principles, really significant development achievements can be reached in the coming decade. The future holds promise for the world of women and consequently, the world of children and men.

ASSESSING THE STATUS OF WOMEN

International Women's Rights Action Watch

The Committee on the Elimination of Discrimination Against Women (CEDAW, 1983, 1988) suggests that reports on the status of women be divided into two parts. Part One should provide a general framework, presenting background information about the country, a description of the institutions charged with enforcing women's rights within the country, the means used to improve and protect the status of women, and the remedies available to women. It is also appropriate to discuss the effect of ratification of the Convention (1980) when applicable. As a minimum, the following information ought to be provided:

A.   Population data, including (1) total population, percent male and female; (2) number of persons per square kilometer or mile; (3) percent male and female by relevant age groups: (cf., 0–14, 15–59, 60 and over); (4) percent total population which is rural, male and female; (5) important changes in population, such as shifts in the percentage of people living in rural and urban areas.

B.   The date on which the Convention came into force and the description of how it is being enforced, where applicable.

C.   The general state of the economy, including the gross national product (GNP), per capita income and distribution by income.

D.   A description of the religions of the country including the percentage of the population and geographical distribution of each, if relevant.

E.   A description of the governmental and non-governmental institutions that promote and protect the advancement of women.

F.   The legal meachnisms, remedies, or resources available to women who have experienced discrimination.

Part Two should examine each article of the Convention (as presented in Chapters 2 through 9 of this book), furnishing specific information about legal and administrative provisions in force, developments that have taken place since ratification, legal or practical obstacles, and any other relevant information. This section should include information on the laws as they are written and as they are administered (IWRAW, 1988). The following general suggestions also will serve to make reporting consistent across nations:

A.   Use statistics whenever possible to provide concrete information on the status of women, including statistics that show changes that have occurred.

B.   Give illustrative examples, where possible, of discrimination and corrective measures.

C.   In addition to laws and regulations, describe the actual, real-life conditions for women.

D.   Discuss obstacles to improving the status of women.

E.   Describe any differences in the status of women from different ethnic groups, socio-economic classes, religions, and geographic regions.

F.   Highlight the effects of particular circumstances, such as war or drought, on the status of women.

The International Women's Rights Action Watch (1988) has taken on the responsibility of documenting this information for CEDAW. Please send your reports to:

International Women's Rights Action Watch
Arvonne Fraser, Director
143 Humphrey Institute
301 – 19th Avenue, South
Minneapolis, Minnesota 55455, USA

*   *   *

Women in Social Work International

(WISWI) is a global feminist resource network for social workers and related disciplines who are working on behalf of women. Founded in 1985 following the Decade of Women conference, the organization contends that the problems of women are the problems of the world. The social justice ethic inherent in social work, therefore, must be applied to the concerns of women. The membership emphasizes a global perspective regarding women's concerns in order to impact personal, professional, research and policy spheres of social work influence worldwide; to promote personal and social development; and to provide visibility and supportive global linkages for women in social work at international meetings.

At the International Association of Schools of Social Work conference in Vienna, Austria in 1988, the Women's Caucus voted to ensure the global ownership of WISWI, allowing the organization to emanate from any region at any time, and to operate as a local support network, as well as an international system. The WISWI Global Feminist Resource Directory includes names, addresses, telephone numbers, and interests in specific issues, curriculum development, research opportunities, and practice consultation, as well as action-oriented activities. As of 1991, over 300 members from 40 countries were listed. Refer to the mailing address below for inclusion in updated directories.

Women in Social Work International
Janice Wood Wetzel
Adelphi University
School of Social Work
Garden City, Long Island,
New York 11530, USA

Appendix

COUNTRIES THAT HAVE RATIFIED THE UN CONVENTION
ON THE ELIMINATION OF ALL FORMS OF DISCRIMINATION
AGAINST WOMEN

As of October 1991, 109 countries have consented to be bound by the provisions of the United Nations Convention on the Elimination of All Forms of Discrimination Against Women:

Angola, Antigua & Barbuda, Argentina, Australia, Austria, Bangladesh, Barbados, Belgium, Belize, Bhutan, Bolivia, Brazil, Bulgaria, Burkina Faso, Byelorussian Soviet Socialist Republic, Canada, Cape Verde, Central African Republic, Chile, China, Columbia, Congo, Costa Rica, Cuba, Cyprus, Czechoslavakia.

Democratic Yemen, Denmark, Dominica, Dominican Republic, Ecuador, Egypt, El Salvador, Equatorial Guinea, Ethiopia, Finland, France, Gabon, Germany, Ghana, Greece, Grenada, Guatemala, Guinea, Guinea-Bissau, Guyana.

Haiti, Honduras, Hungary, Iceland, Indonesia, Iraq, Ireland, Israel, Italy, Jamaica, Japan, Kenya, Lao People's Democratic Republic, Liberia, Libyan Arab Jamahiriya, Luxembourg, Madagascar, Malawi, Mali, Malta, Mauritius, Mexico, Mongolia, Napal, New Zealand, Nicaragua, Nigeria, Norway.

Panama, Paraguay, Peru, Philippines, Poland, Portugal, Republic of Korea, Romania, Rwanda, Saint Christopher and Nevis, Saint Lucia, Saint Vincent and the Grenadines, Senegal, Sierra Leone, Spain, Sri Lanka, Sweden, The Netherlands, Thailand, Togo, Trinidad & Tobago, Tunisia, Turkey, Uganda, Ukranian Soviet Socialist Republic, Union of Soviet Socialist Republics.

United Kingdom of Great Britain and Northern Ireland, United Republic of Tanzania, Uruguay, Venezuela, Viet Nam, Yugoslavia, Zaire, Zambia, Zimbabwe.

(Source: U.S. Congressional Record and the National Committee on the United Nations Convention on the Elimination of Discrimination Against Women.)

Courtesy of Billie Heller, Chair of the National Committee on the United Nations Convention on the Elimination of Discrimination Against Women (520 North Camden, Beverly Hills, California, USA 90210–3302), an advocacy group working to achieve U.S. ratification or accession.

Bibliography

Academia Mexicana de Derechos Humanos (1989). Personal Interview (*Mexican Academy of Human Rights: Filosophia y Letros Mexico*), Mexico City, Mexico.

Acosta Vargus, Gladys (1988). "Los Derechos De las Mujeres En las Constituciones Politicas," *NASA: Revista Cultural de Indes*, 3:3 (December), 28–39.

—— (1989). "Los Derechos Humanos y los Derechos de las Mujeres, Encuentro "La Mujer in la Defensa de los Derechos Humanos," organizado por el Colectiveo Profuest y la Asociacion Calandria, Lima, Peru (February).

Acosta Vargus, Gladys with Norma Gamarra Sedano (1988). "The Rights of Women in Political Constitutions," *MASA*, 3:3 (December), 28–39.

Acosta, Mariclaire (1989). Personal Interview (Academia Mexicana de Derechos Humanos, Mexico City, Mexico (June).

Ahmed, Shaheen (1989). Personal Interview (Women for Women), Dhaka, Bangladesh (February).

Alcoholism Center for Women, Los Angeles, CA, USA.

Alejandre, Virginia, Maria C. Galante, and Paula Sesia-Lewis (1986–1989). Personal Interview (Groupo de Estudios Regionales de Oaxaca), Oaxaca, Oaxaca, Mexico.

American Association for International Aging (1988), *Reports*, 6:2, (Spring), 5.

American Association of Retired Persons (AARP) and the International Federation on Aging (IFA), (1989). *Statement for the UN: Social Development Commission* (March 13–22).

Andia, Bethsake P. (1989). Personal Interview (Aurora Vivar), Lima, Peru.

Angulo, Carmen D., Mariella Sola, Marisa Godinez, Diana T. Meloslanok, Sylvia Loli, and Rosa Guillen (1989). Personal Interview (Flora Tristan: Centro de la Mujer Peruana), Lima, Peru.

Anstey, B, Eleanor (1986). "Pesticide Poisoning: Payment of Women in Developing Countries," *Canadian Woman Studies*, Vol. 7, Nos 1 and 2, Spring/Summer, 175–177.

—— (1988). "Pesticides and Women: Protecting Yourself and Your Family," Booklet for Rural African Women, Iowa City: The University of Iowa.

Apodaca, Lourdes and Eugenia Lizalde, interpreter (1989). Personal Interview (Universidad Nacional Autonoma de Mexico), Mexico City, Mexico.

Apuzzo, Virginia M. (1988). "Leadership: The Essential Element in the Control of Global AIDS and the Protection of Human Rights of HIV-Infected, Persons," Keynote at World AIDS Day Special Symposium on AIDS and Human Rights, United Nations, New York City, New York, USA.

Arken, Susan Hardey, Karen Anderson, Myra Dinverstein, Judy N. Fensink, and Patricia MacCorquodale, Eds (1988). *Changing our Minds*, Albany, NY: State University of New York Press.

Asian Women's Resource Center on Culture and Theology, Personal Interview, Kowloon, Hong Kong (January).

Associated Press (1989). "Women Gain Ground in Wages, Study Shows," *The New York Times* (February 9).

Associated Press (1989). "Women Struggle for Equality," *South China Morning Post* (January 9).

Association for the Advancement of Feminism (1988). Personal Interviews, Wan Chai, Hong Kong (January).

Association for the Promotion of the Status of Women (1988). Personal Interviews, Bangkok, Thailand (February).

Association for Women in Psychology (1985). "An International Feminist Mental Health Agenda for the Year 2000," working paper presented at the Non-Governmental Organization World Meeting for Women, Nairobi, Kenya (July 10–19).

Ballou, Mary and Nancy W. Gablac (1985). *A Feminist Position on Mental Health*, Springfield, Illinois: Charles C. Thomas.

Barrow, Dame Nita (1988). "Testimony of a Convert," *World Health*, (August/September), 26–29.

Barry, Kathleen, Charlotte Bunch, and Shirley Castley, Eds (1984). *International Feminism: Networking Against Female Sexual Slavery*, NY: International Women's Tribune Centre, Inc.

Beatty, Ned (1989). "Suppose Men Feared Rape," *The New York Times* (May).

Berlin, Sharon (1982). "The Woman Question: Does Social Work Have an Answer?," NASW Regional Conference – Empowering Women for Survival and Change, Minneapolis, MN (May).

Bermudez, Tesse (1989). Personal Interview, Lima, Peru (June).

Bernard, Jessie (1987). *The Female World from a Global Perspective*, Bloomington and Indianapolis: Indiana University Press.

Bernstein, Aaron (1988). "So You Think You've Come a Long Way, Baby?," *Business Week* (February 29).

Bhanti, Raj (1988). "Role of Women in Drought," Unpublished Monograph, Udaipur, India.

Bhowmik, Usha (1988). "The Dowry System in the Context of the Present Social Order and the Need for a Social Structure Based on Equality, Liberty and Peace," Unpublished Monograph, Bombay, India.

Birkeland, Ingunn (1988). Personal Interview (Norwegian Housewives Association), United Nations: New York, NY, USA.

Blakey, Virginia (1985). "Women's Health and Family Planning," International Planned Parenthood Federation, Monograph, Cardiff, Wales: University College of Population Centre.

Boulding, Elise (1980). *Women: The Fifth World*, NY: Foreign Policy Association.

Bourque, Susan C. and Kay B. Warren (1989). *Learning About Women: Gender, Politics and Power*, in Jill Conway, Susan Bourque, and Joan Scott, Eds, Ann Arbor: University of Michigan Press, 173–197.

—— (1987). "Technology, Gender and Development," *Daedalus*, 116:4, (Fall), 173–197.

Branch for the Advancement of Women, Centre for Social Development & Humanitarian Affairs, United Nations Office at Vienna (1988), Data Highlights No. 2: "Age Structure of the Female Population and Dependency and Caring Ratios."

Brawley, Edward A. and Ruben Schinder (1986). "Paraprofessional Social Welfare Personnel in International Perspective: Results of a Worldwide Survey," *International Social Work*, 29:2 (April) 165–176.

Brooke, James (1991). "Honor Killing of Wives is Outlawed in Brazil," *New York Times* (March 29).

Broudy, Harry (1980). "Tacit Knowing as a Rationale for Liberal Education," in Douglas Salon, Ed., *Education and Values*, NY Teachers College Press.

Bruin, Janet, Ed. (1988). *Pax et Libertas*, 53:2, Women's International League for Peace and Freedom (June), 1–16.

—— (1988). *Pax et Libertas* 53:3 (September), 1-16.

—— (1989). *Pax et Libertas*, 54:1 (March), 1-16.

Bunch, Charlotte (1987). *Passionate Politics*, NY: St. Martins Press.

Bunch, Charlotte, Kathleen Barry, and Shirley Castley, Eds (1984). "Global Feminist Workshop," Rotterdam, The Netherlands.

Bunch, Carolotte and Sandra Pollack, Eds, *Learning our Way: Essays in Feminist Education*, Trumansburg, New York: The Crossing Press Feminist Series, 49–58.

Campfens, Hubert (1988). *Women Organizing in Latin American Shanty-towns: Issues and Research*, Unpublished Monograph, Wilfred Lourier University, Waterloo: Canada.

Catpo, Abelina G., Carmen Nakasato, Maria Lug Y. Casas, and Irene Buendia (1989). Personal Interview (Orientacion Legal a La Mujer), Villa el Salvadore, Peru (June).

Centre for Social Development and Humanitarian Affairs (1988). "Distribution of the Female Population in Rural and Urban Areas," *Data Highlights*, No. 3.

Centro Latin Americano de Trobajo Sociale (1989). Personal Interviews, Miraflores, Peru (June).

Chamnavej, Wimolsiri (1980). "Legal Aid Projects in Thailand," *Women and the Law* (June).

Cheung Choi Wan (1989). Personal Interview. (Association for the Advancement of Feminism), Wan Chai, Hong Kong (January).

Chodorow, Nancy (1978). *The Reproduction of Mothering: Psychonalysis and the Sociology of Gender*, Berkeley: University of California Press.

Christian Conference of Asia (1988). Personal Interviews (Ecumenical Peace Program), Kowloon, Hong Kong (January).

Chueca, Marcella, Norma Rottier, Margareta Rosa, Esperanza Reyes, and Monica Escobar (1989). Personal Interviews (Centro Latin Americano de Trabajo Social), Miraflores, Peru (June).

Committee for Asian Women (CAW) (1988). Personal Interviews, Kowloon, Hong Kong (January).

Committee for Chilean Inquiry (1989). *Chilean Freedom: Annual Report Newsletter* (Fall).

Convention (1980). *The Elimination of All Forms of Discrimination Against Women*, New York, NY: United Nations.

Corneyjo, Maryza F. (1989). Personal Interview (Pontificia Universidad Catholica), Lima, Peru (June).

Dahlin, Yvonne (1989). Personal Interview (Asian Women's Resource Centre), Kowloon, Hong Kong (January).

Davies, Anne G. Ed. (1989). *Reports*, Vol. 76 (Winter).

Davis, Susan (1989). Personal Interview (The Ford Foundation), Dhaka, Bangladesh (January).

d'Epinay, Christian J. Lolive (1985). "Depressed Elderly Women in Switzerland: An Example of Testing and Generating Theories," *The Gerontologist*, 25:6, December, 597–604.

Desai, Armaity S. (1988). "Curriculum Imperatives for Social Change," Eileen Younghusband Memorial Lecture at the 24th International Congress of Schools of Social Work, Vienna, Austria, July 17–23.

—— (1989). Personal Interview (Tata University Institute of Social Sciences), Bombay, India (February).

Dewey, Arthur E. (1988) "Interview: We have to be Tenacious in Our Protection Efforts," *Refugee*, 56 (September), 19–20.

Dhamabutra, Chalermasri (1989). Personal Interview (Appropriate Technology Association), Northeast Province, Thailand (January).

Dixon, Ruth (1980). "Assessing the Impact of Development Projects on Women," Washington, DC, Women in Development, AID. Program Evaluation Paper No. 8, PN-AAH-725, Bureau for Program and Policy Coordination: Agency for International Development.

Dolon, P. and E. Apostol Eds (1988). "International Policy on Health," *International Policy Papers*, Geneva: International Federation of Social Workers, 32–35.

Donovan, Rebecca (1987). "Home Care Work: A Legacy of Slavery in U.S. Health Care," *Affilia,* (Fall), 33–44.

—— (1989). "Work Stress and Job Satisfaction: A Study of Home Care Workers in New York City," *Home Health Care Services Quarterly*, Vol. 10, No. 1/2, 97–114.

Dougher, Christine, Dorriece Pirtle, and Janice Wood Wetzel (1976). "Feminist Theory and Social Work Practice," paper presented at 50th Anniversary of George Warren Brown School of Social Work, Washington University, St. Louis Missouri, USA.

Driscoll, John S., Ed. (1988). "Giving Back to the Care-givers," *The Boston Globe* (November 24), 30.

Duley, Margot I. and Mary I. Edwards, Eds (1976). *The Cross-Cultural Study of Women: A Comprehensive Guide*, New York: Feminist Press.

Dunfee, E. J. (1987). "A Hot Time in Hatyai," *Asia Magazine* (May), 24–29.

DuPont (1988). *In Good Company*, "A Guide to DuPont's Seminars on Meeting the Challenges of a Diverse Work Force."

Duvall, Ann (1989). Personal Interview (Women's World Banking), New York, NY, USA.

Ecumenical Peace Program (1988). "Life for the People; Peace With Justice in Asia," 1:3 (September–December).

Eisler, Riane (1987). *The Chalice and the Blade*, San Francisco: Harper & Row Publishers.

Enloe, Cynthia (1985). *Radical America*, "Bananas, Bases, and Patriarchy: Some Feminist Questions About the Militarization of Central America," 19:43 (July/August), 7–23.

Epstein, Susan, Ed. (1988). *International Labor Organization Information: U.S. Edition*, 16:4 (October), 1-8.

Erlanger, Steven (1988) "In Thai Camps, Forced Labor and Military Rigidity Under Khamer Rouge," *The New York Times International* (November 20), 3.

Escobae, Monica (1989). Personal Interview (CELATS), Miraflores, Peru (June).

Escuela de Trabajo Social (1989). Personal Interview, Pontifica Universidad Catolica, Lima, Peru (June).

Escuela de Trabajo (1989). Personal Interview, Universidad Nacional Autononoma de Mexico, Mexico City, Mexico (June).

Estes, Richard J. (1988). *Dilemma in International Development: Implications for Social Work Education for the Year 2000 and Beyond*, presented at 24th International Congress of Schools of Social Work, Vienna, Austria (July 19).

—— (1988). *Trends in World Social Development*, NY: Praeger.

Evans, Sarale (1964). (Uganda Council of Women), Uganda, Africa.

Fedele, Nicolina and Jean Baker Miller (1988). "Putting Theory into Practice: Creating Mental Health Programs for Women," *Work in Progress*, No. 32.

Ferguson, Marilyn (1980). *The Aquarian Conspiracy: Personal and Social Transformation in the 1980's*, Los Angeles: J.P. Tarchet, Inc.

Fine, Michelle and Adrienne Asch, Eds (1988). *Women with Disabilities: Essays in Psychology, Culture and Politics*, PA: Temple University Press.

Finlay, J. M. (1986). "Transcending Equality Theory: A Way Out of the Maternity Debate," *Columbia Law Review*, 86 (October),1118–1182.

Fiske, Edward B. (1989). "The Global Imperative," *The New York Times*, (April 9), 18–20.

Flora Tristan: Centro de La Mujer Peruance (1989). Personal Interviews, Lima, Peru (June).

Ford Foundation Annual Report (1987). New York, New York, USA, (October 1, 1986 to September 30).

Foundation for Women (1988). Personal Interviews, Bankok, Thailand (January).

Foundation for Women, *Prostitution: Thai-European Connection – An Action Oriented Study*, Bangkok, Thailand.

Freire, Paulo (1970/1982). *Pedagogy of the Oppressed*, New York: The Continuum Publishing Corporation.

—— (1973/1981). *Education for Cultural Consciousness*, New York: The Continuum Publishing Corporation.

Freire, Paulo and Donaldo Macedo (1987). *Literacy: Reading The Word and the World*, MA: Bergin and Garvey Publishers, Inc.

Friedan, Betty (1989). "Not for Women Only," *Modern Maturity* (April/May) 66–71.

Galdos, Susana and Frescia Carrasco (1989). Personal Interviews (Manuela Ramos), Lima, Peru (June).

Gerstel, Naomi, "Same Differences," *The Women's Review of Books*, VI: 9, June 1989.

Ghai, Dharam (1984). *An Evaluation of the Impact of the Grameen Bank Project*, Dhaka, Bangladesh: Eastern Commercial Service, Ltd.

Gilkes, Cheryl T. (1981). "From Slavery to Social Welfare: Racism and the Control of Black Women," *The Control of Black Women*, 289–300.

Gilligan, Carol (1982). *In a Different Voice: Psychological Theory and Women's Development*, Cambridge, MA: Harvard University Press.

Glenn, Evelyn N. (1985). "Racial Ethnic Women's Jobs: The Intersection of Race, Gender and Class Oppression," *Review of Radical Political Economics*, 17:3, 86–108.

Goldberg, Gertrude Schaffner and Eleanor Kremen, Eds (1990). *The Feminization of Poverty: Only in America?* New York: Praeger.

Goldstein, Howard (1986). "Education for Social Work Practice: A Cognitive Cross Cultural Approach," *International Social Work*, 29:2 (April), 149–164.

Goleman, Daniel (1989). "The Self: From Tokyo to Topeka, It Changes," *The New York Times* (March 7), C1, C6.

Group for the Support of Ethnic Development (1989). Personal Telephone Interview, Grupo de Estudios Regionales de Oaxaca, Oaxaca, Mexico (June).

Hartman, Heidi (1988). "Help Families Pay for Child Care," *The Texas Observer* (July 15).

Haynes, Karen S. and James S. Michelson (1986). *Affecting Change: Social Workers in the Political Arena*, NY: Longman.

Health Commissioner Talks About AIDS," *Action for Children*, 3:4, 2.

Health Resources and Services Administration (1987). "Report of the Social Workers Task Force on AIDS," *Proceedings of the Multidisciplinary Curriculum Development Conference on HIV Infection* (September).

Healy, Lynne M. (1986). "The International Dimension in Social Work

Education: Current Efforts, Future Challenges," *International Social Work*, 29:2 (April 1986) 135–148.

Heisel, Donald (1989). "Women and Population," *NGO Committee on the Decade for Women* (April 20).

Helping Hand of Hong Kong (1989). Personal Interview, Wan Chai, Hong Kong (January).

Helping Hand (1987–1988). *Report of the Executive Committee of Helping Hand*, Wan Chai, Hong Kong.

Hillyer, Barbara (1989). "Blueprint for an Alliance," *The Women's Review of Books*, VI: 6 (March), 10.

Hobbs, Mary Kay (1989). Personal Interview (Christian Conference of Asia-Ecumenical Peace Program), Kowloon, Hong Kong (January).

Hoffman, Starr (1981). *National Association of Social Workers International Social Work Program Plan*.

Holtzman, Elizabeth (1989). "Rape – the Silence is Criminal," *The New York Times* (May 5).

Hongskrai, Boonchean and Wasana Suskasan (1989). Personal Interview (National YWCA of Bangkok), Bangkok, Thailand (January).

Hood, Janice C. (1989). "Why Our Society is Rape-Prone," *The New York Times* (May).

Hoskins, Irene, Ed. (1988). "XIIth International Congress of the European Federation for the Welfare of the Elderly (EURAG): Focus on Older Women in Europe," *Network News: A Newsletter of the Global Link for Midlife and Older Women*, 3:2 (Summer/Fall), 12– 15.

Hossain, Mahabub (1986). *The Impact of Grameen Bank on Women's Involvement in Productive Activities*, Dhaka, Bangladesh: Zenith Packages, Ltd.

Hossain, Mahabub and Rike Afsar (1988). "Credit for Women's Involvement in Economic Activities in Rural Bangadesh," mimeograph, BIDS (December).

Hui, Cynthia and Kalei Inn (1989). Personal Interview (Helping Hand), Wan Chai, Hong Kong (January).

Hunter College Women's Studies Collective (1983). *Women's Realities, Women's Choices: An Introduction to Women's Studies*, New York: Oxford: University Press.

Huperg, Margit (1988). Personal Interview (Violetta Clean). West Berlin, West Germany (presently Germany) (July).

Huq, Jahanara, Johan Roushan and Hamida Akhtar Begum (1985). *Women and Health*, Bangladesh: Brac Printers.

Hutchins, Loraine (1988). "Gabriela Leite Promotes Human Rights for Prostitutes: Opens New Avenues of Dialogue in Brazil," *Action for Children*, 3:4, 1.

Imre, Roberta Wells (1982). *Knowing and Caring: Philosophical Issues in Social Work*, Washington, DC: University of America.

Inter-African Committee (1988). *Inter-African Committee on Traditional Practices Affecting the Health of Women & Children*, Newsletter, No. 6, Inter-African Committee Newsletter, Addis Ababa, Ethiopia (September).

International Planned Parenthood Federation (1985). *Women's Health and Family Planning Centre*, Wales.

International Labor Organization (1989). Personal Correspondence, Washington, DC.

International Women's Tribune Center New York, NY, USA.

—— (1988). *Women Share-Funding Newsnote*, Issue No. 1 (July), New York, NY, USA.

International Workshop on Women and the Unpaid Work (February 19–22, 1987), Norwegian Housewives Association, Oslo, Norway.

Isaacs, Stephen, Renee Holt and Andrea Irwin (1988). *Assessing the Status of Women*, New York: International Women's Rights Action Watch, Columbia University.

Jadhav, Philip (1989). Personal Interview (Asian Alliance of YMCA's), Kowloon, Hong Kong (January).

Jang, Winnie and Chee Liu Chin (1989). Personal Interview (Senior Citizens Programme, Ministry of Community Development), Singapore (January).

Jeffrey, Patricia (1979). *Frogs in a Well: Indian Women in Purdah*, London: Zed Books, Ltd.

Johnson, Julie (1989). "Elderly Suffer Mental Ills Without Hope of Aid, Congress Panel Told," *The New York Times* (March 7).

Josephs, Barbara, Susan Lob, Peggy McLaughlin, Terry Mizrahi, Jan Peterson, Beth Rosenthal, and Fran Sugarman (1989). "The Community Organizing From Women's Perspectives: Developing of Feminist Theory-Based Practice Model Through the Building of A Women Organizer's Network," Unpublished Manuscript (March).

Kakir, Sandra Mostata (1989). Personal Interview (Bangladesh Women's Health Coalition), Dhaka, Bangladesh (January).

Kendall, Katherine A. (1988). "The Evolving Family: An International Perspective," *International Social Work*, Vol. 31, 81–93.

Kerkar, Amol (1988). *Violence Committed by Younger Generation Daughter and/or Son-in-Law. Son and/or Daughter-in-Law on Elder Generation Females*, Unpublished Mmonograph, Dadar, Bombay.

Khandekar, Shuba (1987). "Yatra," *Femina: Applause* (March 23–April 7).

Kleinman, Carol (1987). "Skepticism Greets Report on Women's Pay," *Chicago Tribune* (November 16).

Klouda, Tony (1988). "Walking on a Fairly Tight Rope: Policy Formation for AIDS in the Family Planning World," symposium on AIDS and Human Rights, United Nations: New York, NY, USA (December 1).

—— (1988). "Working at a Crisis: Family Planning AIDS and Human Rights," Symposium on AIDS and Human Rights, United Nations: New York, NY, USA, (December 1).

Kolata, Gina (1989). "Growing Movement Seeks to Help Women Infected with AIDS Virus," *The New York Times Health Section* (May 4), B16.

Kooi, Loh Cheng (1988). Personal Interview (Committee for Asian Women (AW), Kowloon, Hong Kong (January).

Kugler, Israel (1987). *From Ladies to Women: The Organized Struggle for*

Women's Rights in the Reconstruction Era, Westport, CT: Greenwood Press.

Kum, Leon Wai (1980). "The Status of Women in Singapore," *Women and the Law* (June).

Lam, Gladys (1989). Personal Interview (Hong Kong Polytechnic-Department of Applied Social Studies), Kowloon, Hong Kong (January).

Lartey, Joyce (1988). *Women's International League for Peace and Freedom Backgrounder*, No. 7 (October).

Leung, Lei Ching (1989). Personal Interview (Association for the Advancement of Feminism), Wan Chai, Hong Kong (January).

Lewis Harold (1982). *The Intellectual Base of Social Work Practice*, NY: Haworth Press, Silberman Fund.

—— (1982). "Morality and the Politics of Practice," *Social Casework*, 53–7 (July), 404–417.

Lily, Jobunnesse (1989). Personal Interview (Save the Children – USA), Dhaka, Bangladesh (January).

Lin, Tsung-yi (1984). "A Global View of Mental Health," *American Journal of Orthopsychiatry*. 54:3, July, 369–374.

Lourdes (1989). Personal Interview (Collectiva MULA), Mexico City, Mexico (June).

Lucente, Randolph L. (1987). "n=1: Intensive Case Methodology Rediscovered," *Journal of Teaching Social Work*, 1:2, (Fall/Winter), 49–64.

Lynn, D. B. (1959). "A Note on Sex Differences in the Development of Masculine and Feminine Identification," *Psychological Review*, 66, 126–135.

Lyons, Cathie (1984). "A Woman's Health is more than a Medical Issue," *Contact*, Number 80 (August), 5/14.

Madeley, John (1989). "It has given a New Dimension to my Life," *United Nations Development Fund for Women UNIFEM*, Unpublished Article, New York, NY, USA.

Mahler, Halfdan (1985). "Women the Next Ten Years," *World Health, Women Health and Development*, United Nations. (April).

Mananzan, Mary John (1987). "Guide to the Analysis of Women's Situation from a Third World Perspective," *Manila, the Philippines*, St. Scholasticas College: Manila, The Philippines.

Mann, Jonathon M. (1988). "Acquired Immune Deficiency Syndrome – A Global Perspective," World AIDS Day, Symposium on AIDS and Human Rights, United Nations, New York, NY (USA, December 1).

Mann, Judy (1988). "The Leave Act's Costs," *The Washington Post* (April 13).

Manuela Ramos (1989). Personal Interviews, Lima, Peru (June).

Mariano, Ann (1988). "Housing Crisis Grips Low-Income Women," *The Washington Post* (October 8).

Martenson, Jan (1987). *Human Rights: Questions and Answers*, New York: United Nations Department of Public Information.

Mason, Diane (1988). "The Hidden Costs of Having Babies," *St. Petersberg Times* (June 3).

Mayor, Federico (1989). "Strengthening Solidarity Between Peoples," *Bangladesh Times* (January 25), 5.

McCalman, Kate (1981). *We Carry a Heavy Load: Rural Women in Zimbabwe Speak Out*, Zimbabwe Women's Bureau (December).

McEwan, Sylvia (1989). Personal Interview (AMNLAE – Instituto Nicaraguense de la Mujer), Managua, Nicaragua (June).

McGinley, Monica, Ed. (1988). "Localizing Health Care in Abuse," *Medical Mission Sisters News*, XVIII:1.

—— Ed. (1988). "Poverty and Pregnancy . . . A Deadly Combination," *Medical Mission Sisters News*, XVIII:3.

—— Ed. (1987). "Brazil's Long Journey to Justice," *Medical Mission Sisters News*, XVII:I.

—— Ed. (1987). "A Healing Presence in the Philippines," *Medical Mission Sisters News*, XVII:3.

—— (1987). Personal Correspondence (Holistic Health Centre), Pune, India.

—— (1987). "Wholistic Health Care in India," *Medical Mission Sisters News*, XVII:5.

—— (1984). "In Search of Refuge," *Medical Mission Sisters News*, XIV:2.

—— Ed. (1982). "Quality of Life," *Medical Mission Sisters News*, XII:2.

McIlliaine, Lawrence, Ed. (1989). *On Beyond War*, Issue 45 (January), Palo Alto, California.

McNeely, Dave (1988). "Women in Workplace Force Changes in Employment Policies," *American Statesman* (April 17).

Mellish, Page, Ed. (1989). *The Backlash Times*, "Feminists Fighting Pornography," New York, NY, USA.

Miller, Jean Baker (1976). *Toward a New Psychology of Women*, Boston, MA: Beacon Press.

Ministry of Social Affairs and Employment (1985). *A Decade of Equal Rights Policy in the Netherlands 1975–1985*, The Hague, The Netherlands. (June).

Mitrakul, Panida (1989). Personal Interview (Bangkok Collins YMCA), Bangkok, Thailand (January).

Mizrahi, Terry et al (1989). Personal Interview (Education Center for Community Organizing), New York, NY, USA.

Morimiento Manuelo Ramos (1989). Personal Interviews, Lima, Peru (June).

Mostafa, Sandra K. (1989). Personal Interview (Bangladesh Women's Health Coalition), Dhaka, Bangladesh (January).

Murphy, H. B. M., E. D. Wittkower, and N. A. Chance (1967). "Cross-Cultural Inquiry into the Symptomology of Depression," *International Journal of Psychiatry*, 3:1, (January), 6–15.

Murthy, Nirmala (1985). "Bring Health Service to Where Women Are," *Women in Development*, United Nations: New York, NY, USA.

Nairobi Forward Looking Strategies for the Advancement of Women (1985). United Nations: New York, NY, USA, 69–70.

Narayanan, K.R. (1988). "International Cooperation for Nation Building and Human Progress," *Darshan* (August), 14–16.

NASW News (1989). 34:2 (February), 3.

National YWCA of Bangkok (1988). Personal Interviews, Bangkok, Thailand (January).

NiCarthy, Ginny, Ed. (1987). *INAVAW* (International Network Against Violence Against Women), *News* (Winter), 3–7.

Ochamowitz, Barbara, Helen Orvig, and Juanita Napuri (1989). Personal Interview (Cendoc Mujer), Lima, Peru (June).

Okeyo, Achola Pala (1989). *Toward Strategies for Strengthening the Position of Women in Food Production: An Overview & Proposals on Africa*, United Nations International Research & Training Institute for the Advancement of Women (UNISTRAW).

Older Women's League (1988). *The Road to Poverty: A Report on the Economic Status of Midlife and Older Women in America* (May).

O'Neill, William (1969). *The Woman Movement: Feminism in the United States, England*, Chicago: Quadrangle Books.

Orientacion Legal a La Mujer (1989). Personal Interviews, Women's Legal Guidance of Villa El Salvador, Villa El Salvador, Lima, Peru (June).

Oxfam America (1988). Personal Communication, Boston, MA, USA *Oxfam America Special Report* (1986/1987). (Winter), 1–8.

Pacsi, Filomena T., Flora Rojas, Patricia Amat, Angelica Medrano, and Esther Hinostroza (1989). Personal Interviews (Services for Women of the Mines), Lima, Peru (June).

Padhye, Mangala (1988). *Violence Committed by the Husband on the Wife (Wife Beating By In-Laws on Daughters-in-Law and on Widows, and on Separated and Divorced Women*, Unpublished Monograph, Deadar, Bombay.

Palmer, George, David E. Morrison, and Carol Peterson, Eds (1988). *Diversity: A Source of Strength.*

Papanek, Hanna (1989). "India's Dowry Murders Mark Rise in Violence Against Women," *The New York Times* (February 11).

Pastizzi-Ferencic, Dunja, Mercedes Sayagues, and Debbie Crowe, Eds (1989). INSTRAW, *Links: A Bulletin for Networking*, Santo Domingo, Dominican Republic.

Pastizzi-Ferencic, Dunja, Krishna Ahooja-Patel, and Mercedes Sayagues, Eds. (1988).INSTRAW, *News: Women and Development*, No. 11 (Winter).

Pastizzi-Ferencic, Dunja (1988). Personal Interview at United Nations (The International Research and Training Institute for the Advancement of Women – INSTRAW), Santo Domingo, Dominican Republic.

Peace, Sheila M. (1981). *An International Perspective on the Status of Older Women*, Monograph, Washington, DC: International Federation on Aging.

Peralta, Asuncion (1986). "The Boss Behaved Like a Petty Dictator: Unions Don't Keep Women Either," in Jennie Clark, Ed., *Wearing New Patterns: Women's Struggle for Change in Asia and the Pacific.*

Perera, Lakshoni (1982). "Women and Work: Background Paper," presented at National Symposium on "New Dimensions in the Role of Women (November. 8–11), Colombo, Sri Lanka.

Petevi, Mary (1988). "Resettlement of Refugee Women at Risk," *Refugees*, 56 (September), 22.

Pokhrel, Durga (1980). "Behind the Bars of Nepal Central Jail," *Manushi*, 6 (July–August), 14–16.

Polani, Michael (1974). *Personal Knowledge: Towards a Post Critical Philosophy*, Chicago: University of Chicago Press.

Pongsapich, Amara (1989). Personal Interview (Social Research Institute, Chulalongkorn University), Bangkok, Thailand (January).

Pontificia Universidad Catholica Escuela de Trabajo Sociale (1989). Personal Interview, Lima, Peru (June).

Press, Robert M. (1988). "Credit Where It's Due: African Women Get Chance at a Better Life," *The Christian Science Monitor International*, (December 30).

Pruekpongsawalee, Malee (1989). Personal Interview (Women in Development Consortium in Thailand), Bangkok, Thailand (January).

Pseawa, Feoni P. (1988). "Values for Policies and Laws Affecting Women: Asia Pacific Forum on Women, Law & Development Regional Conference," *Forum News* 1:2 (December 11 14).

Pureo, Prema (1989). Personal Interview (Annapurna Women's Center), Bombay, India (February).

Quanine, Jannat (1989). Personal Interview (Grameen Bank), Dhaka, Bangladesh (January).

Rahman, Qiyamak and Ginny Nicarthy, Eds (1988). Internatiuonal Network Against Violence Against Women, *INAVAW, News* (Winter).

Raje, Shri Parag (1988). *Annapurna Mahila Mandal Report of Activities*, Bombay, India: Arem Printers (October 1–September 30, 1986).

Rao, Vijaya (1988). *NGO Committee on Aging*, Minutes, Vienna, (September Meeting).

—— (1988). "Sharing of Domestic, Parental and Other Family Responsibilities in Developing Countries," Working paper for Expert Group Meeting on Social Support Measures for the Advancement of Women, Vienna, Austria (November 14–18).

Rawls, John (1971). *A Theory of Justice*, Cambridge, Massachusetts: Harvard University Press.

Reilly, John (1988). "Parental Leave Laws Don't Hurt Business, Study Says," *The Ann Arbor News* (September 2).

Rich, Adrienne (1979). *On Lies, Secrets and Silence: Selected Prose*, New York: W.W Norton.

Rich, Spencer (1988). "Study Details Income Lost in Giving Birth," *The Washington Post*, The Federal Page (March 15), A21.

Robyn, Kathryn (1990). Personal Communication (Alcoholism Center for Women), Los Angeles, CA, USA.

Rodriquez, Helen (1988). World AIDS Day Symposium on AIDS and Human Rights, United Nations, New York, USA (December 1).

Rogers, Barbara (1984). *The Domestication of Women: Discrimination in Developing Societies*, London and New York: Tavistock Publications.

Rohland, Carman (1989), Personal Interview (Women for Life), Santiago, Chile.

Rosemond, Yvon (1988). "Economic, Social and Cultural Rights in the Context of AIDS As a Disease of Poverty, Discrimination and Disadvantage," Symposium on AIDS and Human Rights, United Nations: New York, NY, USA (December 1).

Rosencranz, Ann (1989). Personal Interview (San Francisco Acupuncture and Healing Arts Center). San Francisco, CA, USA.

Rosenthal, Elizabeth (1989). "Different but Deadly," *The New York Times Magazine* (September 17).

Salem, Deborah A., Edward Seidman, and Julian Rappaport (1988). "Community Treatment of the Mentally Ill: The Promise of Mutual Help Organizations," *Social Work*, 33:5 (September/October), 403–408.

Sandra, Joanne and Anne S. Walker, Eds (1989). *The Tribune: A Women and Development Quarterly*, Newsletter, 40.

Sathe, Sharada (1989). Personal Interview (Stree Mukti Sanghatana), Women's Liberation Organization, Bombay, India (February).

Schaef, Ann Wilson (1981). *Women's Reality: An Emerging Female System in A White Male Society*, Minneapolis, Minnesota: Winston Press.

Schmidt, Peggy (1988). "Women and Minorities: Is Industry Ready?" *The New York Times* (December 16).

Seager, Joni and Ann Olson (1986). *Women in the World: An International Atlas*, NY: Simon & Schuster, Touchton Book.

Segall, Edith and Winifred Norman (1988). Committee on the United Nations Decade for Women, Minutes of October 20 meeting.

Sesia-Lewis, Paula, Virginia Alejandre, and Maria Christina Galente (1989). Personal Communication (Group for the Support of Ethnic Development), Oaxaca, Oaxaca, Mexico (June).

Sevilla, Rebecca (1989). Personal Interviews (GALF – Grupa du Auto Consciencia Lesbiano Feminista), Lima, Peru.

Shrier, Sally, Ed. (1989). *Women's Movement of the World: An International Directory and Reference Guide*, United Kingdom: Keesings Publications.

Siddigui, Kamal (1984). *An Evaluation of the Grameen Bank Operation*, Booklet, Dhaka, Bangladesh: Eastern Commercial Service.

Siemens, Maria (1988). "Protection of Refugee Women," *Refugees*, 56, (September), 21-22.

Sivard, Ruth L. (1985). *Women . . . A World Survey*; Washington, DC: World Priorities.

Smith, Dorothy E. (1987). *The Everyday World as Problematic: A Feminist Sociology*, Boston: Northeastern University Press.

Sparks, Caroline H. and Bat-Ami Bar Or (1985). "A Social Change Approach to the Prevention of Sexual Violence Toward Women," *Work in Progress*, No. 83–08.

Spivek, Roberta, Ed. (1989). *Peace and Freedom*, 49:1 (January/February), 1-27.

Stamatopoulou, Elsa (1988). "AIDS and Human Rights," Symposium on

AIDS and Human Rights, United Nations: New York, NY, USA (December 1).

Stoiber, Susan (1989). "Parental Leave and Woman's Place: The Implications and Impact of Three European Approaches to Family Leave Policy," *News from WREI* – Women's Research and Education Institute, (February).

Strobanek, Siriporn (1989). Personal Interview (Foundation for Women: Rural Women's Education Media), Bangkok, Thailand (January).

—— (1988). *Violence Against Women in the Family*, Bangkok, Thailand: Foundation for Women.

—— (1985a). *Umbrella-Plan for Women's Development in Thailand*, Bangkok, Thailand: Foundation for Women.

—— (1985b). *Appropriate Technology for Rural Women*, Bangkok, Thailand: Foundation for Women.

Strobanek, Siriporn and Mantana Ithinanthaweerachai (1989). *Power of Media and Subordination of Women*, Bangkok, Thailand: Foundation for Women.

Sukop, Sylvia (1988). "Bangladesh Floods," *Oxfam America News* (Autumn).

Suzuki, Kazue (1989). "Japanese Companies Slow on Child Care," *The Strait Times*, Singapore (January 19), 16.

Taft, Ronald (1977). "Coping with Unfamiliar Cultures" in Neil Warren, Ed, *Studies in Cross Cultural Pathology*, Vol. I, New York: Academic Press, 121-153.

Takenaka, Masao (1988). "Theme Presentation," *Working for Justice, Making Peace*, Kowloon, Hong Kong: Asia Alliance of YMCA's.

Tata Institute of Social Sciences (1988). *A Draft Report of the Training Needs for Social Welfare Development Personnel in the North Eastern Region*, Deonar, Bombay (November).

Teltsch, Kathleen (1988). "Foundations Expand Family Planning Aid Abroad," *The New York Times* (September 5), 1, 7.

Teufel, June (1988). "African Women Farmers – a Key to Ensuring the Continent's Food Security and Economic Viability: "Lessening the Burden for Women, and the Role of Non-Governmental Organizations (NGO's)," *UN Radio: Women*, No. 25 (October).

—— (1988). "The UN Social, Humanitarian and Cultural Committee Discussions on Women's Issues – The Need to Find Greater Expression in Political Life: A Tribute to MargaretSnyder, Director, UNIFEM, The UN Development Fund forWomen," *UN Radio: Women*, 31 (November).

Thammasat University (1988). Personal Interviews, Bangkok, Thailand (January).

Towle, Charlotte (1945). *Common Human Needs*, Washington, DC: NASW.

Tuttle, Leslie and Haleh Wunder (1989). "Women Creating a New World," *Oxfam America: Facts for Action*, #3.

Uchitelle, Louis (1989). "U.S. Businesses Loosen Link to Mother Country," *The New York Times* (May 21).

UNICEF (1984). *The State of the World's Children*, New York: Oxford University Press.

UNICEF (1988). "The Seven Sins: Bedevilled Development," *Development Forum* (January–February) 24.

United Nations (1987). *Global Strategy for the Prevention and Control of AIDS,"* Note by the Secretary General, prepared in response to General Assembly: Economic and Social Council Resolution, (October).

United Nations (1983). Report on the Investigation of World Wide Prostitution.

United Nations Centre for Social Development and Humanitarian Affairs (1988). "Participation of the Elderly in Developing Technical Guidelines for Programme and Project Planning," Vienna, Austria.

United Nations Development Fund for Women (1988–1989). *Strength in Adversity: Women in the Developing World,* New York, NY, USA.

United Nations General Assembly (1988). "Alternative Approaches and Ways and Means Within the United Nations System for Improving the Effective Enjoyment of Human Rights and Fundamental Freedoms," 43rd Session, (October 18).

United Nations General Assembly (1988). "Office of the United Nations High Commissioner for Refugees," 43rd Session, Agenda item 102 (b), (August 31).

Universidad Centroamerican Escuela de Trabajo Social (1989). Personal Interview, Managua, Nicaragua (June).

Vajrathon, Mallicia (1989). Personal Interview (United Nations Population Fund: Gender Role Analysis), New York, NY, USA (August).

Van Dyk, Carla (1989). Personal Interview (Foundation for Social Aid and Consultation), Amsterdam, The Netherlands (February).

Van Walsum, Sarah (1989). "Rights of Women in The Netherlands: the Clara Wichman Institute," Amsterdam, The Netherlands.

Varde, Sudha (1989). Personal Interview (Women's Vigilance Committee), Bombay, India (February).

Viswanathan, N. and Janice Wood Wetzel (1992). "Concepts and Trends in Mental Health: a Global Perspective," *International Mental Health* (working title). Deonar, Bombay: Tata Institute of Social Sciences (in press).

Wakefield, Jerome C. (1988). "Psychotherapy, Distributive Justice and Social Work," *Social Services Review*, Part I (June).

Walker, Anne S., Ed. (1984). *The Tribune: A Women and Development Quarterly*, Newsletter, 29.

Weinberg, Joanna K. (1988). "Autonomy as a Different Voice: Woman, Disabilities and Decisions," in Michele Fine and Adrianne Asch, Eds, *Women with Disabilities*, PA: Temple University Press.

Wetzel, Janice Wood (1987). "Mental Health of Rural Women: An International Analysis," *International Social Work*, 30:1 (January) 43–59.

—— (1986). "Feminist World View Conceptual Framework," *Social Casework*, 6–3 (March), 166–173.

—— (1986). "Global Issues and Perspectives on Working with Women," *Affilia: Journal of Women and Social Work*, 1:1 (Spring), 5–19.

—— (1986). "The World's Women Unite in Diversity," *Canadian Woman Journal*, 7:1 & 2 (Spring/Summer) 11–14.

—— (1985). "Forum '85 Spurs World's Women to Unite for Restructuring Society," *The Journal of the National Association of Women Deans, Administrators, and Counsellors* (October).

—— (1984/1991). *Clinical Handbook of Depression*, New York: Gardner Press, Inc.

White, M. E. (1904). "Work of the Woman's Club, "*Atlantic Monthly*, 93.

Wilkinson, Benjamin (1988). Personal Correspondence regarding DuPont's Diversity Program.

Williams, Juanita (1977). *Psychology of Women: Behavior in a Biosocial Context*, NY: W.W. Norton.

Women for Women (1988). Personal Interviews, Dhaka, Bangladesh (January).

Women's Action Alliance (1988). *Alcohol and Drugs are Women's Issues: What are You Doing About Them?*, New York, NY, USA.

Women's Alcohol & Drug Education Project (1989). Personal Communication, New York, NY, USA (August).

Women's Equity Action League Educational Defense Fund (1975). World Plan of Action for the Decade of Women, Washington, DC, USA.

Women's Information Center (1988). *Rural Women's Education Media*, Bangkok, Thailand: Foundation for Women.

Women's Self-Help Center (1989). Personal Communication, St. Louis, Missouri, USA.

Women's World Banking (1989). Personal Commmunication, New York, NY, USA.

Yih, Katherine (1988). "Bangladesh Floods: Behind the Headlines," *Disaster Background* (September).

Youssef, Nadia H. and Carol B. Hetler (1985). "The Women Who are Head of Rural Families," *ILO and Working Women 1980–1985*, Geneva: International Labor Office, p. 11.

Yunus, Muhammad (1987). *Credit for Self Employment: A Fundamental Human Right*, Pamphlet, Grameen Bank, Bangladesh: Al-Falah Printing Press.

—— (1984). *On Reaching the Poor*, Unpublished Paper, Dhaka, Bangladesh.

Yunus, Muhammad (1982). *Grameen Bank Project in Bangladesh – A Poverty Focused Rural Development Programme*, Pamphlet, Dhaka, Bangladesh: The Imperial Press.

Index